THE ATTENTION ECONOMY

THE
ATTENTION
ECONOMY

Understanding the New Currency of Business

THOMAS H. DAVENPORT
JOHN C. BECK

HARVARD BUSINESS SCHOOL PRESS
BOSTON, MASSACHUSETTS

Library of Congress Cataloging-in-Publication Data

Davenport, Thomas H., 1954–
    The attention economy : understanding the new currency of business / Thomas H. Davenport and John C. Beck.
       p. cm.
    Includes index.
    ISBN 1-57851-441-X (alk. paper)
    1. Personal information management. 2. Attention. I. Beck, John C. II. Title.

HD30.2 .D38 2001
303.48'33--dc21

                                                                                            00-054269

The paper used in this publication meets the requirements of the American National Standard for Permanence of Paper for Publications and Documents in Libraries and Archives Z39.48-1992.

CONTENTS

PREFACE

W E FIRST DISCUSSED attention in a setting both personally and geographically dramatic. We were having breakfast in the dining room of the Cliff House in Ogunquit, Maine, which looks out over craggy rocks and crashing waves. It was our first meeting in about twenty years. We'd worked together as student (John) and not-much-older professor (Tom), and now we were going to be colleagues in an Accenture (then known as Andersen Consulting) research center. "What do you want to do research on, John?" Tom asked between bites of Raisin Bran. "I'm really interested in attention," John replied with some trepidation—thinking that the issue was unlikely to be at the top of any business researcher's list. "That's amazing—so am I," Tom quickly interjected. "In fact, I've booked myself to talk to five hundred people about attention in about a month, and I have no idea what I'm going to say." Our collaboration began that August morning in 1998 and has continued (at least) through the writing of this book.

We became interested in attention from very different perspectives. Tom has spent his career looking at topics like knowledge management, process redesign, and the management of information technology. John has been working in the areas of strategy, international business, and leadership. Partly because of the diversity of our backgrounds, we were convinced that attention is an important and pervasive concept.

If the topic appealed to us, we suspected that it might appeal to a broad group of businesspeople. This realization motivated us to pursue a research project and eventually a book on this topic. As we explored the topic, we realized that it was "in the air"; many people whose ideas we respected said that attention was important. Several even noted that we live in an attention economy. But none clearly spelled out what an individual or an organization might do about attention.

While we believe this is the first book to examine in detail the business implications of attention, we know we're not the first people to think or write about the subject. The topic was first introduced to John by Mitchell Wade, who was leading a project to reposition the strategy of Rand Corporation in the newly emerging information economy. Wade suggested that human attention might be one of the most restrictive limitations to the promise of the Internet. The first that Tom read on the topic was a short article in the September 1997 issue of *Wired* magazine by consultants Tom Portante and Ron Tarro (a friend of Tom's). In "Paying Attention," the authors argued that attention had become the scarce resource of the information economy. Portante and Tarro mentioned a book by Richard Lanham called *The Electronic Word: Democracy, Technology, and the Arts*. Lanham, then a professor of rhetoric at UCLA, was the first scholar we know of to think about the implications of information technology for human attention management. His book includes a particularly memorable discussion about how black-and-white text can ever hold the attention of a generation of children brought up on the dancing and singing letters and numbers of *Sesame Street*.

We think it was also Tarro who pointed us to the Web-published work of Michael Goldhaber, whom we have not met. We've only read an article based on a presentation he gave, but he inspired the title of our book, *The Attention Economy*, and gave us the idea that the Internet is a fantastic market for attention.

We're grateful to our intellectual predecessors for their ideas on attention, but their published comments have only scratched the surface of the topic. We're also pleased that we have contemporaries in this emerging field (soon movement?) of management research. Less than a week before we sent our final manuscript off to Harvard Business School Press, Ken Sacharin sent us a copy of his book *Attention!* in galleys. While Sacharin's book is primarily concerned with advertising, we believe it contributes to the buzz, breadth, and credibility of the field. The more books on this topic the better. We hear, also, that Goldhaber has a book manuscript on the topic, and we hope someone will publish it soon.

At the Accenture Institute for Strategic Change we've been able to pursue this topic in substantial depth, even without its immediate relevance to the firm always being clear. We're grateful to the two generations of firm leaders who made this possible, including first Peter Fuchs and George Shaheen, and later Mike May, Steve James, and Joe Forehand.

Several people read all or parts of the book along the way, or discussed attention with us in detail, and helped us sharpen our perspectives on the attention issue. They include Warren Bennis, Allan Cohen, Dave De Long, Steve Denning, Jeanne Glasser, Morten Hansen, Al Morrison, Al Preble, Larry Prusak, Chuck Sieloff, Mitch Wade, and Tom Waite. Martha Beck and Julia Kirby were incredibly helpful in thinking and even writing at the early stages of the book. Our colleague Patrick Lynch did a lot of work on the AttentionScape tool, and Lawrence Tu helped get it online. Margaret (Gosia) Stergios, our intrepid knowledge manager, found us lots of external knowledge to incorporate in the book. Jim Wilson came on during the later phases and played a heroic role in pulling everything together—particularly the "meta-text" (a term he coined) in the margins and sidebars.

Three anonymous reviewers and one who named himself, Bill Jensen, gave us constructive criticism about the first draft of the book. Sarah Cliffe, our editor for an article on attention in the September–October 2000 *Harvard Business Review*, helped us think clearly about the implications of attention for senior executives. Our literary agent, Rafe Sagalyn, gave us much encouragement and eventually escorted us back to our old friends at Harvard Business School Press. Our editors at the Press, Hollis Heimbouch, Genoveva Llosa, and Barbara Roth, kept us on time and on point. They were almost always calm as we continually prodded them to help us produce a book that was a little more attention-getting than average. We are very pleased with their efforts and those of Hyun Kounne, designer, in the final look of the book.

Most of all we thank our families: Tom's (Jodi, Hayes, and Chase) and John's (Martha, Kat, Adam, and Liz). They are the subject on which we most enjoy focusing our own attention!

THE
ATTENTION
ECONOMY

CHAPTER 1

A NEW PERSPECTIVE ON BUSINESS

Rob Lippincott is starved

for attention. As senior vice president of an online learning network in Boston, he spends virtually every minute of his day working or catching up on family business—he has nothing left for "hobbies," a term that has come to seem quaint. At home, he's devoted to his wife and school-age daughters, but even so he feels compelled to check voice mail and e-mail on a regular basis.

At work, the scarcity of attention is palpable. About thirty-five people work for him—software developers and content experts—and all of them feel the need for more of Rob's attention. They and his peers in the company often ambush him on his way to the bathroom. Sometimes the best he can do is to offer someone who wants a meeting with him a shared wait in the cafeteria line. His office is surrounded by great restaurants, but he rarely has enough spare time and attention to visit them. Rob spends the great majority of his day in meetings; in between he answers e-mails and voice mails. He and his colleagues often resort to instant messages because regular e-mails aren't attention getting enough. Even his commutes are consumed by cell-phone conversations or voice mail. Occasionally Rob will put the top down on his convertible on sunny days so that the wind noise will dissuade callers from long conversations.

As the information assault persists, Rob worries about the implications of his attention deficit. Is he giving his family all the attention it deserves? As a manager, does he owe more attention to the employees who report to him? Does his inability to reflect quietly mean that he'll overlook something important in his business? These concerns persist, and Rob has no idea how to address them. No massive infusions of free attention seem to be forthcoming.

If this situation sounds familiar, you are not alone. We all know a person like Rob Lippincott (though, in fact, he is a friend of ours). He is your boss, your neighbor, your spouse—or perhaps even you. His experience represents today's most pressing problem: not enough attention to meet the information demands of business and society.

Rob and the rest of us live in an attention economy. In this new economy, capital, labor, information, and knowledge are all in plentiful supply. It's easy to start a business, to get access to customers and markets, to develop a strategy, to put up a Web site, to design ads and commercials. What's in short supply is human attention. Telecommunications bandwidth is not a problem, but human bandwidth is. At one point, software magnates had the ambition to put "information at your fingertips." Now we've got it, and in vast quantities. But no one will be informed by it, learn from it, or act

Taking Stock

Insider trading is one of those rare Wall Street practices, or malpractices, in which investors want to stay beneath the attention radar. But here's what draws a blip on the Securities and Exchange Commission (SEC) screen:

• An unusually large amount of shares trade hands, particularly in companies about to take part in a promising, yet unannounced, merger. Of the forty-nine instances of insider trading that got the SEC's attention in 1998, twenty-seven involved mergers and acquisitions.

• A company that has received a downgraded rating, or has falling or flat share prices, gets a sudden spike in the amount of shares. The spike occurs just days before the company's discovery of, say, Prozac, or its equivalent, is announced.

Source: Steven Mufson, "Regulators Crack Down on Insider Trading," *Washington Post*, 26 February 1999.

Prominence as Wealth. "It is becoming popular in our affluent society to rank income in attention above money income. When rising numbers of people are able to afford the insignia of material wealth, then the desire for distinction will create a demand for attributes which are more selective than a large money income. In accordance with the law of the socialisation of luxuries, such attributes will be found among privileges which are still élitist. The undisputed common denominator of present-day élites is prominence—and prominence is nothing but the status of being a major earner of attention."

Source: Georg Frank, "The Economy of Attention," *Telepolis*, 12 July 1999, <http://www.heise.de/tp/english/special/auf/5567/1.html>.

on it unless they've got some free attention to devote to the information. Unfortunately, most organizations have precious little attention to spare. This leads us to a key principle of attention management.

DEFICIT PRINCIPLE: Before you can manage attention, you need to understand just how depleted this resource is for organizations and individuals.

> Understanding and managing attention is now the single most important determinant of business success.

What is it that makes the economy hum, but is not growing? What's the limiting factor behind all those Web pages, business plans, strategies, books and articles, marketing initiatives, partnerships and alliances, and expansion initiatives? An attentive human mind. Attention is the missing link between the "bloomin' buzzin' confusion" (to use the phrase of William James, an early fan of attention) of the world around us and the decisions and actions necessary to make the world better.

Today, attention is the real currency of businesses and individuals. Purist economists may take some umbrage at our calling attention a "currency." But it does have many attributes of a monetary instrument. Those who don't have it want it. Even those who have it want more. You can trade it; you can purchase it—any job description that falls under the "consultant" category exemplifies this. People work to preserve and extend what they already have—just look at the proliferation of caller ID devices and e-mail filtering software. And attention can be converted into other currencies, like accumulating enough "e-points" by viewing online ads to "earn" a DVD player.

In postindustrial societies, attention has become a more valuable currency than the kind you store in bank accounts. The vast majority of products have become cheaper and more abundant as the sum total of human wealth increases. Venture capital dollars have multiplied like breeding hamsters. The problems for businesspeople lie on both sides of the attention equation: how to get and hold the attention of consumers, stockholders, potential employees, and the like, and how to parcel out their own attention in the face of overwhelming options. People and companies that do this, succeed. The rest fail. Understanding and managing attention is now the single most important determinant of business success. Welcome to the attention economy.

Information Glut

Previous generations of citizens didn't have an attention problem, at least not compared to ours. They didn't have the Internet with its ever-increasing number of Web sites. At most, they had a few channels of broadcast television, a local newspaper, and a few magazines—*Life*, perhaps, which was mostly pictures, or *Time* or even *Reader's Digest* if they were particularly ambitious. Given the explosion of information sources since then, these previous objects of our attention seem rather paltry.

But even those sources are voluminous compared to what our earlier ancestors consumed. The Sunday *New York Times* contains more factual information in one edition than in all the written material available to a reader in the fifteenth century. In 1472, for example, the best university library in the world, at Queen's College in Cambridge, housed 199 books. Francis Bacon complained of the available books in English that "the whole stock, numerous as it appears at first view, proves on examination to be but scanty."[1] Back in the days before Gutenberg, it took months or years for a few dedicated scribes to create a single copy of a single book. A literate medieval person, provided he or she was not interrupted by the Inquisition or bubonic plague, could probably read the book as fast as your typical modern American high school student. The problem was not finding time to read, but finding enough reading to fill the time. Information was a seller's market, and books were considered far more valuable than, say, peasants.

But now it's difficult to imagine how we could possibly devote enough attention to all the information in our society. Think about all the text in those 60,000 new books that spew out of U.S. presses every year, or the more than 300,000 books published worldwide. Think about the more than 18,000 magazines published in the United States alone—up almost 600 from the year before—with more than 225 billion pages of editorial content. There were more than 20 billion pages of magazine editorial content about food and nutrition alone![2] Consider the 1.6 trillion pieces of paper that circulate through U.S. offices each year. Try scanning the 400,000 scholarly journals published annually around the world. If you

> The Sunday *New York Times* contains more factual information in one edition than in all the written material available to a reader in the fifteenth century.

The Role of Control. "To control attention means to control experience, and therefore the quality of life. Information reaches consciousness only when we attend to it. Attention acts as a filter between outside events and our experience with them. How much stress we experience depends more on how well we control attention, than on what happens to us."

Source: Mihaly Csikszentmihalyi, <http://www.thousandmonkeys.com/cs060499.html>.

prefer lighter reading, peruse some of the 15 billion catalogs delivered to U.S. homes in 1999, or the 87.2 billion pieces of direct mail that reached U.S. mailboxes in 1998.[3]

If you believe that print media are obsolete, consider the more than 2 billion Web pages in the world, a large chunk of which can't even be found with the best search engine. A U.S. government study estimates that the amount of Internet traffic doubles about every hundred days.[4] And online information is not restricted to the Internet. A 2000 University of Illinois study revealed that there are 11,339 distinct electronic databases on the market (up from 301 in 1975).[5] If you like to sit in front of larger screens, you have 80 percent more feature films to watch today than were released in 1990.

Of course, information arrives not only in the form of words and pictures. Every new product or business offering is a form of information that requires attention to be comprehended and consumed. During the 1990s, for example, 15,000 new products were introduced in grocery stores each year.[6] Today the average grocery store stocks about 40,000 different items, or stock keeping units (SKUs). So, how do they get attention when the average household buys only 150 SKUs per year? How does a single brand of salsa attract your attention when two hundred other brands are available? The answer in the attention economy is to buy attention with money. Grocery manufacturers in the United States spent $25 billion on trade promotions in 1999; this money went for stocking allowances for new products, advertising, coupons, end cap displays, and so forth. The number of dollars spent buying attention, interestingly, is about five times all the profits made by U.S. grocery chains in 1999.

Until the beginning of the twentieth century, most people still had enough wherewithal to learn an enormous percentage of the information available to them. In 1900, a well-educated person could still grasp the

---

Ignored Business Travelers Unite!

Have baggage handlers lost your Samsonite lately? Ever tried filing a lost luggage claim? Ever called Air Uganda's toll-free customer-service number? How do you say, "Do you speak English?" in Swahili? The crescendoing whines of an unprecedented number of business travelers has grabbed the attention of the National Business Travel Association (www.nbta.org), which is, in turn, trying to grab the attention of business travel service providers with its new complaint-sharing Web site (www.biztraveler.org). Input from the community of violated business travelers is cataloged and posted on airlines, hotels, car rental agencies. *Now* can I have my new golf clubs back?

Source: Joe Sharkey, "Horror Stories about Life on the Road Are Getting Some Attention That Could Make a Difference," *New York Times*, 20 October 1999.

Sheets to the Wind. "Accumulating productive capacity has always been the means by which economies grow, from seed corn to factories to mutual funds. Now the focus is shifting to your knowledge capital and relationships. Capital, too, is connecting, picking up speed, and becoming intangible. As it does, its future capability to create value becomes far more important than its cost. Productive capacity will be bought and sold at auction, rather than built on a balance sheet. And the most productive resource isn't even connected yet: attention."

Source: Stan Davis and Christopher Meyer, *Blur: The Speed of Change in the Connected Economy* (Reading, MA: Addison-Wesley, 1998), 175.

existing knowledge in almost every field of science and the arts (in fact, this was what a college education was supposed to provide). Human knowledge was still increasing at a rate that a single human brain could handle.

Then the size of humanity's information base zoomed sharply upward, as those pesky geometric growth curves are wont to do. Scientists, increasing in both population and specialization, uncovered more and more new knowledge about the nature of the physical universe. This allowed them to create new technologies that, in turn, sped up the search for knowledge. The technologies were used to communicate more information to more people, who then went on to create even more knowledge, which then had to be communicated to other people within the organization, thus creating the need for more bandwidth, and so on, and so on. This simultaneously virtuous and vicious cycle got us where we are today.

How much does an attention deficit cost us on the job and at home?

BANKRUPTCY PRINCIPLE: If you run an attention deficit too often or too long, there will eventually be serious psychological and organizational consequences.

We all understand the attention deficit problem at some level; we live it every day, even if we don't quite understand how to manage it. But what are the consequences of our individual and organizational attention deficits? One possible concern is the psychological impact of feeling constantly overwhelmed by the imbalance of information over our available attention. Such *info-stress* is not uncommon. In an Institute for the Future study describing a two-hundred-message-per-day communications environment, 71 percent of white-collar workers said they felt stressed by the amount of information they received each day; 60 percent felt overwhelmed.[7] And yet we question how serious info-stress really is. Certainly no one has ever shot up an office or held coworkers hostage while claiming that info-stress had motivated the rampage. Info-stress, then, may not be enough for the average CEO to address the attention issue in a serious way.

Members Only. "In modern industrial societies, a growing percentage of the individual's social life occurs in 'secondary' relationships. . . . People must seek to satisfy their basic needs—including attention—in interactions governed directly or indirectly by the market. Attention has become increasingly available as a commodity to be purchased from people who give attention in the course of their work and expect to be paid for their services. Members of the dominant classes are best able to afford attention of this kind and consume the greatest amount."

Source: Charles Derber, *The Pursuit of Attention* (New York: Oxford University Press, 2000), 59.

So what other rationale is there for doing something about attention? How much does an attention deficit cost us on the job and at home? With a couple hundred messages zinging by every day, how do we know what's important? If we believe that humans work best when they have some time to reflect before acting, we need to assess how much room we have for concerted attention and reflection. There can't be much reflecting going on in an info-glut environment. And if we were all honest with ourselves, we could think of occasions when we could have reacted earlier to information in our environments. Without so much information bombarding us every day, we could have headed countless problems off at the pass. Further, it's unlikely that any project can get the concerted, long-term attention it needs if everyone is so busy responding to incoming e-mails and flashing voice mail lights. Any ambitious initiative in business needs substantial attention over substantial periods. Yet we're becoming used to skipping from topic to topic like fairy sprites. Can we focus organizational attention and stretch the organizational attention span when we need to?

> Because attention is one of those slippery intangible assets, it's difficult to document its presence (though its absence is surely felt).

Just as attention deficit disorder is diagnosed with increasing frequency in individuals (production of Ritalin, the primary drug used to treat ADD, is up ninefold since 1990),[8] organizations can suffer from "organizational ADD."

Failures of attention management are undoubtedly responsible for many business catastrophes, but because attention is one of those slippery intangible assets, it's difficult to document its presence (though its absence is surely felt). How many executive teams have been justifiably accused of being asleep at the switch while a major business or competitive trend was overtaking them? How many managers can claim that their attention has been focused laser-sharp on the truly important issues to their businesses and careers? All of us make the tacit—and, we believe, correct—assumption that when managers and professionals devote attention to a business problem or issue, it will usually be resolved or get better. But what if there simply isn't enough attention to go around? What if attention is going to the wrong topics?

Symptoms of Organizational ADD

1. An increased likelihood of missing key information when making decisions

2. Diminished time for reflection on anything but simple information transactions such as e-mail and voice mail

3. Difficulty holding others' attention (for instance, having to increase the glitziness of presentations and the number of messages to get and keep attention)

4. Decreased ability to focus when necessary

The risks of not managing attention carry opportunity costs for individuals and organizations. If you want to be successful in the current economy, you've got to be good at getting attention. If you want to keep your employees, you need to catch and hold their attention. If you want to sell products and services, at some point customers will have to direct some attention your way. If you run a public company and want your stock value to rise, you've got to attract the attention of investors and analysts. In other words, it's no longer sufficient to be a solid, competent organization; you have to stir the brain cells—and the hearts—of your intended audience.

> If you want to be successful in the current economy, you've got to be good at getting attention.

Objects of Our Attention

Over the past several decades, we've witnessed an information revolution in business. The amount of internal electronic information available to managers has grown enormously. With the advent of the Internet, a manager has more external information handy at the click of a mouse than he or she could ever deal with. At the same time, the volume of noncomputerized information has continued to increase—volumes of phone calls, faxes, and paper mail are all up.

At earlier stages of the information revolution, we could continue to point to the need for more and better technologies as the primary shortcoming in managing information effectively. "Access to information" was the rallying cry that justified the expenditure of trillions of dollars on hardware, software, and telecommunications. But we've won the technology war. New technologies will continue to emerge, and they'll offer nifty new features that promise to make our information environments better. But if the past is any indication, they'll create an even greater need for attention. Computer scientists have prophesied the rise of *filters* and *agents*—tools for limiting and personalizing the amount of information someone receives—for decades now, but any progress in this direction has been woefully outstripped by progress (if you can call it that) in techniques for information

Blazing Attention Trails While Truckin' up to Buffalo

The Grateful Dead allowed its audiences to make bootleg tapes of their live shows since the late 1960s. This innovation got the attention of the free lovin' (and then, free bootleggin') hippies and never hurt the band's ticket sales. Many within earshot of a bootleg became ticket buyers. When Jerry Garcia died in 1995, the Dead was the largest grossing concert-draw in history. The bootleg idea was an effective, "free," noncoercive attention getter. The Dead's counterintuitive and revolutionary stance toward intellectual property was attractive to antiestablishment types. Anyway, the tactic fueled the Dead's primary profit vehicle—the live concert.

distribution and access. The Internet and e-mail alone have increased by several orders of magnitude the amount of information an individual can access easily. Most of us have learned the hard way that the answers to the attention deficit depend not on better technology or simply more information but on finding better ways to manage attention.

MARKETS PRINCIPLE: **As with any other scarce and valuable resource, markets for attention exist both within and outside an organization. As with other markets, some people do a lot better than others in the attention markets.**

Economies based on any scarce good have certain recognizable characteristics. For example, every economy has markets in which its key goods are bought and sold. No, there's no New York Attention Exchange, but markets for attention do exist both inside and outside organizations. Both on the Internet and in more traditional media like television, viewer attention is exchanged for money thousands of times a day. Anyone who wants to sell something or persuade someone to do something has to invest in the attention markets. If I want the attention of a large group of customers, I try to get it by paying to monopolize their TV screens, Web pages, mailboxes, and ultimately their brains.

Another fundamental principle of an economy is that the currency has to be scarce. When the currency becomes too widely available (as in Weimar Germany, for example), it becomes worthless. We're unlikely to see an inflationary rise in attention. The biggest risk to the attention economy would be that individuals could expand their attention at will—that they could engage in unlimited multitasking with no loss of comprehension or meaning. But we're not worried. True, our children sometimes make this argument when they try to do their homework while simultaneously watching television, listening to music, and sending instant messages over the Internet. But as much psychological research attests, attention has its definite limits. What is spent in one place cannot be simultaneously allocated elsewhere. Automobile safety researchers tell us that cell-phone users in cars are four times more likely to have accidents.[9] Other studies suggest that heavy Internet users spend less time doing other things—watching television, for example, and more importantly, spending face-to-face time with other human beings.[10] The American

Overheard. "We are the first society with ADD."
Evan Schwartz, "Interrupt-Driven"

Academy of Child and Adolescent Psychiatry suggests that children who watch a lot of television have lower grades in school, read fewer books, and exercise less.[11] There is only so much attention to go around, and it can only be increased marginally by somehow exercising the brain or by adding new sentient beings to the planet.

> There is only so much attention to go around, and it can only be increased marginally by somehow exercising the brain or by adding new sentient beings to the planet.

Like other markets, some people and topics do a lot better than others in the attention economy. In *The Entertainment Economy*, consultant Michael Wolf argues that more attention is devoted to the entertainment industry now than in the past, and within that industry, the supply of attention goes to a small group of performers (think Gwyneth, Julia, and Tom Cruise).[12] Entertainment-oriented information is flourishing; the year 1998 brought thirty-nine new magazines about media personalities, more than any other type of content. Certainly the public attention seems focused on a small number of sports figures: Michael Jordan, Tiger Woods, Wayne Gretzky. Even in the political sphere, only the leading presidential candidates seem to get any attention or votes. During the 1990s, for example, the number of presidential election stories in four major newspapers published fifteen months before the relevant election almost doubled compared with the number published during the same period in the 1980s.[13] When there is contention for attention, those who seek it turn to the most reliable attention getters: sex, hierarchy, calamity, and so forth.

Every economy has organizational and individual participants, and the attention market qualifies as an economy in this respect. Organizations participate when they want to attract attention from their customers, business partners, investors, or employees. But every individual in business is also an actor in the attention economy. We're all information providers, trying to attract attention to our memos, e-mails, projects, presentations, and careers. Although we know of no sociological study relating the ability to mobilize attention to career success, it's business common sense that those who get noticed get ahead.

Economies have currency and measurement systems. This has long been true for attention in a metaphorical sense, as we are always talking about "paying" attention. Since attention is invisible within human brains, we'll probably never have formal attention currency. But in this

---

Overheard. "Rule Number One is to pay attention. Rule Number Two might be: attention is a limited resource, so pay attention to where you pay attention."
Howard Rheingold, *Virtual Community*

book, we will describe several ways in which attention can be measured, either though self-reporting or more invasive techniques like brain wave or eye movement analysis.

In the absence of precise attention currency, we often use the proxy of time. I can't know for sure if my customer is paying attention to my advertisements, but I can at least determine the likelihood that he or she was watching during the time it appeared. I don't know if anyone is actually attending to my Web site, but I can measure the total time it was displayed on someone's screen. We'll show in chapter 2 that time is not the same as attention and is sometimes a poor proxy for it, but you measure what you can in this world.

> **Like airplane seats and fresh food, attention is a highly perishable commodity.**

All economies have both producers and consumers, supply and demand. The attention economy qualifies in spades. As noted, we're all producers of information, seeking the attention of consumers. But we're all information consumers as well, with only a limited amount of attention to bestow upon the world. To consume information, we must also be investors of our own attention portfolios. The payoff for allocating my attention in a specific direction can be great—I can learn something, change something for the better, fix what's broken, or gratify another human being.

But remember that if attention goes one place, then it can't go another. As a consumer of information, I have to be very careful about my attention allocation. And like airplane seats and fresh food, attention is a highly perishable commodity. Once a moment's attention is gone, it can never be brought back. Just as airlines have created "yield management" systems to maximize the value of their perishable seats, perhaps we need similar approaches to optimize the use of our attention.

Certainly the attention economy has laws of supply and demand. The most obvious one is that as the amount of information increases, the demand for attention increases. As Herbert Simon, a Nobel prize–winning economist, put it, "What information consumes is rather obvious: it consumes the attention of its recipients. Hence a wealth of information creates a poverty of attention."[14] Yet the supply stays constant or even shrinks if there are fewer people available to attend to vastly more information. As more women have entered the workforce, for example, the number of people who watch daytime television or receive door-to-door salespeople

Overheard. "In the end it may turn out there's a cash market for human attention, the most coveted commodity of all."

Thomas Weber, "With Cash for Clicks, Web Marketers Turn Advertising on Its Head"

has decreased. The mismatch of demand and supply has already led to a widespread attention deficit that can only get worse. More information will be ignored, and many key business issues will not receive the benefits of concerted human attention.

As with stock and commodities markets, some segments of the attention economy are hotter than others. As the century turned from twentieth to twenty-first, the hottest attention market was the Internet and the world of electronic commerce. In this environment, attention was at a premium. Internet companies were highly motivated to get attention from Web users; the area has been called a gold rush. The real rush, however, was for user attention. To get it, firms were willing to spend several times their annual revenues on Super Bowl advertisements (e.g., Computer.com), give away millions in sweepstakes and lotteries (iWon.com, Freelotto.com), or sell goods at or below cost (buy.com).

One other law of attention economics is worth mentioning here. Like many other aspects of the "new economy," attention involves "increasing returns." The more we have of it to begin with, the easier it is to get more. If I'm a rock star, anything I do will attract attention. If I'm a very well known politician or CEO, any pronouncement I make will be covered by the press. Those who are rich in attention seem only to get richer. Even as media outlets proliferate, they all seem to be covering the same celebrities and the same issues. With so much contention for their readers' attention, they all pursue the most attention-getting topics they can find.

> More information will be ignored, and many key business issues will not receive the benefits of concerted human attention.

Internal Attention Markets

Just as the broad economy around us can be thought of in terms of attention, every organization has its own internal attention market. Although it overlaps somewhat with the external market, it's composed of internal information providers and consumers who either need attention or have it to give.

Here as in the external markets, there is an attention deficit. The sources of information supply have multiplied, whereas the sources of attention supply have not expanded and may even have shrunk. Many large firms have become leaner through reengineering and personnel

Overheard. Of those who access the Internet at work, 50 percent use it for personal business.
The UCLA Internet Report, "Surveying the Digital Future"

reductions, and there are fewer people around to do the same or more work. In an economy based primarily on physical labor, increases in the amount of work done while a business employs fewer people should lead to unequivocal celebrations of productivity gains. In an attention economy, however, one has to wonder how the numbers all add up. How can we be paying attention to all the information flying around our organizations when there are fewer people to do so?

We believe that the numbers balance in internal attention markets because of two factors. One is the increase in the hours worked by professional and white-collar workers. Although analysts debate whether U.S. workers in general are working more hours, most agree that professional and managerial workers are working more hours. And many knowledge workers now devote considerable "off-hour" attention to work-related information. Remember Rob Lippincott, checking voice messages and e-mail at home? Do you listen to voice mail messages on a cell phone in the car to and from work? Do you check e-mail after dinner? Ever talk to coworkers while at home? And the wireless Web is only going to exacerbate the problem—imagine being able to access broadband anywhere, anytime. All these behaviors are means of coping with attention deficit in business—unfortunately at the expense of our private lives and families. Given the need to sleep, eat, and spend some time in social interaction with family members or friends, this strategy has limits—and many of us have already reached them.

> Since few of us have a good sense of how to process vast amounts of information effectively, we're bound to allocate attention ineffectively.

The other factor that balances the supply of information against the limits of attention is more focus on, and more rapid processing of, informational messages. Even though much of our workday is now spent processing various types of messages, we cannot possibly spend as much time on each individual message in a two-hundred-message-a-day world as we did in the past. As a result, we delete e-mails based only on their headings, skim the contents of messages, and skip big chunks of voice mail messages. We also spend major chunks of our so-called home lives processing messages. Since few of us have a good sense of how to process vast amounts of information effectively, we're bound to allocate attention ineffectively. We don't devote enough attention to some messages, and we spend too much on others. And we have virtually no attention left for reflecting on what all the messages mean.

Any internal attention market has several definable roles. The market maker should be the leader of the organization. He or she determines who gets attention for what and controls the resources that can create attention-getting information. The CEO generally controls the resources and should be able to mobilize the attention of whomever he or she wants within the firm. After all, the CEO has power, money, and the communications department at his or her disposal. The leader of an organization also has to be attuned to what things other people in the organization are paying attention to. If they're paying attention to the wrong things (as judged by the leader), the organization will be unlikely to move in the direction the leader desires. If the CEO wants my attention focused on cost control, but it's actually on deciphering politics after a merger, costs are unlikely to decline much.

> **One way to get attention from customers, of course, is to give them attention.**

The primary consumers of an organization's information can be employees or parties external to the organization, namely, customers, suppliers, investors, and so forth. We've all worked in organizations that sometimes seemed more interested in the attention of customers than that of their own employees (of course, this is not all bad). Firms totally preoccupied with market value may be overly focused on getting and managing the attention of investors or investment analysts. How much attention from these different groups should a firm be seeking? The right proportions will vary across organizations, although almost every organization should be seeking attention from a mixture of audiences.

It is getting more difficult both to capture the attention of your employees and to get a sufficient amount of your customers' attention at the same time. Your customers are just as distracted by all the things going on in today's complex information environment as the people in your own firm. One way to get attention from customers, of course, is to give them attention. Suppliers must use all the means at their disposal, including personalization technologies that provide retail-level attention at wholesale costs, to persuade customers that they are getting attention. "Satisfy the customer" has new meanings in a society in which technology is enabling companies to give attention to customers at an unprecedented level. In yet another "new economy" book, *The Experience Economy*, Joe Pine and Jim Gilmore argue persuasively that organizations need to offer

Overheard. "To get attention you really have to be different, it's not enough just to be good."
Paul Schulman, quoted in Kyle Pope, "NBC Entertainment Chief Says Network Will Tone Down Shows' Explicit Content"

rich and compelling experiences to their customers if they want to attract their attention. Of course, creating those experiences itself requires a great deal of attention.

New Lens

As these examples suggest, the study of attention provides a new lens on business. Many business topics people thought they understood already look substantially different when the attention lens is placed in front of their previously naïve eyeballs. In our approach to the topic, we first describe attention's many facets, examining four perspectives that are particularly relevant in the business context: the measurement of attention, its psychological and biological dimensions, the technologies that attempt to structure and protect attention, and, finally, the industries in which attention management has become high art. These four perspectives illuminate familiar business activities. They also elucidate several business domains in which attention becomes a particularly critical element for success: electronic commerce, project and process management, organizational leadership, strategy, and information and knowledge management. The later chapters will address how managing attention can transform these and other business domains.

To close this chapter, we'll return to our friend Rob Lippincott, otherwise known as Attentional Everyman. Will the demands on Rob's attention decrease in the coming years? Will his attention somehow become less valuable to himself or his organization? Absolutely not. Rob's problem is hardly going to disappear, and it's likely to get worse. If it's going to get any better, Rob will have to become a diligent manager of attention. He'll have to use the tools of economics and measurement, technology, and psychobiology and apply the lessons from the attention industries to manage his own attention and that of his organization. As an e-commerce executive, he's playing in the most competitive attention market on earth. He needs help, and fast. Come to think of it, we'd better get him an advance copy of this book!

CHAPTER 2

ATTENTION, THE STORY SO FAR

Every business is an engine

fueled by attention. In the farms and fields of primitive societies, and in the factories of the Industrial Revolution, physical manpower drove the economy. In the information era, knowledge was power—the more a company had, the more successful it could be. But now, as flows of unnecessary information clog worker brains and corporate communication links, attention is the rare resource that truly powers a company. Recognizing that attention is valuable, that where it is directed is important, and that it can be managed like other precious resources is essential in today's economy.

Although a large body of literature on attention exists in the fields of psychology and physiology, very little has developed about the systematic understanding of attention in the context of business or management. As early as the nineteenth century, academics have assumed that the definition of attention was self-evident. O. S. Munsell, a prominent early psychologist and president of Indiana Wesleyan University, put it this way: "On attention itself, it is needless to discourse at length; its nature and conditions are familiar to every thoughtful student."[1] William James (to whom both of us have a certain devotion, since we both spent much of our student careers in William James Hall), who devoted a significant portion of his life's work to the topic, defined attention this way: "Everyone knows what attention is."[2]

Yet the definition is complicated, as the word seems to mean something slightly different to almost everyone. Early psychologists were some of the first to study and define attention as one of the bedrocks of the entire discipline. The first psychology experiments on attention were all about sound. Scientists were fascinated by how the mind worked when a subject was trying to grapple with stereo sound: Which ear would the brain pay attention to, the left or the right? (It turned out that the particular ear doesn't matter much; more importantly, attention almost always is given to one's own name and to loud sounds.)

Mixed Messages

Early studies by Donald Broadbent in 1954 asked experimental subjects to listen to two or more messages simultaneously and then answer questions about, or repeat back, the messages they were hearing. These competing messages were delivered from loudspeakers or stereo headsets. In general, Broadbent found that the farther apart the sound sources (left and right headset speaker instead of both messages from the same speaker), the greater the attention listeners would give to both messages. About the same time, E. Colin Cherry began to study how subjects listen to two messages, one for each ear simultaneously, and then restate the messages. As it turned out, when the subjects were asked to pay more attention to one particular message (i.e., the right versus the left), they were very good at repeating the message they were asked to listen to. The conflicting sounds in the other ear didn't distract them too much—in fact, most couldn't even recall if the speaker in the nonattention ear was speaking English or if the recording was played backward. They could, however, report if the nonfocus speaker was a male or female or if the speech was replaced by a tone. In other words, as long as the subject was processing similar messages that were processed in similar parts of the brain, attention was limited. But when the direction of the sound or the type of processing required changed (tones replaced by speech), attention could be more effectively split.

In more recent experimental designs on attention, the maxim is that "the eyes don't lie." If you want to know what people are paying attention to, follow what they are looking at. Now we all know that this is not entirely true. Who hasn't feigned interest in a business meeting by staring directly at the speaker while thinking about plans for the weekend?

THE EYES DON'T LIE

THE BULK OF RECENT RESEARCH on attention psychology has been experiments in visual attention. Since the experts argue that the "eyes don't lie," researchers have designed tests to understand how quickly the eye can focus on a particular object in a visual field. Drawing from these experiments, we find better ways to manage attention in organizations. By maximizing both speed and attention, companies will create more competitive, more satisfying homes for their employees.

Employees must attend to a variety of inputs throughout the day. Getting attention is a function of the mind's singling out specific items or issues from the distractions or "noise" in the surrounding environment. Experimental psychology has taught us several ways to get attention most effectively:

• *Pop-out effects:* In attention experiments, search times (the time necessary for the eye to find a given target) are longer when features of objects are similar. (It is easier to find an "S" than an "I" in a field of "T's.") Consequently, it would make sense that if you are trying to direct your employees' attention, you should have unique features that stand out in the world around them. Similarly, in the exhibit shown here, people find the slanted lines in a field of straight lines faster than they find the straight lines among slanted lines. Researchers hypothesize that we are more accustomed to processing "straight lines"—it is easier for our minds to recognize the abnormal in a familiar field than to pick out the normal in an unfamiliar setting.

• *The boy-who-cried-wolf effect:* An extension of the pop-out experiments showed that novel features among a set of different novel features ("flankers") do not gain a performance benefit. In other words, the company that is always doing something new and different will not gain any advantages by doing something new and different yet again. In these cases, novel has become expected and therefore yet another novel notion or initiative will gain little if any natural attention.

• *Counterintuitive role of distracters:* Evidence shows that attention getting is most effective when the field has other distracters, and that directed attention has no benefit when only one stimulus is presented within a visual field. Attentional benefits (enhanced performance) of directed attention occur only in the context of distracters. We've all met managers who try to keep their employees focused on the work and let some strategic planning group think about the external, competitive world. But the attention psychology literature suggests that employees will pay more attention to their work if they understand it in the context of the competitive world.

In other fields of study, attention has come to be related to a variety of different concepts. In political science, attention is closely related to the notion of agendas.[3] In sociology, economics, and organization theory, attention is central to the study of search and decision making.[4] The point is that every discipline takes its own cut at attention. Since our attempt in this book is to convince you that attention is the most important concept in the economy today, perhaps we need to present our own definition.

Attention involves understanding how to work despite an overabundance of "information competition."

Let's look at the word *attention*: Notice that its root word is *attend*. To attend to something is to tend it—to take care of it. A typical employee in today's world is expected to take care of more things than a worker would have at any other time in history. That is what makes this topic important. So much information and so many activities, people, and places are vying for our attention today that the mere *management* of attention has become one of our most important activities. Attention involves understanding how to work within an overabundance of "information competition," whether you are interfacing with customers, coworkers, or your own priority list. We do not necessarily notice the ticking of the clock or the sound of the noisy streets just because they are there. As discussed in chapter 1, frequent complaints about time pressures and information overload suggest that individuals have more things to do than they have the time and mental resources to do them. Thus, priorities must be established.

Our Definition

Our simple definition of attention is this: *Attention is focused mental engagement on a particular item of information. Items come into our awareness, we attend to a particular item, and then we decide whether to act.* Attention occurs between a relatively unconscious *narrowing phase*, in which we screen out most of the sensory inputs around us (we are aware of many things, but not paying attention to them), and a *decision phase*, in which

Laser Guidance. "The focused beam of light generated by a laser is hundreds of times more powerful than an ordinary light beam from the 100-watt bulb in a desk lamp. Ordinary, incoherent light consists of waves of many frequencies, in all phases, and moving in all directions. Light waves in the laser beam are coherent, organized at the same frequency and phase, and traveling in the same direction. This gives a laser the power to cut through even very dense materials that are normally difficult to penetrate with precision. This power and precision comes from the organization of its individual light waves. . . . the remarkable thing is that the light waves organize themselves."

Source: Suzanne Kelly and Mary Ann Allison, *The Complexity Advantage: How the Science of Complexity Can Help Your Organization Achieve Peak Performance* (New York: McGraw-Hill, 1999), 3.

we decide to act on the attention-getting information. Without both phases, there is no attention. A causal relationship exists between awareness, attention, and action. For example, attention is a link in the decision-making chain prior to the decision to buy, move, or otherwise act. If you do not get to the point at which you are considering some kind of an action, you really have not given an item your attention. The action may be as simple as telling someone that you thought about the topic, or that you simply thought about writing it down, or that you made a mental note to yourself to remember it. Whatever the topic, our definition of attention requires some consideration of action, or at least a willful decision not to take action. In the end, you may or may not act, but your consideration of the action suggests that you gave the matter some degree of attention. Exhibit 2-1 shows the relationships between awareness, attention, and action.

Exhibit 2-1: A Graphic Model of Attention Processes

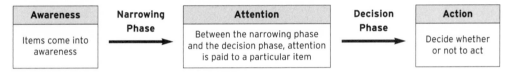

Beyond Advertising

Although it is fairly obvious that there are links between advertising and attention (links from which we'll draw some important lessons in later chapters), the concept of attention management is far broader than advertising alone. Leaders of organizations, for example, must manage attention on several levels: They must direct their own attention to particular projects and information, they must focus the attention of their employees on the most profitable activities, and they must attend to the most important buyers, suppliers, and other stakeholders. Equating attention management to advertising or customer-relationship management is like equating the motion picture industry with the selling of popcorn.

Bull's-Eye

Nor is attention management the same thing as simple awareness, a conscious recognition of a piece of information. The word *awareness* often is substituted erroneously for *attention*. The two terms are not interchangeable, but are linked in a mental sequence. Awareness is a precursor of attention. *Awareness becomes attention when information reaches a threshold of meaning in our brains and spurs the potential for action.*

You can throw oodles of information into a person's awareness. The problem is that *everybody* is doing it. Awareness is vague, general information, and doesn't by itself catalyze any action. Attention is targeted and specific. It gets people moving. In a simple analogy, awareness is the target, and attention the bull's-eye.

TYPES PRINCIPLE: Six basic units of currency are exchanged in an attention market, each emphasizing a specific facet of focused mental engagement.

Now that we have a sense of the meaning of attention, we can move toward a more nuanced understanding of it. Six types of attention can be paired into three dimensions. Each pair contains two opposing kinds of attention: (1) captive or voluntary, (2) aversion-based or attraction-based, and (3) front-of-mind or back-of-mind (exhibit 2-2).

Exhibit 2-2: Paired Opposites: Types of Attention

The first two types of attention—*captive* and *voluntary*—have to do with choice. Attention is driven by rules concerning what is relevant and what is not, and who is permitted to attend to what and when. Although attention is often expedient, it can also be driven by curiosity, a desire to learn, or sometimes a desire to escape from the demands of the environment. People pay attention not only to things they *have* to pay attention to, but also to what they *want* to pay attention to. You pay voluntary attention to things you find innately interesting, things you'd focus on even if doing so were explicitly forbidden. Captive attention, on the other hand, is thrust upon you. The inordinate amount of attention people pay to car accidents or other such tragedies exemplifies voluntary attention. The attention that "speeding school" attendees pay to a film on the tragedies caused by speeding and poor driving, on the other hand, illustrates captive attention. Of course, the coercion involved in captive attention may be much more subtle than an explicit command. For example, the teasers and slide-show ads projected on a movie screen before the main event are examples of forced attention. If you're going to see the movie, you'll have to sit there letting the cinema trivia questions rot your brain until you actually start caring about the answers.

The second category of attention, *aversive* versus *attractive*, has to do with carrot-and-stick motivation. We pay attention to some things because we wish to avoid negative experiences (aversive attention), whereas we pay attention to other things because we think they may bring us positive experiences (attractive attention). For example, Michelin tires advertisements elicit aversive attention. Television commercials show adorable babies using empty tires like sleds, while a voice-over proclaims, "Michelin. Because so much is riding on your tires." The underlying message is that if you do not buy Michelin tires, you will jeopardize your children's safety. Conversely, a car with a dubious safety record might be pitched exclusively on attractive attention: Ads would encourage consumers to remember that the machine is sleek, powerful, and prestigious enough to make any driver irresistible to members of the opposite sex, while downplaying the car's unfortunate tendency to burst into flames at speeds over thirty-five miles per hour.

Finally, attention may be *front-of-mind* or *back-of-mind*. Front-of-mind attention is conscious, focused, and explicit. You use this kind of attention to write reports, pay your taxes, read magazines, and have conversations. At the same time, your remarkable brain is paying back-of-mind attention to dozens of other subjects—things that will never even come into your conscious awareness unless something unexpected occurs. For example, you could be paying highly focused, front-of-mind attention to a cell-phone conversation while paying back-of-mind attention to driving home from work.

When you are first learning a skill or confronting new information, you will usually need to devote front-of-mind attention to it. But psychological research suggests that when tasks become familiar, they can often be relegated to back-of-mind (or, as some psychologists have called it, automatic) attention, freeing up more focus for challenging tasks. Processing information in the back of the mind, or automatically, seems to free up front-of-mind attention.[5] This suggests that organizational phenomena that currently require too much attention could be made routine through practice.

Combinations

In our research, we've found that the paired opposites for each aspect of attention are *not* mutually exclusive. In other words, the attention you're paying to any given item may be both captive and voluntary, both avoidance- and attraction-based, and both front-of-mind and back-of-mind. Think about it: You may be sitting in a dark theater, waiting for your movie to start, when a trailer for another film appears on the screen, demanding captive attention. However, the trailer may be pretty interesting—so much so that within a few seconds you're happily giving it voluntary attention as well. The trailer has created in you captive and voluntary attention. If a car manufacturer develops a gorgeous automobile that also gets high safety ratings, the firm could simultaneously pitch its advertising toward both aversion-based attention ("This car could save your life . . .") and attraction-based attention (". . . and women love it!"). A mountain climber may be paying back-of-mind attention to using his gear properly, while focusing front-of-mind attention on the path ahead or the gorgeous view. Different parts of his mind may be attending to different elements of the climb, but climbing is his sole focus.

> We love to have our attention totally saturated, to an extent that some of us risk our lives for the experience.

Because the effect of combining extremes is additive, the ultimate attention-getter draws all six extremes of attention at once. This type of all-consuming attention seems to be a feature of what psychologist Mihaly Csikszentmihalyi calls *flow experiences*.[6] Flow experiences characterize the most intensely rewarding and enjoyable moments of our lives, and we

---

The Power of Purpose. "When you want a thing deeply, earnestly and intensely, this feeling of desire reinforces your will and arouses in you the determination to work for the desired object. When you have a distinct purpose in view, your work becomes of absorbing interest. You bend your best powers to it; you give it concentrated attention; you think of little else than the realization of this purpose; your will is stimulated into unusual activity, and as a consequence you do your work with an increasing sense of power."

Source: Grenville Kleiser, <http://www.geocities.com/Athens/Acropolis/7025/desire.html>.

human beings have a tendency to seek them out or create them. Extreme sports are good examples of activities that elicit captive and voluntary, avoidance and attractive, front-of-mind and back-of-mind attention. Bizarre as it sounds, many people devote enormous amounts of time, energy, and money to things like jumping out of airplanes so that they can fall like rocks, only to be rescued at the last second by pieces of nylon tied to their backs. We love to have our attention totally saturated, to an extent that some of us risk our lives for the experience.

One and Many

Another definitional issue is whether attention is an individual or a group phenomenon. Obviously, at its most basic level, attention is a physiological, sensory, orienting response in individuals. Early psychological treatises on attention asked readers to notice how they were holding their heads or positioning their eyes to figure out what was holding their attention. One of the early psychologists who studied attention at the turn of the twentieth century, W. B. Pillsbury, noted that "there is no act of attention that is unaccompanied by some motor process."[7] We constantly position our bodies to be able to "attend" to the most important external stimuli. For example, dogs cock their ears in the direction of a sound, and people generally orient their eyes so that a perceived image falls within the fovea area of their retinas. Other signs of sensory attention—as identified in Pavlov's famous experiments—include increased muscular tension and other physiological changes detectable with instruments.

Obviously, focusing only on the physical aspects of attention limits the usefulness of the concept. We can pay attention without even opening our eyes or moving our heads. Attention is about psychology more than physiology; it is a selective, cognitive process through which we absorb selected information. Attention principally has been studied at this individual level—and that is where attention (in its basic forms) must be understood. Some researchers, however, have suggested that attention can be studied at the group level as well.[8] William Ocasio of the University of

Examples of Collective Attention

- Everyone in a theater is usually facing and paying attention to the screen.

- As professors, we often teach in lecture rooms with squeaky chairs. When the noise levels of the squeaky chairs goes up, we're certain that the collective attention to our lectures wanes.

- Members of the Secret Service scan crowds for individuals looking in a different direction from the rest of the crowd—an indication of attention's departing from the social norm.

- Workers in U.S. steel factories in the 1950s were much more likely to pay attention to the quality of their output, whereas Soviet workers of the same era focused more on quantity.

Michigan brought the collective nature of attention into the executive suite by arguing that corporate strategy can be understood as a "*pattern of organizational attention*, the distinct focus of time and effort by the company on a particular set of issues, problems, opportunities, and threats, and on a particular set of skills, routines, programs, projects and procedures."[9] We'll discuss at greater length in chapter 10 how strategy relates to attention.

When a group of individuals is brought together, each person with his or her own focus of attention, an aggregated, collective attention is likely to exist. Of course, organizational attention is fundamentally related to individual attention in that organizations are no more than groups of individuals. Like the individuals who form them, organizations are limited in their information-processing and decision-making capacities. As the political scientist Graham Allison pointed out after studying the Cuban missile crisis, "Companies are physically unable to possess full information, generate all alternatives . . . the physical and psychological limits of man's capacity as alternative generator, information processor, and problem solver constrain the decision-making process of individuals and organizations."[10] Although it is possible for people and organizations to "buy" additional attention resources through delegation and specialized intelligence units, the organization is still allocating attention to one thing and not another, just as individual attention has to be rationed.

Clearly, there are problems with taking a concept that is best understood at an individual level and applying it to an organization. Organizations are complex social systems that cannot be fully understood when analyzed solely in terms of an aggregation of their individual components. People come and go, but organizations preserve some forms of knowledge, cognitive systems, memory, and intelligence, as well as a capacity to learn and adapt to rapid environmental changes.[11] While organizational attention is fundamentally *embedded* in individuals, it can nevertheless be studied successfully at the group level. Furthermore, we believe that attention comes to be *institutionalized*—that is, a consensus builds around what employees should be paying attention to and how they should be doing so—in organizations. Once institutionalized, corporate attention is more than a mere aggregation of individual attention. Though collective attention might seem somewhat unusual, it actually is a common phenomenon.

Overhead. "When the rate of change outside an organization is greater than the rate of change inside, the end is near."

Jack Welch, quoted in Nick Campbell, "Building Job Security"

Structural Distribution

In short, organizational attention involves rich, parallel processes, whereas individual attention is based on sequential processes. Organizations set up social, economic, and cultural structures, routines, and procedural and communication channels that link organizational members to one another and to the environment. Consequently, the organizations govern the allocation of the decision makers' attention in their decision-making activities. Thus, organizational attention is not a shared activity of a collective mind, but an activity structurally distributed throughout the company's context.[12] Companies learn to allocate attention—marketing will focus on *this* set of issues, the Japan office will think about *those* customers, and Jim in the mailroom *always* plans the parties. A division of labor in organizational attention allows a group of people to pay attention to complex systems in ways that no individual could do alone.

PUNCH-THE-CLOCK PRINCIPLE: **Attention management is not time management.**

One misconception must be dealt with right up front, or it will haunt us through the book. We repeat the principle for emphasis: *Attention management is not time management.*

We know that the field of time management has practically exploded with popularity since the 1960s. Time, like attention, is a limited resource and irretrievable once spent. The current profusion of books, articles, personal planners, and handheld organizers demonstrates the popularity of time management tools. These tools underscore how important it is for us to avoid "wasting time." Many Americans experience frustration if forced to spend time away from desired tasks or a sense of guilt if they use time to relax. Organizations, managers, and employees, however, are seeking to be more *effective*, which requires more than an allocation of time to tasks. Effectiveness is defined as much by what is accomplished, and how, as by when it is accomplished.

Blinding Flash

Certainly, something to which people allot a good deal of time in practice can receive minimal attention. Anyone who has been in school probably knows the feeling of sitting through a lecture for what seems hours on end, while thinking about something totally unrelated. (Since we both teach, we know that a number of our students do this, and we are not surprised: Dating, a forthcoming party, and even lunch can be much more interesting and attention getting than the topics covered in classrooms.) Conversely, a huge amount of effective attention can be given to something in a small amount of time. One blinding flash of insight or a compliment to a coworker may not take much time, but may result in focused attention worth a whole year's worth of work. People truly successful at managing their time may not be very good attention managers. Companies that succeed in the future will be those expert not in time management, but in *attention management*.

> **Companies that succeed in the future will be those expert not in time management, but in *attention management*.**

Compensation Calculus

But, you say, what about the adage "Time is money"? Like all axioms, this one is grounded in truth—or at least in the truth of the twentieth century. During your lifetime, the general rule of business has been that the more time you logged, the more money you made. This simple equation worked very nicely in the industrial age.

The image of Charlie Chaplin hanging off a clock in his classic movie *Modern Times* is perhaps one of the best metaphors for the industrial age. Before the industrial age, people were paid for output produced, not time logged. Output received attention and money because it was scarce. In the Dark Ages, people had a lot more free time (in their relatively short lives) than they had output. A European peasant who produced twelve bushels of wheat could trade his harvest for a new pig, or the reassurance that the baron wouldn't kick him out of his home, sell his children, and marry his wife. A Japanese artisan who forged a nifty new sword could trade it to the samurai for, say, the promise that the samurai wouldn't use it to lop off his head. If you were faster at producing the wheat or sword, and if the quality was the same, all the better. You made even more money. The rub was that if you produced nothing, you received nothing, no matter how much time you logged.

Then came the industrial age, and no longer was one individual responsible for the entire manufacture of a product. In this Adam Smith division-of-labor world, a new compensation calculus had to be devised.

Time became a useful proxy for output. People began punching clocks and were paid for the amount of time they spent on the job, regardless of output. From this grew the seemingly perpetual struggle between labor and management to increase productivity while keeping employees happy. Just as this battle was heating up, along came Henri Fayol and Frederick Taylor, the first management consultants or business gurus. They introduced time and motion studies as a means of procuring more product in a given block of time. Additionally, employees were offered benefits, often in the form of time off—coffee breaks, vacation time, sick pay, maternity leave, and so forth. In the industrial system, the only limiting factor to output was time—if you had enough time, you could produce anything. Our world became all about the clock, and our attention and rewards systems switched to time. We came to measure our financial success in terms of dollars per hour. During this period, business developed the first piecework incentive systems, which rewarded workers for jobs completed within specified time limits.

> In the industrial system, the only limiting factor to output was time—if you had enough time, you could produce anything.

In the current age, the utility of such a system has long since disappeared, although the time-based system has become deeply ingrained in our culture and work practices. Professional service employees still think about their hourly billing rate, and employers still prefer to pay employees by time rather than output, even though this limits both of them in terms of money and output.

Billionaires and Paupers

In this new century, both time and output likely will become less important. After all, what do either time or weight (of output) really have do with this emerging era that has been variously described as the century of Internet time, knowledge capital, or networked commerce? In a world in which speed, knowledge, and creativity are vital, doesn't it seem odd that most of us are still paid for how long we take to complete a job or how much the deliverable weighs, rather than the attention paid to the project?

Now that the "time century" is over, we have begun to formulate a new equation for measuring the worth of workers and their companies—shareholder value. It is an appealing measure because it is relatively simple and is measured "objectively" (at least according to economists). In a free market, investors (just about everyone with a spare dime these days) decide how much value is in all the time input, product output, and everything else in a company; then they pay money to have a stake in the future of the firm. Owners of the company have devised an interesting new reward method for their employees as well—they offer stock options to the workers. Stock options tie compensation to the future worth of the company, so that all the employees are motivated to pay attention to the things on which stockholders are willing to spend money. As long as shareholders pay increasing amounts of money for their pieces of a firm, the stock options are as good as platinum. As soon as shareholders become disappointed in the performance of the company, however, the stock options lose value, turning "paper billionaires" into paupers overnight.

Essentially, analysts of shareholder value try to measure the *quality* or *value* of ideas. Rather than receiving payment for time logged or output generated, employees are now paid for the *usefulness* of their ideas. Already we are beginning to implement this new system. Whether acknowledged or not, many companies retain, promote, and award bonuses to their employees based on their employees' ideas and their ability to implement those brainstorms. And there is always room for ideas, regardless of the type of work an individual is performing. The salesclerk who comes up with a new way to sell shirts should be rewarded for the idea—especially if that new method is passed on to others and improves the firm's overall sales ability.

But quality ideas are not enough. Ideas need to be disseminated throughout the organization so that not only the originator, but all the employees in the company pay attention to the idea and incorporate it into their work. We want every customer to feel the effect of the idea and buy more products or seek more service from our company.

Niggling

For a closer consideration of the relationship between time and attention, let's consider a real-life financial-services technology consulting firm (in the interest of anonymity, we'll call it FinByMe). The leadership of FinByMe wanted to know how the members of the firm collectively and individually divided time and attention—particularly the split between

> Rather than receiving payment for time logged or output generated, employees are now paid for the *usefulness* of their ideas.

innovative technology-development projects and business logistics issues. Employees had complained that too much of their days were wasted on niggling issues (e.g., copying each other on memos, tracking down people inside the client organization with whom they needed to talk, making sure their computers were loaded with the latest versions of the software they were developing). These distractions began to take away from their ability to innovate as effectively as they had in the past. Because the leaders of the firm felt that their key to success was innovation, they wanted to see if this was one group's view or a widely held belief.

Management could have followed the employees around with a stopwatch, or they could have asked them to keep a log of their time for a few days. Instead they went for the easy approach and asked people in the firm to state what percentage of their total time they were devoting to "busy work" versus more creative technology development.

The results showed that FinByMe's team was spending about 6 percent of its total time on "housekeeping" activities versus 20 percent on innovation. Although routine work can perhaps be reduced from 6 percent to 4 percent, it can never be banished completely. Managers figured that things were fine as they were and decided not to take any action. A little later, however, on our recommendation, they went back and surveyed the employees on how much attention they were spending on housekeeping (logistics) and innovation. It turned out that the actual percentages were almost inverse from what the employees had reported earlier: They now showed 18 percent on logistics and 8 percent on innovation and technology development.

Given that attention precedes all motivated action, the prognosis for FinByMe was grim. We figured that the firm was unlikely to maintain a high level of innovative activity by devoting such a small amount of attention to it each day. Management was confused by our findings and even more befuddled when it came to thinking up solutions to an attention deficit in their firm.

Here are some of the solutions we suggested:

- *Create attention agendas.* If our world is not about time anymore, why continue to run our meetings around time? A few enlightened (by our definition) executives have started to work with *attention agendas.* Quite simply, this means taking the total amount of attention you expect your attendees to spend on meeting topics. Considering this amount 100 percent, you then arrange the agenda accordingly. Figure it this way: I want 50 percent of their attention to go to this topic, 30 percent to this topic, 15 percent to the next idea, and 5 percent to the last. Most attention probably will be given to the first and last topics of the meeting. The middle topics of the meeting should be subjects that demand less attention. Manage the meeting by asking participants questions: "Have we given enough attention to this topic?" "How can I get more of your attention on this issue?" "Are we putting enough of our attention toward this to get it accomplished?" Don't assume that, like time, you know where attention is going— you don't! You have to ask questions to understand attention and influence it.

• *Focus attention on novel ideas and their implementation.* Because of our output- and time-based heritage, we tend to think that paying attention to the time we put in and the products we produce will be enough to get the results we want. In today's world, that just isn't the case. As an entrepreneur, you can spend your entire life putting in fifteen-hour days efficiently producing slide rules and, apart from a few novelty items, you are unlikely to sell anything. As an employee, you may be hired to make slide rules (fifteen hours a day with great output); you will be paid for your services until the company goes out of business—which it will. As a consultant, you may spend a year producing a 2,500-page report (in four colors with accompanying PowerPoint presentation) that recommends your client make slide rules. The company that takes your advice will probably end up suing you. But in most cases, you will just be laughed out of the room, acquire a poor reputation, and find yourself clientless. You and the others around you must focus on innovation and implementation. If most of your attention lies outside these two categories all the time, you are doing everyone around you a huge disservice. Reward people for having ideas and for actually implementing those ideas. Drive this notion down to the very lowest levels of your organization. You may no longer be able to exercise "control" as you

---

Innovation and Differentials. "The only way to survive and thrive is by paying attention to new ideas from any source. Look at the engineering slant: differentials make the world go 'round, literally. High pressure at one point in a pipe and a low pressure at another point create a high differential and high fluid flow. Electricity is similar: high difference equals high potential equals high current flow. Knowledge transfer works exactly the same way."

Source: Jane M. Howell and Christopher A. Higgins, "The Impact of Flexible Scheduling on Employee Attendance and Turnover," *Administrative Science Quarterly* 35 (June 1990): 317.

could in a time-based or output-based company, but you'll gain the loyalty of your employees and your customers.

- *Pay for attention.* As employee, contractor, and corporate values evolve, so too must recognition and reward criteria. Managers must try to ascertain where employee attention is going, and reward those who are focusing their mental engagement on the issues that really matter to the success of the organization.

- *Create attention guards.* In the case of FinByMe, one of the most important recommendations we made (and one the company followed with some success) was to make sure that a division of attentional labor would allow people tasked with innovation to concentrate on it more effectively. FinByMe hired an extra assistant to manage the logistics of the firm. This new position took away the other employees' burden of having to remember bits and pieces of logistics issues, and it put the burden, instead, directly on one person. Having been freed from their worries that these issues might somehow fall between the cracks (or the even larger attention drains of "cleanups" after they fell between the cracks), almost everyone in the firm was freer to focus on innovations and creative work.

Companies, both start-ups and multinational empires, are interested in ushering ideas from start to finish in the most efficient way possible. Attention—not time, not ideas (without implementation), not implementation (without ideas), not awareness—is indispensable for that efficiency.

CHAPTER 3

DOING
A NUMBER
ON YOU

THE MEASUREMENT OF ATTENTION

No matter how well informed

or earnest your attempts to manage attention, you can't know how well you're doing or improve your performance—or that of your organization—unless you can measure the results of your efforts. Until the late 1990s, measuring attention has been a rather awkward affair dependent on self-reporting techniques, sound perception, or eye movements. We'll take a look at the early days of attention measurement and the state of the art in attention monitoring.

A Brief History

It should be no surprise that first radio and then the television industry led the way in attention-measuring approaches. If you're paying big bucks for commercial time, you want to know who's listening or watching. Although neither very accurate nor technologically sophisticated, the earliest invention for monitoring attention was the diary. Families selected in samples (called panels) by such firms as Nielsen Media Research dutifully recorded every TV show they watched. But if Sis missed *Lassie* (and more importantly, the commercials surrounding it) because of a telephone call from her boyfriend, her absence probably didn't make it into the diary. Diaries are still used in smaller TV markets and outside the United States. Advertisers in newspapers and magazines also learned—more or less—whether readers were paying attention through diaries.

> In the short run, attention will be much more easily and practically measured through nontechnical self-reporting approaches.

More recently, a few organizations have combined diaries with paging systems to reduce the amount of recording necessary. If your goal is to determine what someone is paying attention to at any given moment, you can beep his or her pager at random intervals and ask the person to record where his or her attention is going. This technique has most frequently been used in psychological research, for example, in the work by psychologist Mihaly Csikszentmihalyi determining when people experience "flow."

Attention measurement took a big step forward with the advent of metering technology, a device invented by A. C. Nielsen. Metering technology took the pencil and paper out of the process. The device attaches to a television set for a panel of households and records when the TV is on and to what channel it is tuned. The data are uploaded daily to Nielsen for aggregation and sale to networks and advertisers. In the United States, metering systems are installed in about twenty thousand households.

Another advance on the monitoring front came when Nielsen introduced the People Meter, an attempt to bring attention monitoring to the level of the individual rather than just the TV. With the People Meter, which is in five thousand U.S. households, each individual in the household is supposed to press a button (on a set-top box or remote control) noting when beginning to watch TV and when ending the viewing session as well. Each household member has his or her own button, and Nielsen tracks everyone's ages and genders. At random intervals a red light flashes on the box, reminding viewers to confirm that they are still present and alive.

The People Meter is undeniably a step forward in monitoring attention, but it has been controversial and is still somewhat primitive. Some

---

Overheard. "How you measure the performance of your managers directly affects the way they act."
John Dearden, "Measuring Profit Center Managers"

advertisers claim that it overstates TV viewing because all that really matters is that the TV is on, not that the "viewers" are actually watching. Nielsen and other firms are working on ways of monitoring attention that provide greater certainty that a certain viewer is in the room, facing the television, and fully attentive to its absorbing content. After all, if Mr. Whipple squeezes the Charmin and no one's looking, it could be argued that the event never really happened. But compared to some other attention-monitoring tools on the horizon, TV attention measurement is in the Dark Ages.

Although better attention-measuring technologies will be broadly available in the future, they're already being explored in laboratories and in limited real settings. The technologies described below will become better understood, cheaper to use, and less obtrusive and will thus be incorporated into many environments in which attention is at a premium. But in the short run, attention will be much more easily and practically measured through nontechnical self-reporting approaches.

"JUST ASK" PRINCIPLE: The most straightforward means of measuring attention is to ask individuals directly.

There are many ways to ask people where their attention is going, from simple to complex. The most commonly used method of measuring attention is time recording—figuring out the number of minutes and hours spent on a task. This is a very crude means of measuring attention, however, and is clearly far more concerned with quantity than quality. Ten seconds of Garry Kasparov's time on a chess move may represent a lot more game-winning attention than ten hours spent by a novice. This is not to say that calculating time is not a useful means of measuring attention, but time and attention are not synonymous, as discussed in chapter 2.

Another way of measuring attention may be *best recall,* simply asking people to write down every topic that has drawn their attention in, say, the past twenty-four hours. Simply completing a best-recall exercise helps managers and employees spot their own errors and excesses in allocating attention. To increase the accuracy of this method, one can simply employ the periodic check-and-record technique. This means stopping at regular

---

Next Step in Measurement: A Leap. As Daryl Simm, head of media at Omnicom, a large ad agency, and a former media executive at Procter & Gamble, put it, "The measurement we use today is very crude. It's an average measurement of the number of viewers watching an individual program that does not even measure the commercial break. When you think about improvements in measuring viewing habits, you think not about incremental changes but great leaps."

Source: Michael Lewis, "Boom Box," *New York Times Magazine,* 13 August 2000, 41.

intervals throughout the day—say every fifteen or twenty minutes—and recording where your attention is directed at that moment. Tedious? Of course it is, but the results are also quite revealing. An additional spin on this technique is having others observe the "subject" and record where they believe his or her attention is directed at the designated intervals.

All these methods can be implemented with minimal effort and can produce enormous benefits. They are not without limitations, however. These methods represent *casual* attention measurements, requiring little training on the part of the subjects or the researchers and no formal instruments. Consequently, the results are subject to interpretation and guesses.

The AttentionScape

We created a tool called the AttentionScape to advance the state of self-reported attention measurement. It assesses—in a more conclusive and rigorous manner than the methods we've described above—how people and organizations allocate their attention. The AttentionScape helps companies diagnose attention distribution problems, determine how the company is directing employees' attention, analyze the attention the company is getting from customers and clients, or complete any task that requires a detailed understanding of attention levels. Essentially, the AttentionScape measures the different types of attention discussed in chapter 2: captive or voluntary, aversion-based or attraction-based, and front-of-mind or back-of-mind. Recall that these attention types can be combined. We often pay captive and voluntary attention, or front-of-mind and attraction-based attention to, say, a task that our boss has given us. Skilled attention managers know how to produce high levels of all six types of attention—sometimes simultaneously, sometimes separately, sometimes without recognizing that they *are* producing these results or even *how* they are doing so. The AttentionScape measures the level and type of attention and explains how to understand and interpret the measurements. This measurement tool, described in the next section, is more rigorous than some of the aforementioned methods and a lot less detailed (and tedious) than other methods described below.

> Skilled attention managers know how to produce high levels of attention—whether simultaneously, separately, or even without recognizing that they are producing these results.

Making the Chart. Want to see how you measure up? Log on to www.attentionscape.net, and test your attention acumen.

Making the List

The first step in using the AttentionScape is to create a list of the items that occupy your attention. If you're interested in looking at your own attention patterns, list everything that has caught your attention in, say, the past twenty-four hours (e.g., three different projects at work, a managerial meeting, an interview with a potential employee, your spouse, your children, your favorite TV show). If, for example, you're using the AttentionScape with your work team, ask participants to enter the names of several issues that you expect are occupying their attention; this will help you determine which ones have a corner on their attention markets, and what types of attention those issues are receiving.

The Test

Once the topics are determined, an AttentionScape participant responds to a set of six statements with answers ranging from "strongly agree" to "strongly disagree." The same six statements are repeated for each item on the AttentionScape. Responding to the sentences shouldn't present much of a challenge to those reared in the age of standardized testing.

Here are the statements:

1. I really concentrated on this, spending quality time on it.

2. I'm excited by this; it is something that makes me happy.

3. I did not feel like I could avoid this; it was necessary or imperative.

4. I might have suffered negative consequences had I not paid attention to this; it was not necessarily positive.

5. This was on my mind, but at a subconscious level; I didn't really have to concentrate on it.

6. I chose to focus on this; it was voluntary.

The Chart

After all the responses have been entered, the AttentionScape program churns out an attractive, full-color attention chart of a respondent's profile (as an example, see exhibit 3-1). Each topic on the list appears as a

---

Overheard. "As far as the laws of mathematics refer to reality, they are not certain; and as far as they are certain, they do not refer to reality."

Albert Einstein, quoted in Jan Emblemsvag and Bert Bras, "Process Thinking—A New Paradigm for Science and Engineering"

circle positioned on a graph. With the AttentionScape, size does matter—the bigger the circle, the more attention that topic is receiving.

The position on the y-axis indicates whether the attention was front-of-mind or back-of-mind. If the attention paid to an item was conscious and deliberate, it will appear on the top half of the chart, whereas something tucked into the back of one's mind will register on the bottom. The x-axis shows the captive or voluntary aspect of the attention: Items that get voluntary attention appear on the right; captive-attention items on the left.

Finally, the level of color of each circle denotes whether that particular topic is getting more attraction-based or aversion-based attention. If someone is focusing on a topic mainly because they are afraid that *not* doing so will bring negative consequences, the circle for that item will be a shade of gray (with white being the most intensely aversion-based). If someone is positively oriented to something they find absolutely fascinating, the circle will be in a shade of green.

Exhibit 3-1: Goode's Chart

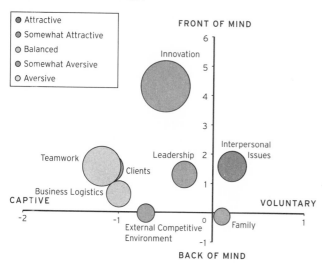

To illustrate the AttentionScape's means of gauging attention, let's take a look at FloppyTech, a high-technology firm whose true identity we will not disclose. FloppyTech executives wanted to know where the attention of their employees and thus the company was directed. They wanted to see whether and how they might make the firm more productive. With the AttentionScape, we showed them the quantity and quality of the attention their employees and company were allocating to various topics.

Working together, the employees and managers decided that they allocated significant amounts of attention to the following items: clients, teamwork, business logistics, leadership, innovation, family, interpersonal relationships at work, and the firm's external competitive environment.

Exhibit 3-1 is a chart from a member of the FloppyTech leadership team whom we will call Shessa Goode. We'll use her as our first example—but remember that aggregated AttentionScapes can yield the same useful information about a group, team, or corporation.

As you can see, each of the items listed in the FloppyTech attention list shows up as a circle on Shessa's AttentionScape chart. The largest share of her attention is going to innovation, an important part of her job. Teamwork runs a distant second, followed by client and interpersonal issues. The minuscule size of Shessa's family circle indicates that a very small portion of her attention actually goes to her family (at least while she's at work).

The colors on Goode's chart indicate that most of her work is motivated by innate interest. Her interest in her interpersonal relationships at work is fairly strong. She focuses mild interest on innovation, clients, leadership, family, and the external competitive environment. Business logistics and teamwork show up light green, which means that Shessa's attention to these topics is balanced between avoiding negative consequences and achieving positive ones.

Almost every item on Shessa Goode's chart appears to the left of center, indicating that Shessa's attention to them is captive—she's focusing because she feels she *has* to. Only family and interpersonal relationships show up as voluntary items. Further, all but two items are in the front-of-mind area on the top of the chart. Even family and the external competitive environment, the two items that make it south of the equator, are only partly back-of-mind.

Thus, we have a picture of Shessa Goode's attention allocation. But how do we interpret this information?

Interpretation

The key to getting useful information from an AttentionScape readout is to remember that the chart is like a bull's-eye target: The most effective attention will go to items that show up near the intersection of the x- and y-axes. In analyzing a layout, the first thing to look for is *imbalance*. Do the items on the chart tend to gather in one area, leaving other areas of the chart embarrassingly naked? In Shessa's case, as we've seen, the answer is yes. Most notably, *all* her attention items appear (at least partially) in the front-of-mind category—none appear to be getting mostly back-of-mind attention. On this dimension, our measures may have a slight bias toward front-of-mind attention. If something is far in the back of someone's mind, but still there nonetheless, then it might not register in the AttentionScape.

Overheard. "If you don't measure it, it won't happen."
Anonymous

Overheard. "One accurate measurement is worth a thousand expert opinions."
Grace Murray Hopper, quoted in Lewis D. Eigen and Jonathan P. Siegel, *The Manager's Book of Quotations*

This means that Goode hasn't been able to "routinize" many aspects of her attention. She goes through her day paying close, conscious attention to almost *everything*, including items like business logistics, which really don't require—or deserve—such a large chunk of her expensive focus. People who keep everything in front-of-mind attention are easily overwhelmed, overworked, and overwrought. (The pathological extreme is a form of schizophrenia; people with this problem are unable to screen out *any* information as unimportant, which makes the noise of the air conditioner or a birdcall outside seem as significant as a discussion with the boss.) Goode's boss needs to find a way to off-load some of her obviously more routine activities, by giving her an assistant to help out, or by helping Shessa realize that some of the "perfectionism" in her work even around mundane activities like business logistics can be completed with more abandon.

> People who keep everything in front-of-mind attention are easily overwhelmed, overworked, and overwrought.

Analyzing the Unbalanced

The box entitled "Correcting Attention Imbalances" delineates the general effect you can expect from the various types of imbalance that may occur in an AttentionScape chart. Remember that the "you" in the descriptions could be either individual or collective—it could refer to you personally, a team you're working with, an entire firm, a group of customers reacting to a sales pitch, or another group.

Individual Items

If you were to map the AttentionScape of someone engaging in an intensely attention-focusing extreme sport, you'd see just one topic (e.g., mountain climbing, skydiving). This topic would be a huge circle, located dead center. Knowing how to get that kind of focus will make you an excellent attention manager. However, being able to direct people's attention isn't going to do you much good if you can't direct it toward the right things.

Attention allocations can also be assessed for a group or an organization by aggregating the AttentionScape scores. For example, let's look at the AttentionScape readout for the combined personnel at FloppyTech (exhibit 3-2). We instructed the computer program to aggregate the scores for the dozen or so individuals whose attention was being measured. For

CORRECTING ATTENTION IMBALANCES

IF YOU FIND that you, your employees, or your company's attention is severely out of balance on an AttentionScape, follow these strategies for correcting the problem.

TOO MUCH . . .

Captive Attention. You feel like a POW. You pay attention, but you resent it. Your devious, subconscious mind is always looking for ways to "escape" by distracting you.

Example: Dinner conversation with your in-laws.

Correction: Use motivational techniques around this issue, remove constraints, replace people who detest a certain job with people who find the task inherently interesting.

Mantra: "I want to, I really, really want to!"

Voluntary Attention. All your attention to a particular item is voluntary, with no captive elements; your ability to stay focused on the item becomes very vulnerable. If "captive attention" items intrude, the voluntary topic vanishes.

Example: Your precious "Give Back to the Community" initiative gets replaced with "more pressing issues" after *Consumer Reports* trashes your company's product.

Correction: Find concrete reasons why an employee must pay attention to this issue; enlist the support of others who will require that employee stick to his or her guns. Alcoholics Anonymous and Weight Watchers groups are examples.

Mantra: "Get thee to a nunnery!"

Back-of-Mind Attention. Your work may be routine to the point of boredom, and you'll probably have a hard time dealing with new data or unexpected occurrences.

Example: Your procurement manager who had developed and perfected the system for "paper-based" buying did not see the Internet coming and doesn't know how to adapt to it now.

Correction: Make the habitual parts of this task more conscious by mixing up the routine and pausing to think about what you really are doing. Teach your task to someone who knows nothing about it.

Mantra: "Once more, with feeling."

Front-of-Mind Attention. You're anxious, stressed-out, and overwhelmed. You dwell on minor details, lose the forest in the trees, and seem absentminded.

Example: When asked why she travels so much, a road warrior executive who has to remember passports, hotel room numbers, and contact names from around the world can't answer why it is necessary for her to be traveling at all.

Correction: Create repetitive systems and procedures. Think about this issue, or participate in this activity often enough that it becomes routine.

Mantra: "An apple a day means you don't have to pay attention to the doctor."

Attractive Attention. You may not fully understand the negative consequences of inaction and, with no negative consequences for misbehavior, your motivation may lag.

Example: After the sinking of the *Titanic*, lifeboat supplies on cruise ships finally started getting as much attention as did the dinner china.

Correction: Add some sticks to the carrots— make this a do-or-die item. Scare yourself with the thought of negative consequences.

Mantra: "When she hit me with the ruler, it made me feel strangely cheerful."

Aversive Attention. Your life is dominated by negative incentives. With a world of sticks and not a carrot in sight, you'll quickly lose interest and motivation.

Example: Another day, another deadline.

Correction: Add some carrots to the sticks. Reward yourself for paying attention to this topic.

Mantra: "I'm going to Disney World!"

FloppyTech, the chart contains good news and bad news. Comparing each item on the AttentionScape against considerations about optimal attention distribution, the team came up with the following conclusions.

Clients

After engaging hundreds of highly paid consultants to conduct an intensive four-year investigation, the FloppyTech leadership team rediscovered a compelling fact—the company's raison d'être was its clients. Building on this concept, the team concluded that clients should also be the main focus of their attention. Happily, the AttentionScape revealed that FloppyTech was generally doing well in this area. The "clients" circle on their AttentionScape turned out to be quite large (meaning that the topic was receiving a good deal of attention) and a light green (meaning that attention to clients was based on a balance of aversion and attraction). The front-of-mind position of the client circle was a good thing too, since client relationships are ever-changing and require a lot of conscious attentiveness. The only real problem with this item was that it lay so far toward the captive side of the diagram. FloppyTech's personnel were paying attention to their clients because they felt they had no choice.

Exhibit 3-2: Good and Bad News for FloppyTech

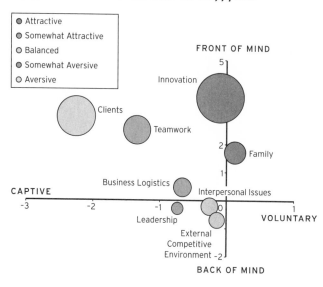

The lesson from this information was that the managers at FloppyTech needed to find ways to make client interaction more appealing. One way to do this was to check individual AttentionScapes to see if some people's interactions with clients showed up as highly voluntary. Then, those people could be given the bulk of the responsibility for client work, whereas people who preferred other activities would lead those activities.

Overheard. "To measure is to know."

James Clerk Maxwell, *Treatise on Electricity and Magnetism*

Overheard. "Whenever parameters can be quantified, it is usually desirable to do so."

Norman Augustine, *Augustine's Laws*

Additionally, FloppyTech decided to create more financial incentives for client interaction and to hold meetings in which consultants who enjoyed client work could share their motivating ideas and techniques with their less enthusiastic coworkers (if that didn't work, FloppyTech planned to hire more consultants).

Innovation

In theory, innovation was the second most important item for FloppyTech employees, although the AttentionScape showed that it commanded more attention than did the employees' attention to clients. Clearly, the team as a whole was more creative and idea-oriented than social and client-oriented. The innovation circle appeared on the chart a vivid green, meaning that FloppyTech person-nel were paying attention to the topic because they were innately interested in it and not afraid of the results should they fail to keep up with cutting-edge ideas. Since creativity tends to be diminished by aversive attention and increased by attraction attention, the team decided that this was OK. Innovation was also very front-of-mind, another good thing when it comes to constantly changing ideas and projects.

> **FloppyTech's personnel were paying attention to their clients because they felt they had no choice.**

After looking at the AttentionScape, the FloppyTech team decided that they needed to redirect some of the attention that was going into inno-vation, so that it flowed instead to client work. They believed that the incentives to increase client involvement (noted above) probably would help. Decreasing slightly the incentives for innovation was a second prong in their approach. After implementing these measures, they planned to run another AttentionScape to see if more tactics were needed.

Teamwork

Teamwork was a big issue for the leadership group, one that received high front-of-mind ratings and mainly captive attention. The medium-green color of the teamwork circle indicated that the FloppyTech group paid attention mainly to the positive effects of functional teams. How-ever, the size of the AttentionScape teamwork circle was something of a

---

Overheard. "All the computer models and fancy forms will quickly lose their appeal (if they had any to begin with) unless top management pays a lot of attention to the results they generate."
Bernard C. Reimann, speech presented at The Planning Forum

Overheard. "Too often people mistake being busy for achieving goals."
Philip D. Harvey and James D. Snyder, "Charities Need a Bottom Line Too"

disappointment to the managers, who feared that they would be outperformed by other corporations. As they discussed the AttentionScape readouts, however, they realized that one reason for diminishing attention to teamwork was that the FloppyTech teams were actually working quite smoothly. They decided to monitor this issue for a while before making any policy changes.

Competitive Environment

The FloppyTech leadership group had decided that attention to the external competitive environment was very important—the fourth most important item on their list. In contrast, the AttentionScape showed that this issue was receiving very little attention, and all of it back-of-mind. The reasons for this reality emerged very quickly from a discussion: No one was specifically assigned or given any incentive to pay attention to the environment. Everyone was supposed to simply "stay aware." In addition, FloppyTech (like any other bureaucracy) had a tendency to become its own little universe.

The group decided to assign small "attention tasks" to put more emphasis on the external environment. People who seemed predisposed to notice environmental conditions would hold a monthly meeting to discuss the latest environmental developments. Every participant would be expected to contribute ideas and information at each meeting.

Leadership

Leadership received less attention than any other issue on the firm's AttentionScape. The team gave leadership attractive attention, but spent almost no mental energy on it. What little focus they did devote to leadership was definitely a "have to," not a "want to." While discussing this issue, the team agreed that their organizational culture gave lip service to developing leadership qualities, but didn't follow through with incentives or recognition. They decided to link leadership to innovation, the big favorite of almost everyone on the team. People who came up with new ideas or procedures would be appointed R&D czars.

Family

The family item was the most voluntary one on the chart, as the FloppyTech team decided it should be. Some members said they'd like to see family issues drop out of front-of-mind and into back-of-mind; others pointed out that this might create personal imbalances that eventually could have negative repercussions at work as well as at home. The family circle was a vivid green, indicating that group members were paying attention to their families because they yielded a lot of positive rewards, not because they were *afraid* that something would go terribly wrong if they didn't.

Logistics

Logistics, universally considered the least important item on the chart, turned out to be receiving far more attention than anyone had anticipated. In a cost-cutting move some months before the managers completed the AttentionScape, FloppyTech had cut most of its office support staff, reasoning that consultants could use new technologies to quickly complete sundry tasks like buying their own airplane tickets, reserving their own hotel rooms, and making their own copies.

The AttentionScape revealed that this assumption was wrong. Business logistics were, in fact, taking up a pretty big chunk of time for even the top-level executives. As a group, FloppyTech people were spending almost as much attention on business logistics as they were on their families—and more than they were allotting to leadership, work relationships, and the external competitive environment. Fortunately, this problem had an obvious, easy fix. The team decided to hire a couple more office assistants, who could take the burden of logistical work and free up the executives for more value-added tasks.

The AttentionScape as a Predictor

To understand if the AttentionScape was a useful tool in predicting or understanding behavior, we (with the help of our colleague Patrick Lynch) decided to study the attention that college students pay to movies. We chose this medium because there is a short fuse to

Lessons from the Movie Study

In the entire movie study, a few lessons stood out:

1. Everyone has an attention sweet spot. Every respondent had a slightly different pattern of attention before seeing a movie. As their self-reported amounts and types of attention moved to this attention sweet spot, they were more likely to go see any given movie.

2. Generally, slightly aversive attention is more likely to result in behavior than attractive attention. Remember, aversive attention means that the respondents are saying to themselves, "If I don't pay attention to this movie, something bad will happen to me." Although the respondents may find one movie less attractive than others, the fear of being left out of the conversation about this movie or being shunned by peers for not seeing a particular movie seems to be a big factor in final behavior.

3. Captive attention is better than only voluntary attention. This was quite a strong correlation to behavior. If respondents felt that a movie's presence was everywhere—"I can't avoid paying attention to it"—they were more likely to go see it. This is probably a combination of advertising, media, and word of mouth that makes a movie unavoidable.

first-run movie attendance. Most movies don't last as long in the theaters as *Titanic* did. Many, in fact, have only a week or two before they disappear from the local scene. Movies are also interesting because in certain populations, particularly young, single people, they are a kind of social capital. It is important to be able to converse about movies, to know what is good and what isn't, to have an opinion. College students use movies as a significant social activity for dating and for more general fraternizing.

Exhibit 3-3: Moviegoer Attention

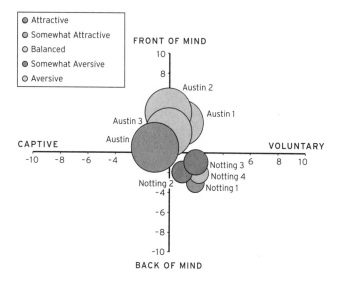

In the summer of 1999, we asked a group of college students to fill out an AttentionScape survey on a daily basis regarding the attention they paid to first-run movies. We also asked them to report when they had actually gone to see a movie. Exhibit 3-3 shows one woman's attention to two movies—*Austin Powers: The Spy Who Shagged Me* and *Notting Hill*—over a four-day period before she saw a movie on the weekend. The numbers with the movie titles signify the attention given a certain movie on a certain day of the survey. For example, the circle labeled "Austin 3" represents the attention she gave the movie *Austin Powers* on the third day of the survey (one day before she saw a movie). Can you guess which movie she finally decided to see?

As you can see, *Notting Hill* gets lots of attractive, voluntary attention. But from the size of the circles, you can also see this respondent is giving *Notting Hill* less attention and less front-of-mind attention than *Austin Powers*. By the day before the respondent actually goes to see one of these movies (on day four), both movies are getting less attractive attention. In fact *Austin Powers* has moved squarely into the "aversive" camp.

In the end, *Austin Powers* wins out. The pattern in this chart is not unlike many others that we studied. Generally, movies for which attention moved into slightly "aversive" and "captive" territory were the ones that the students were most likely to go see.

Overheard. "Things difficult to quantify are inconvenient for analysts to credit."
George Will, "Navy Loses a Warrior"

WIRE 'EM UP PRINCIPLE: **The most accurate and useful attention measurements will ultimately be produced by direct access to physiological phenomena.**

As we (and Peter Drucker) have noted, if you can't measure it, you can't manage it. Let's give this cliché a futuristic twist, one that will provide a segue to the next chapter on attention technologies. Given the increasing economic premium placed on knowing whether the receiver of information is paying attention, we expect that attention-monitoring technologies hold the most promise in delivering accurate and real-time attention measurement.

In the not-too-distant future, attention monitoring will be a feature of most settings in which important information is transmitted. Almost every television and radio programmer will know who's watching and listening. Every automobile will note where your eyes are pointed, and will ensure that they're open. Purveyors of Internet information will know exactly where your attention has gone; even someone who sends you an e-mail message will know not only whether you've read it, but also how long you spent reading it and what you did with it. And any information provider who's serious about how its audience reacts to the information will have done some brain-wave monitoring to see where your attention is really going. But don't worry—you'll be able to turn off all these devices when you want your attention hidden.

> Almost every television and radio programmer will know who's watching and listening.

The Eyes Have It

Attention to visual information is probably best assessed through the eyeball itself and the movements, or lack thereof, of the head in which it resides. If you're supposed to be paying attention to something straight ahead, and your eyes or head are turned to the side, it's a pretty good bet that your attention has strayed as well. If we had little devices that monitored head and eyeball movements, we could have a good indication of whether you are attending to different aspects of the visual field.

The good news is that we do have such devices. The bad news is that they are a bit obtrusive, resembling something you'd wear in an ophthalmologist's exam room. At the moment, they are best confined to the laboratory, where

Overheard. "A new study reveals that sexually transmitted diseases are the leading cause of statistics."
Anonymous

they can measure visual attention in experimental settings. For example, the U.S. Air Force uses these devices extensively to measure "situational awareness"—its term for attention—among pilots. It is very useful to know, for example, whether a pilot can still attend to instruments while flying upside down, or after a couple of barrel rolls. The laboratories employ virtual-reality screens in flight simulators and allow the close monitoring of attention.

Military researchers employ attention monitoring to understand the impact of training and to help in designing cockpit information flows. For example, U.S. Air Force researchers concluded from pilot attention monitoring that there were more instruments in jet cockpits than there was attention to go around. This finding led both to the "heads-up" display of key information on windshields and to the current preference in cockpit design for displaying as much information as possible through one central, computer-like monitor, in both military and commercial aircraft. Military researchers are also focused on how human attention works in the context of virtual-reality simulations, and how personnel allocate attention to new display technologies. For example, a U.S. Army researcher is studying how helmet-mounted information displays affect the soldier's ability to divide his or her attention among competing informational stimuli.

Automobile firms also are concerned with how drivers allocate their attention to visual information; it's bad for business if too many people are gazing intently at their car radio dials when a big truck is crossing the intersection ahead. Several automotive firms, including DaimlerChrysler, General Motors (GM), and Nissan, conduct extensive research on how drivers allocate their attention to objects within and outside the car. At GM, the attention research led to the adoption of the heads-up display. Researchers at DaimlerChrysler are working on technologies that would monitor the driver's attention while he or she is driving; one feature would sound an alarm if the driver's eyes weren't focused straight ahead for too long a time.

At Nissan's Cambridge, Massachusetts, Basic Research organization, researchers are monitoring attention through eye movements for several different purposes. They're trying to understand driver fixation patterns, or how drivers focus their visual attention as the driving situation changes. The researchers are also addressing "The Need for Attention to See Change" (a project name), a key conclusion of which is that "to see an object change, it is necessary to attend to it" (which certainly confirms our own hypotheses).[1] Nissan employs both head- and eye-tracking technology to monitor visual attention.

Computer-oriented researchers are also beginning to monitor eye movement to understand how consumers of computerized information process information on a screen. Some research, for example, suggests that "banner" advertising on Web pages doesn't guarantee that the viewer's attention will be grabbed. Apparently, experienced users' eyes quickly learn how to avert themselves from ads on the screen. Our brains seem to have some built-in attention-protecting features that this attention-monitoring tool has revealed.

Some designers of person–machine interfaces would like your computer to respond not to a keyboard or to a mouse click, but directly to your attention. Microsoft, for example, is working on technologies that would make your PC respond to your eye movements. Screens would be redrawn based on where you're looking. Microsoft researchers call this a perceptual user interface (PUI—we don't think this will catch on as an acronym, but then we didn't think much of "GUI" either).

Similarly, a project at our firm's CSTaR (Center for Strategic Technology Research) is also monitoring attention in order to act on it. The project employs virtual-reality goggles; when the user puts them on and looks at something in a previously mapped visual environment (e.g., the booths of a trade show), a computer inserts labels into the visual field. If you can't find the booth for that tiny little vendor as you look over a crowded convention hall, just put on your goggles.

Brain Waves

As we noted briefly in chapter 2, since attention is a cerebral phenomenon (with only some relationship to external phenomena such as eye movement), the best way to monitor it is directly through capturing and analyzing brain waves. Thus the ultimate in attention-monitoring technology is an approach developed by the National Aeronautics and Space Administration (NASA) and licensed to a company called Capita Research Group. The technology uses conventional electroencephalograms (EEGs) and the NASA technology to analyze the size, shape, and speed of electrical activity in the cognitive sections of the human brain. The brain activity, measured through a special headset, is used to construct an *engagement index*—in the words of the company, "a measure of attention, interest and involvement recorded from the test subjects."

The Capita technology is already being used in several different contexts.

In 1998, for example, it was applied to television viewing and TV advertising. The study, funded by an advertising agency, found that commercials are more likely to be attended to within the context of a TV program that interests the viewer. This was surely reassuring, since the link between program interest and attention to ads forms the basis of ad sales in television. The Capita technology has also revealed that viewers pay more attention to some programs than the shows' low Nielsen ratings would suggest. Presumably a show that had low viewership but high attention would be interesting to some advertisers.

The Capita technology has also been used in contexts outside of television. A company called V2 has linked up with Capita to offer testing of pharmaceutical sales aids and presentations. In this approach, the headsets are donned by a small group of physicians, who are then subjected to various sales materials from pharmaceutical and health-care companies. The brain wave patterns tell the tale of whether the doctors are bored stiff, totally engaged, or somewhere in between for each second of the test information content. In the V2 example, the poor physicians appeared to be flat-lining at the words, "worldwide experience with confirmed efficacy on a wide range of patient types" (and who could blame them?), whereas the phrase "simplifies patients' treatment regimen" got their rapt attention.

> The brain wave patterns tell the tale of whether the doctors are bored stiff, totally engaged, or somewhere in between for each second of the test information content.

Our own brain waves hit new peaks when we thought about the applications of this technology in other contexts. Imagine wiring up focus groups to learn what consumers of information really think of political speeches, the CEO announcing a new mission statement, or the motivational speech by a highly paid guru. (As teachers, we quake at the prospect of our students wired so that someone could determine an "engagement index.") If this technology becomes pervasive, we can count on a much higher level of brain wave activity in measured settings for all of us in the future.

Measurement Settings

The measurement of brain waves and eye movements are powerful ways to measure attention, but the more invasive ones are applied only in certain settings described below. Outside of those settings, self-reported measurement makes much more sense.

Physiological attention measurement has been applied thus far—and will continue to be used—in two major contexts. One is when the lack of attention is life-threatening, as when a person is driving a motor vehicle or flying an airplane. In these situations, it will be a major step forward when attention monitoring moves from the laboratory to the day-to-day driving or piloting experience.

The other critical setting for attention measurement is when information providers must pay for informational messages (e.g., advertising over a medium such as the television and the Internet, which are free to the consumer). In these circumstances, the information provider will want to know who is actually paying attention to the messages, and someone will put forward an attention-measuring technology.

Where the consumer pays for the medium, measuring attention is not generally at issue. If someone buys a book, we either assume that she will actually read it and pay attention to it, or more likely, once we have her money we don't really care. The same idea generally applies to other paid media such as movies, magazines, and newspapers; paid admissions or circulation is taken as a "good enough" proxy for attention. The only time attention measurement is used with a paid medium is when a company wants to allocate eyeball-based revenues, as with America Online. Then the service provider will want to know what information the consumer actually looked at so that it can pay the creator of the information.

Attention measurement, of course, can be intrusive. Thus far, people have measured attention only with the consent of the measured. We hope and expect that this will continue to be the case; you won't have your brain waves monitored, for example, unless you consent to put on a headset. In many cases, just as we increasingly pay for attention, we'll pay for measuring attention at the same time. Even if attention-measuring devices become sufficiently inexpensive and unobtrusive so that they proliferate widely and covertly, new technologies would probably arise to prevent unwanted monitoring.

CHAPTER 4

FROM AMOEBAS TO APES

You cannot train an ape

if you insist on pretending it is really a calculator. Likewise, the first step in effective attention management is to stop insisting that people function "logically," and accept the *bio*logical realities that dominate the human brain. We can learn much from simply accepting the animal nature of our attention psychology.

In the mid-1990s, a group of business academics gathered to analyze and discuss the phenomenon of attention, which they all agreed was becoming more and more important to corporate success. In virtually every panel discussion, the experts concluded that a full understanding of human attention would necessarily begin with facts about its psychological and biological origins. The question, "Is there a psychobiology of attention?" was raised in several panels and speeches, but answered in none.

It turns out that there is indeed a psychobiology of attention, and that understanding its basic origin, structure, and function is an invaluable aid to managing in the attention economy. While most businesspeople hold—and will continue to hold—unarticulated, inaccurate assumptions about attention, those who learn how it truly works will gain a distinct competitive advantage as the age of attention progresses.

Rational Model

The psychobiology of attention may seem an esoteric topic for businesspeople, but every business discipline, from economic forecasting to corporate strategy to marketing, relies on assumptions about this very topic. Many businesspeople have an unexpressed concept of attention that approximates the Enlightenment image of humans as purely individualistic, "rational" beings. In this view, each individual is supposedly motivated by opportunities to maximize his or her material advantage. Accordingly, our attention is captured and held by anything that holds out the promise of some physical reward. In business, this mainly refers to monetary rewards.

This idea has shaped corporations since the Industrial Revolution. It was the concept of human nature assumed by the creators of assembly lines, where individual workers were employed, literally, as cogs in great manufacturing machines. In the late nineteenth and early twentieth centuries, titans of industry and efficiency experts broke production tasks into minute divisions, isolating each small function and assigning it to one worker, who repeated the same actions hour after hour, day after day. At Henry Ford's automobile plants, the aim was to make each job so simple and repetitive that it could be learned within minutes by immigrant workers who spoke no English. Ford, whose legendary secretiveness amounted to genuine paranoia, liked it that way. The workers did not.

Although their initial job satisfaction was high (because of quick training and relatively high wages), assembly-line workers in Ford's factories soon found it intolerable to focus all their attention on endless iterations of one simple task. Few employees stayed at their jobs longer than two years. According to the models of human motivation that dominated academic thinking at this time, the solution to this problem should have been simple: provide higher rewards for workers' attention. Like a pigeon that could be induced to peck a lever thousands of times if rewarded with enough food pellets, human workers were supposed to direct their attention to whatever task promised a big enough material payoff. But the longer the industrial era continued, the less its participants reacted like the predictable machines they were supposed to be.

Worker satisfaction mattered less in manufacturing, where new workers could be quickly hired and trained to replace those who left, than it did in management. The knowledge base and interpersonal skills required in managerial tasks cannot be broken into isolated fragments of repetitive behavior (though efficiency experts certainly tried). The metaphor of the corporation as a huge machine, in which human beings reacted as reliably as particles in a Newtonian universe, simply didn't work. The corporation-as-machine failed, largely because it is almost impossible to fit anyone's attention, whether it's from a customer, an employee, or a CEO, into a purely "rational" framework. Attention is not mechanical, but organic. It is shaped not only by elegant cost-benefit analysis, but by the erratic forces of evolution. Human attention did not emerge to fit the logical calculus of an idealized societal model, but evolved out of the psychobiological realities of an environment that predated civilization by thousands of years.

> **Attention is not mechanical, but organic.**

The Inner Ape

Most of us would like to think of corporations as groups of sophisticated, intelligent, logical people, ranking "a little below the angels" in attitudes and actions. The blunt truth, however, is that any business—in fact, any human group—is basically a troop of apes. Ninety-six percent of our genetic makeup is identical to that of baboons; 97 percent, identical to that of gorillas. Our closest relatives, the chimpanzees, share 98 percent of our genetic code and are more closely related to us than they are to gorillas. It is believed that humans and chimpanzees split off from a common ancestor as little as five million years ago, the blink of an eye in evolutionary terms. The behaviors and reactions coded into our genes developed because they enabled our ancestors to survive and propagate in forests and grasslands, not cubicles and offices, and these evolutionary origins still dominate the way we give, get, and hold attention.

First Intent

Consider how this evolutionarily ancient coded behavior played out in the "people as economic actors" concept that underlay the structure of the nineteenth-century factory. The rational ideal was that if you paid a person well to focus his or her attention on a single task, the person should do it happily and indefinitely. Although we humans will indeed pay attention to anything that helps us survive, *the psychobiological design of our attention allocation is such that we are in a wild, premodern environment.* The idea of focusing on a highly specific, repetitive task to earn money that can be exchanged for food and shelter is a construct of society, and a fairly elaborate one, at that. Aristotle called money a "good of the second intent," meaning that it is worthless unless it can be exchanged for "goods of the first intent," or things we actually use. Over the long run, it is virtually impossible for goods of the second intent to hold our attention over goods of the first intent. Anyone who hopes to manage attention successfully must understand the way our nature prioritizes our mental focus.

> Anyone who hopes to manage attention successfully must understand the way our nature prioritizes our mental focus.

TAP OR BOTTLED PRINCIPLE: **The most important function of attention isn't taking information in, but screening it out.**

We have already discussed how attention is a finite resource; no human being can pay attention to an infinite number of things. Surprisingly, research on the structure and function of attention indicates that this restriction isn't because of a limitation on our ability to perceive information. Our brains have amazing receptive capacity. We observe millions of "bits" of data, with all our senses, simultaneously. In fact, we can observe far too much for our own good.

The problem is that we can only perform one or two *actions* at a time. We can direct our eyes in only one direction, reach for only one point in space, and run along only one course at a time. For this reason, we (along with other animals) have evolved what researchers call a *bottleneck* in our ability to focus on information. The bottleneck allows very limited information to become conscious at any given moment. It also creates a delay function (known as the Hicks effect after the psychologist who discovered it), so that if we see two things in quick succession, we take longer to focus on the second item. In fact, if the second stimulus appears too soon after the first, we may not become aware of it at all. This is not a flaw in our brains, but a highly successful adaptive trait, selected by evolutionary pressures. It thus appears that *the most important function of attention isn't taking information in, but screening it out.*

Information Jams

The ability to ignore almost everything in favor of a clear, narrow attention focus is obviously useful to any animal in the wild. A hunting predator may see a whole herd of deer, but to make a kill, it must focus on just one target. This is why many prey animals, from fish to fowl, evolved herd behavior in the first place. Far from giving the predator an easy opportunity, the overwhelming abundance of similar animals swamps the attention-limiting capacity of the predator's brain. Too much similar information jams the predator's attention bottleneck, so that it loses the capacity for *any* clear, effective action.

Think about the implications of this phenomenon in a business environment. An executive who tries to capture the attention of customers or coworkers by flooding them with e-mails, phone messages, or direct-mail letters is actually creating the conditions that disperse attention and paralyze action. The flood of information washing across executive desks is not only immense, but monotonously similar. A "herd" of fifty virtually identical memos is almost guaranteed to jam the reader's attention bottleneck. Each additional voice-mail message makes it more difficult for the listener to focus on any single bit of information. It would be far more effective to send one very unusual message than a thousand typical ones.

Demanding that people "Pay attention!" in the face of such an information flood is no solution to the problem because this feat is often beyond our conscious control. The brain's attention bottleneck operates at a *pre-conscious* level. Without our being aware of it, we consider an enormous amount of the information in our environment, weigh the evidence, and decide which issues deserve our attention. Only then does the brain allow selected information into consciousness. For example, subjects who are asked to focus on a spoken or written word will generally not perceive other words flashed briefly across the visual or auditory field. They don't simply ignore the extraneous words, they literally *do not perceive* them. The more focused they are on the target word, the more the subjects display this "inattentional blindness."

Even if inattentional blindness means that we miss a good deal of what happens around us, it seems to bode well for our ability to stay focused on a single task. We should be able to home in on a particular job to the exclusion of all else, the way assembly-line workers were supposed to do. The problem is that we—at least our conscious minds—don't control what manages to get through the attention bottleneck and into awareness. For example, if you take one of the attentional-blindness subjects of the afore-mentioned experiment and flash the subject's own name across the perceptual field, he or she is likely to spot it immediately and lose track of the other word. (This quick recognition of the very familiar is known as the cocktail-party phenomenon. Most people are familiar with the way their attention can be pulled away from a conversation in a crowded room if they hear their names spoken somewhere else.)

Search Image

Obviously, the brain has priorities about attention allocation, and we don't choose them according to good intentions or corporate policies. To some extent, we can tell ourselves to focus on certain subsets of information, and go "attentionally blind" to others. For example, if you were looking for your favorite brand of shampoo on a grocery-store shelf, you would actually "set" your attention bottleneck to screen out bottles that look different from your favorite brand, as though you were programming a computer to notice bottles that matched certain specifications. You wouldn't have to carefully scrutinize every bottle on the shelf (unless all the bottles were visually very similar). You'd let your eyes scan the shelf, paying little attention to most of the shampoo, zeroing in quickly on the one you wanted. The mental operation that allows for this efficient allocation of attention is called a *search image*, which almost all higher animals seem to use. They scan their environments for the particular sight, scent, sound, texture, or taste that says "Food!" or "Danger!" Anything that matches the specifications gets full attention, whereas other images fade into the background or never make it into conscious awareness at all.

> We are actually *unable* to focus on something relatively unimportant to survival when a clear and present threat to our safety comes onto the scene.

Your own conscious control of your attention bottleneck, however, is still subordinate to the brain's built-in priority system. If, as you were searching for shampoo, you suddenly saw a threatening stranger walking toward you down the grocery-store aisle and waving a gun, you would not "go blind" to the intruder—no matter how strenuously you tried to keep your focus on the shampoo. You'd forget all about shopping and pay full attention to the gun-toting stranger. If you didn't, most people would say you were unusual to the point of insanity. The bottleneck that shapes our attention evolved by directing our mental focus toward whatever was most likely to help us survive and propagate in a natural setting. This means that we are actually *unable* to focus on something relatively unimportant to survival when a clear and present threat to our safety comes onto the scene.

SURVIVAL PRINCIPLE: **We pay the closest attention to things that would be most useful to the survival and propagation of the species; once these are satisfied, our attention flows to less pressing matters.**

The priority structure by which the brain determines which information will get through the bottleneck is similar to the hierarchy of human needs described by Abraham Maslow in the 1950s.[1] Other psychologists have created variations on the same theme, but the general consensus is that some needs take priority over others, with physical survival needs topping the list. Only after these needs have been met will the brain turn its attention to needs like social connection; only after social needs have been met will attention go to abstract learning; only then will we turn to aesthetic expression; and so on.

In evolutionary terms, the attention priorities that dominate our genetic code are those that allowed our ancestors to survive and breed successfully: finding food, avoiding predators, mating, caring for young. Since we humans are a highly social species whose young are helpless for a long time after birth, our inherited survival-and-propagation equipment also includes powerful drives toward certain social factors, which we will consider in more detail later on. On its most fundamental biological level, a brain is not rational, but is primed to pay first-order attention to things that would be useful to primitive cave dwellers or hunter-gatherers.

For example, automobile drivers generally instruct their brains to pay attention to their location on the road, the relationship between the way the car moves and the feel of the steering wheel, the relative positions and trajectories of other cars, pedestrians, and so on. Drivers may also be focused on the destination they are trying to reach. All of this is quite logical. It is not so logical that traffic invariably slows near the site of an accident, because most drivers can't resist paying enormous attention to the wreckage as they go by it. This is especially true if someone has been hurt in

---

Schadenfreude. German for "harm" plus "joy," *Schadenfreude* describes a psychological state in which we take joy in the suffering of others. It has its origins in the peculiarly Teutonic combination of aversion-based and attraction-based attention. Seen any good car wrecks lately?

the accident. Though most of us would be reluctant to admit it, we find death and carnage horribly fascinating, so much so that it hijacks at least part of our attention away from driving.

Homicide

The fascination with catastrophe exists in all human cultures. Perhaps focusing intense attention on various forms of violent death is an attempt to learn how to avoid ending up in a similar predicament. Whatever the reason, lengthy, detailed stories of deadly battles, fatal accidents, and executions are prime attention grabbers in every society. We are similarly fascinated by the subject of murder; if you were to judge by the number of television dramas, movies, and books that center on homicide, you would think that it far outstripped every other cause of death in the real world. Large predators also get our rapt attention, even though they no longer represent the slightest threat to the vast majority of us. People who have never so much as visited the beach are riveted by movies like *Jaws* or *Lake Placid*, in which enraged animals tear victims to shreds.

Put a pit viper into a conference room, and even the most committed manager on the scene would immediately stop focusing any attention on the bottom line, and pay undivided attention to the snake. All primates, from lemurs to humans, are biologically programmed to focus on snakes in this way. Most species have a distinct snake call, a sound they make only when a serpent is spotted nearby. The response to this call is not to run away, but to gather near the snake and watch it with utter fascination until it goes away. Sociobiologist E. O. Wilson notes that all human children over the age of five, in every culture studied, have this reaction to snakes. He hypothesizes that this may be the reason snakes play a pivotal role in many cultural myths, like Eden's serpent in the Judeo-Christian tradition.[2] Like accidents and predators, snakes loom large in our built-in attention priorities.

The Power of the Wild. The power of death and mayhem to grab our attention far exceeds any conscious attempt to keep our minds on "goods of the second intent." Long-term financial planning will be bumped right out of the attention bottleneck by the intrusion of, say, a deadly wild animal. Consider the following quotation, from humor columnist Dave Barry's parody of a business letter:

Dear Mr. Blenther,

It has come to our attention that you failed to respond to our invoices of February 16, February 28, and March 8, and that when we sent Miss Bleemer around to discuss the matter with you, you locked her in a conference room with a snake.

Most readers find the letter amusing precisely because snakes grab our attention much more dramatically than do business interactions.

All of this jibes with what savvy advertisers have always intuited about the best ways to capture a human's attention: Don't think logically, think biologically. You can make roughly accurate predictions about human attention patterns by figuring out where a given data bit might fall on Maslow's hierarchy (exhibit 4-1). Anything that would allow an early human to avoid danger, live longer, and have more children, and anything that would assure that those children survived until they were able to reproduce themselves, is going to get through the attention bottleneck, shoving less crucial information out of consciousness.

Exhibit 4-1 lists some topics that might cross an average person's perceptual field on any given day. According to Maslow's hierarchy, the issues associated with the more basic levels of need would co-opt attention from less essential levels. Items that might get *aversive* attention ("Danger! Bad! Stay away!") are on the left; those that might be seen as *attractive* ("Safety! Nourishment! Reproduction!") are on the right. Note that an item will get attention whether it's attractive or aversive, as long as it falls at a basic level on the hierarchy of needs.

Bread, Sex, Tsunami

A comparison of exhibit 4-1 with, for example, the topics of the most successful motion pictures now playing, or the most appealing advertising on television, will show that the attention-as-evolutionary-advantage model holds up fairly well. Food, sex, children, and health are surefire attention grabbers. So are natural disasters, freakishly bad weather, threat from hostile enemies, and other "safety needs."

Exhibit 4-1: Maslow's (Attention) Hierarchy

Psychological Needs (Survival and Reproduction)

Aversive Attention	*Attractive Attention*
Hunger and thirst	Food and water
Sexual rejection	Sexual activity
Any threat to one's children	Caring for children
Disease	Good health

Safety Needs

Aversive Attention	*Attractive Attention*
Suspicious strangers	Trusted friends and family
Weapons (other people's)	Weapons (one's own)
Bad weather (hurricanes, blizzards)	Shelter from the elements
Natural disasters (fire, earthquake)	Resources to cope with disaster

"Belongingness" and Love Needs

Aversive Attention	*Attractive Attention*
Loneliness	Intimacy
Ostracism	Popularity
Disagreement	Consensus
Cruelty	Kindness

Esteem Needs

Aversive Attention	*Attractive Attention*
Subordination to others	Authority over others
Captivity	Freedom
Low rank	High rank
Bad reputation	Good reputation

Need to Know and Understand

Aversive Attention	*Attractive Attention*
Boring or repetitive facts	New or interesting facts
Information about unknown	Information about self
Incorrect information	Accurate information
Lies	Truth

Aesthetic Needs

Aversive Attention	*Attractive Attention*
Ugly objects	Beautiful objects
Traffic noise	Music
Tasteless food	Haute cuisine
Bad fashion sense	Stylishness

Self-Actualization

Aversive Attention	*Attractive Attention*
Ignoring personal potential	Developing talents
Refusing to go out	Seeking adventures
Fearing new ideas	Expanding mind
Clinging to social labels	Defining individual identity

Transcendence

Aversive Attention	*Attractive Attention*
Unethical behavior	Ethical behavior
Massive inner conflict	Perfect inner peace
Self-destruction	Personal enlightenment

Note: The usual "pyramid of needs" is reversed here, so that the most basic needs are shown at the top, instead of the bottom.

This kind of issue is likely to override most people's attention when compared to topics like artistic nuance, ethics, or personal enlightenment—even though these things may be immensely important to someone whose more basic needs are all being met.

Does this mean that to manage attention, businesspeople should start centering all interactions around their associates' interest in sex, violence, and food? Not necessarily—though we're not ruling it out. Marketers, salespeople, advertisers, media producers, and others responsible for gaining consumers' attention may want to spend their whole careers appealing to these basic interests. At the other end of the spectrum, it's quite possible to motivate groups of scientists to focus intensely on learning esoteric facts just for the joy of it. Many executives focus considerable attention on purely philanthropic tasks, motivated by their ethical sensibilities and need for self-actualization. These people have met virtually all the needs on the low rungs of Maslow's hierarchy, so that their attention is focused entirely on the most rarefied, final steps.

> Most managers in any organization will find that a frustratingly high percentage of their employees' attention goes to political scheming, brooding, arguing, and gossiping.

The most typical situation in a business organization, however, is one concerning people whose survival and safety needs are being met, but who aren't yet fully confident on the next levels—the so-called belongingness and esteem needs. These people have stopped thinking in terms of merely keeping themselves and their children alive, which is the reason they took jobs in the first place. Once hired, they quickly become preoccupied with the interplay of human relationships in the organization, and their individual places in the prestige rankings. This is why most managers in any organization will find that a frustratingly high percentage of their employees' attention goes to political scheming, brooding, arguing, and gossiping. We'll call this domain *social attention*.

BEEHIVE PRINCIPLE: **Highly social humans pay enormous amounts of attention—sometimes too much—to social factors.**

When a foreign immigrant took a job at Henry Ford's Model T factory, he was likely thrilled to get a decent wage for a simple job in a new and unfamiliar country. His attention was fully absorbed by survival and safety needs, and that was enough to keep his mind focused on the monotonous work—for a while. As soon as his basic needs were being reliably met, the line worker's unruly brain would begin switching his attention to issues like his social status (low), organizational rank (rock bottom), and level of job autonomy (near zero). Though such a man might have earnestly tried to keep his attention on the work, which was, after all, feeding his family, he probably could not help focusing on the negative aspects of his social position. This, in turn, would have had a disastrous effect on his well-being—not just mentally, but biologically.

Rank Stress

That people suffered stress as a result of their job rank was dramatically demonstrated in a famous long-term study of British civil servants, conducted by Michael Marmot in 1958. Marmot's research showed that the rank of a worker's job was more predictive of stress-related illness and death than any other variables, including obesity, smoking, and high blood pressure. Several other large-scale, long-term studies yielded the same conclusions in the United States. Low rank and lack of autonomy lead to astronomical increases in physiological markers of stress. In other words, no matter how much a factory line worker is being paid, the person's lack of status or self-direction may prove literally deadly. No wonder so many employees, in so many firms, spend so much time brooding about turf wars and power plays. Whatever logic may say to the contrary, biology tells us that these issues are surpassed only by survival and reproductive issues in the attention that they warrant.

> No matter how much a factory line worker is being paid, the person's lack of status or self-direction may prove literally deadly.

We humans pay attention to rank, again because we are social primates. Our apish ancestors survived by banding together, and the higher-ranking members of each band survived longer, bred more frequently, and so passed on their genetic behavioral code. And who were the higher-ranking members? They were the individuals who spent the majority of their time asserting dominance or cementing alliances. Attention to tasks was probably a secondary issue: Preoccupation with social interaction spelled evolutionary success.

This dynamic has been observed over and over in wild primate groups. One long-term study of baboons, for example, showed that an ape could ensure access to the best food and mates in two ways. One was to exercise power over weaker, less aggressive individuals. The other was to make a lot of friends. (The research scientists used this term literally, not metaphorically or anthropomorphically. Baboon friendships are very much like human ones: Friends will protect each other, share food, offer comfort in times of stress, and help care for sick or injured buddies.) Baboons who didn't manage either of these strategies—the seizing of power or the making of friends—suffered from heart disease, ulcers, chronic respiratory infections, a lowered immune response, and many other health conditions we associate with "executive burnout." These less social or less powerful baboons had a higher mortality rate and left fewer offspring than more social or powerful baboons. In other words, evolutionary pressures are even now producing baboons who pay more and more attention to issues of rank and belonging.

Laid-Back

Anyone who has spent more than a week in a corporate job knows that jockeying for power and building useful friendships are as important to businesspeople as these activities are to baboons. Among both groups, aggressive, dominant types storm up the status ladder, stepping on others' toes or heads if necessary. (A word of caution: Baboon leaders who come to power this way are generally tormented by younger baboons as soon as the dominant ape's physical strength begins to decline.) More laid-back individuals are likely to spend a lot of time around the water hole or watercooler—take your pick—establishing rapport and creating informal alliances. Those who are ousted from high-ranking positions may become depressed, brooding, and hostile. Some may even leave the organization (troop), though they have trouble gaining access or acceptance in any other group after midlife.

In business settings, almost the only thing that humans do that other social primates don't do is business. Organizational behavior enthusiasts, impressed by the type of research we've just mentioned, sometimes suggest that since humans are such intensely social beings, virtually *all* organizational attention should go to the personnel issues. After all, this is how most ape troops operate. On the other hand, few baboon groups manage to design, manufacture, and sell a decent automobile. Seeking social rank and affiliation is the ultimate goal on the African savanna; for a baboon, relationship orientation and task orientation are the same thing. This is not true for most businesspeople.

Multitasking Mirage. Research conducted in British textile mills in the early 1950s by Benson and Cox dealt with the relationship between productivity and attending to several tasks at once. They deflated the idealistic argument (one that many today take for granted) that workers can successfully multitask.

F. Benson, "Further Notes on the Productivity of Machines Requiring Attention at Random Intervals," *Journal of the Royal Statistical Society* 14, no. 2 (1952): 200–210.

A Sacrilege Summary

The challenge for today's managers is to use their knowledge of attention to maximize productivity in any number of tasks for which human beings are rather poorly designed. The industrial-era approach is ineffective because it ignores the way that attention works; the industrial-era view is that human beings will focus on any task for a simple reward. The strategy of the information age—deluging every individual with enormous amounts of information—is wildly counterproductive, overloading workers' built-in attention bottleneck and thwarting productivity. In the "attention economy," managers must recognize and accept the effect of human biology on attention. But they must also work with that knowledge to draw as much attention as possible to tasks that make companies productive. Our more frustrated or sacrilegious readers might want to define attention management as "the process required to convince a bunch of apes to build a car."

Primate Training

Bio-logic tells us that it would be futile to simply insist that employees stop thinking about interoffice rivalries, turf battles, and the various weaknesses of their corporate superiors—we all evolved with attention priority systems that put these issues at the front and center of our minds. Bio-logic also tells us that ruthlessly dominating or micromanaging our subordinates, though possibly effective in the short term, almost certainly will focus workers' attention on reasserting their own dominance and "deposing the dictator." Likewise, negotiators who try to shame or bully other parties into agreements will pull everyone's attention away from the matter at hand, creating small wars between conflicting personalities and reputations.

On the positive side, accepting the psychobiology of attention puts managers in a position to find the most powerful attention motivators, many of which you will find in this book. For instance, the "apes" who have the most genuine, mutually satisfying interpersonal connections are in the best possible position to direct others' attention wherever it needs to go.

Ape Behavior

If someone's attention is wandering, and you want it, psychobiology tells you to try the following:

1. Offer very few pieces of information at a time.

2. Make your bid for attention as different as possible from anything around it.

3. Address the most basic needs possible (try holding a snake as you give your presentation).

4. Remember that all the people around you are looking for acceptance, autonomy, and admiration before they orient their attention toward a task.

Some managers have always appealed to the animal side of management. Consider the mission statement of Nike: "To experience the emotion of competition, winning, and crushing competitors." Although this is a thoroughly human sentiment, it also describes a sensation that chimpanzees and gorillas know and love. On a lighter note, we primates love play and group coherence. This may explain why companies like Southwest Airlines, or the California consulting company Playfair, can keep employee morale high despite modest compensation packages. Matt Weinstein, founder of Playfair (his official title is "Emperor") concentrates on keeping employees in a warm, inviting, and creative environment. He realizes that these conditions are even more effective than money when it comes to enhancing worker creativity and innovative thinking, which require extended and intense attention.

IT'S-ALL-ABOUT-ME PRINCIPLE: Narcissism is a powerful factor in focusing individual attention.

One way in which humans differ from other primates in their attention psychology is the glorification of the self. Sure, apes can be caught grooming themselves in the mirror, but no species compares to *Homo sapiens* in the importance of me, me, me. Perhaps this was always true, but we'd argue that humans have become increasingly narcissistic in recent years. So does sociologist Charles Derber, in an interesting book called *The Pursuit of Attention*.[3] Derber feels passionately that mass culture and consumer capitalism have led to an inordinate desire for individual-level attention. In his view, this is a highly destructive trait. We can't even carry on a decent conversation anymore, he argues, because people only want to talk about themselves. (But enough of his views; what do we think about the issue?)

> Apes can be caught grooming themselves in the mirror, but no species compares to *Homo sapiens* in the importance of me, me, me.

Derber is undoubtedly right that people are narcissistic, and probably right that it's destructive. But we're both realists, not social critics. How can an enterprising individual take advantage of the narcissistic nature of his or her peers?

The answer is somewhat paradoxical. If you want to get any attention, you've got to give attention. To get a person to pay attention to your information, the information has to be about that person. As much as possible, the theme has to be, What's in it for me? How does this information tell me what I need to know? How is it tailored to my situation? If a message sheds new light on that most fascinating of subjects—me—then I will probably find it fascinating.

The strong move toward personalization in Internet marketing is largely about such narcissism. So is the move to local news in television, radio, and print journalism. So is the proliferation of highly specialized cable channel content. As much as possible, organizations try to create personalized information without using human attention to create it. So-called one-to-one marketing, collaborative filtering, and the many "My . . ." offerings (MyYahoo!, MySAP.com, etc.) all employ computer-based techniques to personalize communications. The question is whether the information receiver is truly fooled by the automated individualism. We suspect that what humans really appreciate is attention from humans, not computers.

Of course, all this works on the individual level. If you want to get the attention of your coworkers or fellow party guests and want the reputation as a fascinating conversationalist, ask them a lot of questions about themselves. Plead with them to tell you their life stories or to retell the scintillating tales of their vacations. You'll get a lot of attention, but you may tire of it.

> **What humans really appreciate is attention from humans, not computers.**

MINDFUL MANAGER PRINCIPLE: Incorporate Eastern meditation wisdom into your attention management regime.

In addition to displaying narcissism, humans are the only species to deliberately train and control attention. Because the image of the rational, materially motivated worker was so dominant in Western thought, few modern Westerners have tried to harness attention by any means other than the carrot-and-stick motivational methods used in Model T factories. Other cultures, however, have spent centuries considering the nature of attention and how to manage it. Moving from the ridiculous to the

---

I Did Inhale. "[T]he meditating brain is in a quiet, but active state. A noise or sensation creates an 'overshoot'—a massive surge of chemicals are released in the brain: acetylcholine and glutamate, dopamine, norepinephrine and serotonin. These chemicals have a cascade effect on the rest of the brain: first they inhibit gabba nerve cells. Gabba nerve cells normally inhibit networks in the front and inner part of the brain that deal with attention and association formation. If the gabba nerve cells are knocked out, these networks are no longer inhibited and are capable of responding in an unusual way, creating the sensation of enlightenment or kensho-satori."

Source: James Austin, quoted in Sanjida O'Connell, "I Think, Therefore I Am Warm," *Guardian* (London), 3 June 1999.

sublime, let us consider a few lessons on the bio-logic of attention that come from venerable, sophisticated traditions.

Asians who practice the meditative and yogic disciplines, such as those characteristic of Buddhism and Hinduism, began analyzing and "researching" the details of attention management millennia ago. Consider this story about a Zen master who lived in China during the fourteenth and fifteenth centuries.

> [A] student said to Master Ichu, "Please write for me something of great wisdom." Master Ichu picked up a brush and wrote one word: "Attention." The student said, "Is that all?" The master wrote, "Attention. Attention." The student became irritable. "That doesn't seem profound or subtle to me." In response, Master Ichu wrote simply, "Attention. Attention. Attention."[4]

This story, like most Zen koans, makes very little sense to people who are not Buddhist devotees. It refers to the discipline of calming and focusing the mind, a process that forms the center of much Asian religious practice. Meditators try to focus all their attention on something like their own breathing, a repeated word, or a visual symbol such as a candle flame. This state of mind is sometimes called "one-pointedness," and maintaining it is said to be incredibly difficult. The brain, which some Buddhists refer to as the "monkey mind," is constantly hijacking the narrow bottleneck that chooses which information filters into consciousness. The meditator's attention wanders off into observations, plans, memories, anxieties, and a host of other issues.

Crate Training

The way to deal with diversion of attention, meditation masters tell us, is to repeatedly *notice* that one's attention has wandered, and then *refocus* on the "one point." It is this noticing and returning, not the absolute (and always futile) insistence on sustaining full, unwavering focus, that allows practitioners to manage their attention. The process is often compared to training a young animal, one that forgets what it is supposed to do and wanders away very easily (hardly the Enlightenment philosopher's view of the mind, but much closer to the truth of human nature). The good attention manager expects this wandering and does not overreact to it but, at the same time, consistently returns attention to the intended target.

Zen students are expected to focus their full attention not only during meditation, but as they go about their daily work. Their attention is supposed to be absolutely task-oriented, since it is the conscious execution of ordinary tasks that leads to fulfillment and sophisticated understanding. The essence of Zen is said to consist of acts like "chopping wood and carrying water," as long as these are carried out with undivided focus. "What tools do we need to use?" wrote a modern Buddhist teacher, "Only one. We've all heard of it, yet we use it very seldom. It's called attention."[5]

Because they are very pragmatic and designed to deal with attention as it really is, rather than as we might wish it to be, sacred Eastern attention-management processes carry over remarkably well into completely different contexts. Businesspeople who remember that every human brain is mainly a "monkey mind" are ahead of others right off the mark. Those who learn to notice their own attention wandering and who learn to refocus it have already begun the self-discipline of managing their attention. Every time they return attention to the task at hand, they gain more mastery of their own mental focus. This, in turn, puts them in a position to understand how to help others direct their own attention: by allowing time and space for the inevitable distractions, then gently but firmly (and at first, often) directing the focus back to productive activity.

> **Businesspeople who remember that every human brain is mainly a "monkey mind" are ahead of others right off the mark.**

Some of the best-known Western psychologists who study attention have turned to the ancient Asian meditation traditions for vocabulary and concepts necessary for describing the effective training and use of attention. Psychologist Ellen Langer brought into the argot of Western psychology the term *mindfulness*, as good a word as any to describe the modus operandi of a good attention manager.[6] Brute force, unctuous praise, financial incentives, lectures, promises, New Year's resolutions—all these will fail to control the obstreperous attention shifting that comes from the bio-logic of evolution. Nature has given us an incredibly subtle and useful instrument in our capacity to pay attention. Working with that nature, rather than trying to deny or change it, is the way to succeed in the business world of the attention economy.

snoitaiveD

Deviations from well-known stimuli, such as words spelled backwards, attract attention. Experiments on a well-known Dutch coffee's packaging suggest a positive relation between the attention that a package gets and the degree of deviation in its appearance. But how do you prevent confusion or preserve brand identity? A trade-off has to be made between (1) the high attention-getting value of the discrepant stimuli and (2) the brain's capacity to identify and categorize the new stimuli.

Source: Jan Schoormans and Henry Robben, "The Effect of New Package Design on Product Attention, Categorization and Evaluation," *Journal of Economic Psychology* 18 (April 1997): 271-287.

CHAPTER 5

LUDDITES BEWARE

ATTENTION TECHNOLOGIES

When it comes to information

technology, most organizations have taken a hair-of-the-dog-that-bit-you approach. Just as alcohol consumption causes hangovers, the widespread use of technology certainly contributes to the information glut and resulting attention deficit. The question is, can technology cure an information hangover and help solve the problem it helped create? We think so, although the cure must go far beyond the "intelligent agents" that have been discussed—but not made useful—for decades.

In this section we'll describe three different types of attention technologies: attention-getting, attention-structuring, and attention-protecting technologies. For the most part, we'll describe applications of familiar information technologies involving hardware, software, and telecommunications.

All attention-oriented technologies, however, need not be plugged into a wall outlet to function. We'll also describe noncomputational tools and other artifacts (like books, catalogs, television, and movies) that have long had a hold on our attention.

COLD WAR PRINCIPLE: Information technology has been used to get attention for years, but it can lead to an unproductive "arms race."

Using technology to bump up the attention levels received by information is an old trick with ever-changing wrinkles. The world is now full of attention-getting technologies that assault all the senses except smell and taste—and these two senses probably will be exploited shortly.

If I call you on the telephone, the ring begs for your attention. Or perhaps I'll page you and buzz your beltline. We're all too familiar with the attention-getting tricks of television and radio—from bumping up the volume during commercials to sound-bite teasers. "How'd the Red Sox do in the World Series? Highlights at eleven!" Visually, from large type to color to clip art to moving images, we've gotten very sophisticated at bidding for attention. Remember when all we had to do to get attention for a presentation was to put a larger-typeface, capitals-only ball on the IBM Selectric? (For trivia buffs, the name of that typeface was Orator.) We've come a long way in the last couple decades with attention-getting technologies.

The problem, of course, is that these technologies instigate a never-ending arms race. The standard for what's attention getting is always being raised; what was dazzling yesterday is boring today. At one point, inserting into your presentation some clip art of a cute cartoon duck bashing a computer with a sledgehammer (conveniently supplied in the PowerPoint art repository) could get your audience's rapt attention, and a few chuckles besides. Now, every person with a computer has the same goofy clips for a presentation, along with the same artful backgrounds, the same (formerly) unusual fonts, and the same snazzy transitions between slides. If you're talking about newsletters, everybody's got the same crisp, PageMaker-supplied, multicolumn formats.

An E-Nose That Knows. DigiScents, an Oakland, California-based company, is perfecting the wayward "Scratch 'n' Sniff" and "Smellovision" concepts of the 1950s through computer technology. The company, founded in February 1999, has been encoding smells and developing its prototype hardware sniffer ever since. DigiScents plans to offer a hardware scent player, called iSmell, that will have applications for anything from video games and shopping sites to test-marketing candies.

Source: Ethan Smith, "Smells and Whistles," *Industry Standard*, 2 October 2000; Alice Hill, "Follow Your Nose," *Industry Standard*, 9 October 2000.

Even video is becoming a commodity. One of us received a videotaped summary of the class year when his son graduated from the fourth grade. The tape came complete with every conceivable type of wipe or dissolve between scenes, moving titles coming from every direction, and appropriate Top 40 tunes as background music. If a fourth-grade teacher can do this all by herself (granted, she's a sophisticated example of the genre), most savvy businesspeople should be able to master it.

Play or Drop Out

So what should the attention-conscious manager or employee do to compete in this rat race? Only two options are truly viable. One is to play a new game entirely. Forget technology altogether, and try to attract attention in some other way. Stand up before your audience, and simply tell a good story. Get your six-year-old to prepare your transparencies using a crayon (John Seely Brown, the chief scientist for Xerox and head of its Palo Alto Research Center, has done something similar: He has digitized his wife's neat handwriting and line drawings, so that his PowerPoint presentations all look hand-drawn). Hire a harpist to play softly in the background as you deliver your strategic plan. Put your memo on a sandwich board, and walk into your boss's office. Granted, some of these strategies may get you more attention than you desire, but at least people won't be bored.

The other option is to engage wholeheartedly in the use of attention-getting technology—a state-of-the-art, sheets-to-the-wind, no-holds-barred effort to manipulate electrons in the service of attention management. At the beginning of the twenty-first century, those on the cutting edge of attention technologies are finding new uses for streaming stored video, high-quality audio, hypertext, distant connections with real humans, and high production values. Tomorrow, for all we know, what constitutes attention-grabbing technology may include holograms, virtual reality, smell-ovision, and teleportation of humans.

The point is that if you want to attract attention to your messages through the innovative use of technology, you'll have to get on the edge and stay there. You

Looking at Attention *as* Bandwidth

Attention has long been understood in terms of metaphor. Here's an updated example:

Ask your secretary or assistant to tape a one-on-one meeting in your office of at least fifteen minutes' duration. The choice of the meeting is up to your assistant—you shouldn't know when it will be.

Then immediately afterwards . . . write down everything you remember about the meeting, in bullet fashion. Then listen to the tape and write down everything you had already forgotten. The ratio of the two— remembered/forgotten—is a measure of your attention bandwidth.

Watts Wacker and Jim Taylor, *The Visionary's Handbook: Nine Paradoxes That Will Shape the Future of Your Business* (New York: HarperBusiness, 2000), 24.

can't compete unless you're willing to spend lots of time, money, and—well—attention on understanding what new technologies are out there for the display of information, and how they can be effectively employed to get your messages across.

Live Action

One way to anticipate what will be required to get attention in business is to look at what's getting the attention of kids at home. Video games, for example, are clearly proficient at getting and keeping the attention of our children's generation. What's more, if you plan to get their attention in the future, PowerPoint is going to be less germane than Doom, Quake, and Tomb Raider. Important messages will have to be embedded in some sort of live-action game. Beating the competition will feel a lot like repelling space invaders. Otherwise, a generation of children raised on realistic and engrossing information will tune out key information.

> Mass e-mailings annoy us all, whereas a customized message intended for you and you alone gets your attention and your mouse click.

Customization

We've pointed out that a key principle for attention management should be "It's all about me." One application of this principle involves using technology to customize the information presented to each individual. The "mass customization" of information is most familiar on the Internet (discussed later in this chapter), but can involve other types of technology as well. Even the lowly ATM should be able to remember (but usually forgets) what language your prefer for your financial affairs and how much cash you typically extract.

Being presented with a hunk of irrelevant information is no doubt an attention turnoff. Moreover, highly tailored information gets attention. Think about your e-mail queue, for example. Mass e-mailings annoy us all, whereas a customized message intended for you and you alone gets your attention and your mouse click. Chapter 12 discusses how mass e-mailings may soon be considered an etiquette faux pas.

If you're seeking attention for your information, go the extra customization mile. Don't send generic, broadcast messages unless you

---

Overheard. "There is much pleasure to be gained from useless knowledge."
Bertrand Russell, headnote to "Three Papers on Useless Knowledge"

absolutely cannot personalize them, and recognize the consequences: that the messages probably won't be attended to. Build information systems that customize the information they present to each customer—without asking for a lot of the customer's attention in the customization process. For example, Corio, a leading application service provider (ASP) that provides access to business information technology applications over the Internet, has developed a product strategy that attempts to minimize the need for the user's attention. The company wants to present an integrated view (iView, Corio calls it) of all relevant information for a particular type of user so that everything he or she needs is easily accessible through a Web browser. "Otherwise, it just takes too much attention," says George Kadifa, Corio's CEO.

Push versus Pull

A few years ago, technologists became excited about the rise of one type of customization: so-called push technologies. With push technology, information in which you once showed an interest is distributed to you without your further intervention. PointCast (now called Infogate) and BackWeb, for example, tailored the information delivered to your screen through the Internet. (We write in the past tense because Web push technologies are no longer hot, to say the least.)

When information is pushed at us— even when we once thought we wanted it— we lose interest rapidly.

Why did this nirvana-like technology fizzle? It violated all principles of attention management. When information is pushed at us—even when we once thought we wanted it—we lose interest rapidly. Whether the information is an e-mailed research summary, a pushed news display as a screen saver, or an automated weekly fax of mortgage rates, pushed information doesn't engage attention well over the long term.

On the other hand, the act of pulling information—deciding that you want it, searching for it, even clicking on it—stimulates your attention. The process of articulating your need and then acquiring the information takes a considerable amount of attention. Because push technologies eliminated this need for attention, they seemed promising in the first place. But having spent attention on getting information, you are a lot more likely to expend a bit more to digest it. To spend considerable effort

---

Overheard. "Any sufficiently advanced technology is indistinguishable from magic."
Arthur C. Clarke, *Profiles of the Future*

getting information and then to ignore it would, in social psychology terms, lead to a high level of cognitive dissonance. In lay terminology, you'd feel like a jerk.

Environmental Attention Gap

Technology for disseminating information is often found where the competition for attention is fierce—in the office, for example, or even in today's highly information-intensive home. One angle for employing information technologies in an attention-getting fashion is to place them in *environmental attention gaps*, that is, situations in which attention is at less of a premium. Where are people bored? In an airport lounge, perhaps? Put a television in there. Nothing to pay attention to in a supermarket checkout line or a doctor's waiting room? Places such as these present other opportunities for a screen to dispense information of various types, including commercials. If there's an environmental attention gap to be found, you can bet that someone will eventually try to fill it.

Seeking out attention-free zones is one of the ideas behind a research technology developed at Accenture's Center for Strategic Technology Research (CSTaR), a research center that's chock-full of computer science Ph.D.'s. One of these smart guys, Luke Hughes, reasoned that one problem with the concept of knowledge management is that too much knowledge is available when you have no time or attention to consult it. He developed *active knowledge management*, a push technology that presents information in categories specified by the user in advance. So far, so ho-hum. The advantages are distinctive, however: The user can select the desired information quickly and easily, and the information isn't delivered to the desktop. It goes to flat screens in your break room or your coffee nook. The information is context-sensitive, so that if you're passing by the Coke machine at 5:52 to pick one up for the way home, the system displays the traffic congestion map for your commute. How does the system know that it's you, Joseph T. Schmoe, who's passing by? It reads a weak radio signal being broadcast by your ID badge. All these component technologies exist already, but to our knowledge they've never been assembled in this sort of attention-getting fashion.

The occasional attention gap can also be found in cyber-environments. Today, with most home Web users downloading pages through a relatively

---

Overheard. "If attention is the most precious resource in a free-tech economy, then it makes sense to throw battalions of cheap bits into capturing a share of it by making products exciting and easy to use."
Neil Gross, Peter Cox, and Otis Port, "The Technology Paradox"

slow 56K modem, much attention is wasted while people are waiting. Advertising agencies are beginning to create Webmercials, or interstitial commercial messages that appear in the five to seven seconds it takes a typical Web page to load.

Limits

As with all arms races, the viability of the technology-enabled attention getting has its limits. Some senior executive will ultimately cry, "Stop the madness!" and will prohibit the use of some expensive but glitzy technology. For example, Scott McNealy, the CEO of Sun Microsystems, forbade the internal use of PowerPoint. Other CEOs have banned color laser printers for internal documents. It's a good idea to consider such steps internally, so that those who seek attention can wage the arms race at a lower level of sophistication and expense. Externally, however, it may be difficult to declare a truce within your entire industry, and if your competitor employs a more attention-getting technology than your salesperson does, you'll probably feel compelled to invest in an even bigger popgun.

> Some senior executive will ultimately cry, "Stop the madness!" and will prohibit the use of some expensive but glitzy technology.

In addition to these limits of expense and energy, the use of attention-getting technologies may also reach the saturation point of human cognition, which in effect shuts down perception in an overstimulating environment. With sufficient sound, light, color, movement, and other sensate stimuli, our poor brains will simply give up. Before long, perhaps many consumers of information will applaud when a meeting presenter announces that she's using no technology, just the sound of her own voice.

SWITCHYARD PRINCIPLE: Technology can switch your attention from one track to another, and back again.

If attention-getting technologies grab your attention in the first place, attention-structuring technologies try to keep it over extended periods and move it from one topic to another. They move the user through a series of attention-getting experiences to structure the flow of attention over time. It's easy enough to get someone's attention momentarily, but much harder to hold it over minutes and hours, or long enough to get your desired message across.

ATTENTION STRUCTURES

WHAT MAKES US KEEP PAYING attention once we've started? Alternatively, under what circumstances does an informational message lose our attention after it's gained it? Below is a set of attention structures that any seeker of long-term attention can take advantage of in providing information:

- *Make a change.* One way to keep attention over time is simply to provide change—in content, format, tone, involvement level, and so forth. If you're a movie or television program director, for example, you'll often cut from one scene to another.

- *Tell a story.* We stay in movies or finish novels partly because we want to find out what happens to the story and its characters. A powerful way to maintain attention over time is by giving the audience a story.

- *Show them the doors.* Even the most compelling information can't hold attention forever. Therefore, attention managers must build in convenient exit and entry points for our attention. This is why books have chapters, and why episodes of television serials are typically broadcast weekly, not back-to-back.

- *Mix it up.* Most attention structures throughout history, including books, movies, and plays, have been linear, starting at the beginning, and ending at . . . well, you can probably guess. Structuring a linear flow of attention is appealing in that it maximizes attention inertia. On the negative side, however, linear flows typically require the information consumer to invest a high level of attention. Nonlinear structures, such as a catalog or hypertext Web sites, typically make it easier for a consumer to enter the information stream and then to leave it.

- *Keep it real.* Informational messages that are lifelike and realistic are more likely to keep attention than those that aren't. This is why movies are more engrossing than television (the picture is more dominant in your visual field, the resolution is higher, and so forth), and why novels with strong characterization are easier to read and stay with.

- *Remember me.* If the story's about me, I'll pay more attention to it than anything else around. An extension of this principle is that if it's about someone I would like to be (a celebrity or a romantic figure), I'll still supply rapt attention.

- *Go for the action.* Passive media (e.g., television) most easily attract at least a surface level of attention; more active media (e.g., books, the Web, board and computer games) engage a higher level of attention.

- *Stay on task.* We more easily maintain a high level of attention if we are attempting to achieve a specific objective or goal that's meaningful to our job or life.

- *Don't stop.* If I have your attention already, I have a pretty good shot at moving it to another topic or location. If you're watching my television program, chances are good that you'll watch a commercial. If I've gotten you to read the first section of my page-one newspaper article, I can probably switch you over to the continuation on page 27.

- *Don't interrupt.* Information consumers need exit points, but interruptions in the information stream should be minimized if you want to keep attention. People are most likely to change television programs, or stop watching all together, during commercial breaks. The longer the commercials, the higher the likelihood of lost attention.

- *Alter the flow.* The most successful attention-structuring tools try to hold our attention to a given message, but also make it easy to change the informational context. One big reason that TV, radio, and the Web are all successful is that it's very easy to "change channels," or alter the flow of the attention stream.

Fortunately, some factors facilitate the long-term structuring of attention. We've all observed the phenomenon of "attention inertia" in ourselves and others. Once our attention has been engaged in a subject for a while, we sometimes have difficulty in removing our attention. This phenomenon is easily observable in terms of television, movies, even novels— when you've started something, you want to keep giving it your attention until it's completed. When, for example, was the last time you walked out on a movie? It's not because every movie is worth your attention, but rather because of attention inertia.

Scripting

At the heart of any technology that attempts to structure attention is a *scripting* program, or a plan for how the information or message is delivered to the consumer over time. Scripting is not so much a stand-alone attention-structuring technology, but a key component of some of the other technologies that structure attention. Just as a script for a play specifies both the information (the dialogue) and the flow of action (stage directions), scripting programs guide the flow of action and information in attention-structuring technologies.

Creators of these technologies, therefore, have to be both programmers and directors in the movie or television-producing sense. A creator of a Web site, for example, must specify a set of "click streams" that a user might conceivably follow to have a meaningful information experience. A designer of a simulation program must similarly specify the branches that a user might follow; to maintain the user's attention and focus, the flow of the information must remain plausible and interesting. The path through such a program may seem to be arbitrary and unique to the user, but if it's a good attention-structured experience, chances are that it's been carefully planned.

Hypertext

The idea of hypertext is commonly associated with the Web, but it was around long before the invention of the Web and has broader applications. Briefly, hypertext—the underlined text on a Web page—brings the ability to move easily from one document or section to another based on relatedness specified by the author. On the Web, of course, it means you can move from one Web page to another related one by clicking on a link pre-specified by the author of the page. Hypertext can also be used within documents (the application for which it was invented), in such contexts as word processing (taking one directly from text to footnotes, for example), or in presentation programs such as PowerPoint.

The value of hypertext is that it allows a nonlinear attention flow. If I want to shift your attention to some other topic or location, it's easy to do if I can get you to click on a link. However, I need to be aware that it may then be harder to bring your attention back to the original information!

Learning

It's difficult to learn something without paying attention to it. The need for attention in learning has not been lost on designers of educational software, who are paragons in the use of attention-structuring technologies. Various forms of educational technologies embody leading approaches to attention management. Most such technologies, for example, contain scripting, or "authoring," languages that structure the flow of attention. Instructional designers carefully map out the flow of the learner's attention through the educational offering, and construct alternative paths based on whether the information has been learned or not.

Accenture, the firm where we work, incorporates several principles of attention structuring for educational technologies used for both internal employees and client engagements. Originally based on a partnership with "learning scientist" Roger Schank at Northwestern University's Institute for the Learning Sciences, this approach uses goal-based scenarios to capture and maintain the learner's attention. That is, the learner uses the program to achieve a specific goal (e.g., preparing a business plan or developing a risk management proposal), and does so within the context of a scenario or story (one of Schank's books, *Tell Me a Story*, reflects the importance of stories in learning and knowledge transfer[1]). Since most of these educational programs are distributed on CD-ROMs, the programs can employ multiple media and offer the user many alternative paths of learning (eventually, with enough bandwidth, all the programs

---

Overheard. "Automation may be great, but nothing speeds up work like a waste basket."

Frank Hodur, quoted in Joe Griffith, comp., *Speaker's Library of Business Stories, Anecdotes, and Humor*

will be on the Web). Although these educational technologies are difficult and time-consuming to create, research suggests that they are substantially more effective than "talking head" modes of instruction, such as classroom lectures.[2] The use of stories, goals, and high levels of involvement between the program-instructor and students ensures that the learner pays attention to the content.

Simulated Attention

Simulations, which have application in both learning and game technologies, offer excellent potential for the structuring of attention. Even simulations that are not terribly realistic (including the Sim series of entertainment-oriented simulations—SimCity, SimAnt, SimEarth, the Sims, etc.) can monopolize a user's attention for hours. Such simulations use personal experience in combination with attention management principles (come to think of it, personal experience is an attention management principle). As a result, the simulations both entertain and get across key ideas. It's a relatively painless way to devote attention to something.

Serendipity

A professor friend once complained to us that she hated electronic library catalog systems because what most attracted her attention in the library (okay, we're paraphrasing . . . the thing she liked most in the library) was the element of surprise from walking past a shelf of books and finding something random. If you want to keep someone's attention over time, providing some element of randomness and serendipity is very helpful.

Few technologies embody this approach, although considerable opportunity exists for doing so. A few Web sites do bring your attention to books or other products that you might like on the basis of other things you've bought. This isn't completely random, but it has some element of indeterminacy. Web search engines already turn up a considerable amount of randomness—perhaps too much—in searching for particular terms and phrases. As search technologies are

> When any sort of search or information requirement is fulfilled too predictably, less attention may be devoted to the result.

refined, it's important that they not be made perfect. When any sort of search or information requirement is fulfilled too predictably, less attention may be devoted to the result.

Standard Attention

People commonly herald the virtues of openness in information technologies, and indeed, openness is useful for consumers when all software or hardware manufacturers in an industry segment adhere to a common standard. Prices generally fall in such situations, and consumers don't have to learn new tools when they change vendors. From an attention management standpoint, however, proprietary technologies may prove much more useful.

> Since the early days of business computing, firms have been tempted to use proprietary technologies to keep their customers' attention (and their money) from moving elsewhere.

Imagine, for example, that you are the CEO of America Online. Are you likely to get more attention for your own content if you adhere to standard, Web-based ways of displaying information, or if you have your own proprietary approach? The answer is undoubtedly the latter. One reason that AOL has prospered to such a degree is that its proprietary standards enable the company to monopolize its customers' attention. If AOL were just another Web site, customers could enter and leave at will—instead of being cocooned within the AOL world, which receives every bit of their attention.

This phenomenon isn't specific to AOL, and it's not new. Since the early days of business computing, firms have been tempted to use proprietary technologies to keep their customers' attention (and their money) from moving elsewhere. With its open standards for information display and transmission, the Internet has certainly been a boon to consumers. On the other hand, the open standards have been tough on content providers, and you can expect to see continual proprietary salvos by companies in attempts to structure and hold their customers' attention streams.

We're just at the beginning of technological attempts to structure and hold attention, and we can expect to see many more of them in the attention economy. If you want to get attention and keep it, you'll need to learn how to employ attention-structuring technologies.

FORCE-FIELD PRINCIPLE: **Use technology to defend your attention resources against uninvited intrusions.**

Given the barrage of information and the scarcity of attention, perhaps the most popular technologies of the future will be those that preserve, protect, and defend your attention. Unless technology begins to come to the aid of (rather than continuing to assault) our attention, we'll all suffer from attention deficit disorder. In the next paragraphs, we'll describe both the current state of the attention-protecting art and much more sophisticated future technologies for obtaining only the information really needed.

Silicon Breastplate

Using technology for protecting attention is a new trend, but hardly a surprise. Bids for attention barrage the normal consumer thousands of times every day—not just at home, but now in supermarkets, airports, and public restrooms. Seekers of attention have employed technology to squeeze information into almost every possible domain. Today, the technology that has facilitated the decimation of privacy and contemplation is beginning to be used to protect our personal space.

The goal, of course, is not to eliminate all information, but just to eliminate the information not wanted at any particular moment. It's a difficult objective, because many of us can't easily specify what kind of information we want. Technologies are giving us increasing choice about what information we want to see and hear, but many of us have only a dim view of what we like until we see it. Attention-protecting technologies will require that we invest attention in our own preferences and then communicate these preferences to machines by selecting among alternatives. The best technologies will learn our preferences by observing us as we make several choices, rather than asking us in general what categories of stuff we like and how much of it we want.

> The best technologies will learn our preferences by observing us as we make several choices, rather than asking us in general what categories of stuff we like and how much of it we want.

Even if we do know our preferences, our desires for information often change over time. If you're preparing for the end of a big project, you may want only the most urgent information; if you're on a very long plane flight with a bad movie, you may devote your attention to almost anything (even the advertisements in the airline magazines!). Any attention-protecting technologies should therefore have the capability of modifying information-filtering instructions based on the availability of the user's attention. If a technology has learned your preferences through observing some initial choices, a good technology can always unlearn or change them easily.

That said, technology alone will rarely, if ever, be the solution in itself to attention protection. Since even the best technologies will not be able to learn your information preferences without some investment of your own time and attention, you will always need to be involved. And the best attention protectors have always been human. Take the fast-vanishing institution, the secretary. Good secretaries or executive assistants have always played an important role in filtering information and determining what messages truly require their bosses' attention. They can still perform this role better than any technology can, and nothing on the horizon will diminish their relative value. We can also combine secretarial help with technology—when, for example, a manager asks a secretary to delete unimportant e-mails or to highlight important ones. Perhaps when organizations begin to realize how scarce and valuable the attention of highly paid employees is, they will provide more secretarial services for those managers and knowledge workers.

> **The best attention protectors have always been human.**

Technology is nowhere near providing people with a more general attention-protecting tool (other than, perhaps, a set of earplugs and blinders). While it's increasingly possible to get all your voice mail, e-mail, and even scanned paper messages in one mailbox (a concept called "unified messaging"), this consolidation just makes you realize how bad the problem is. For now and the foreseeable future, all available technologies protect attention within specific information domains (e.g., e-mail, telephone, television).

E-Mail

Attention protection for e-mail has been discussed for many years, but it's still in its infancy. We've been told for decades, for example, that intelligent filters and agents for e-mail are just around the corner. Yet they stubbornly refuse to arrive in a useful form. The filtering capabilities that do exist require a high level of user attention and still aren't intelligent enough to meet the needs of a complex e-mail environment. You can filter out all outside messages, for example, from anyone not on your correspondent list, but what if the potential outside e-mailer is a headhunter offering you a great new job? Even the so-called bozo filter, which automatically trashes messages from people you've previously identified as being unworthy of your attention, can occasionally eliminate something worth your attention. And then there's the problem with human nature: our desire not to miss anything important. Even if filtering devices correctly eliminated 99 percent of extraneous messages, many of us would be paranoid about the 1 percent of valuable items that we missed. Perhaps we simply don't value our attention enough yet. A final problem—that of our changing preferences for how much e-mail information we want—was discussed above. No single filter setting is likely to suffice for our ever-changing preferences.

> **Perhaps what we need are not utopian systems that would filter our attention for us, but rather tools that would let us become the protectors of our own attention.**

The good news in filter and agent research is that researchers are beginning to think seriously about the attention problem. At Microsoft, for example, a team of researchers led by Eric Horvitz is attempting to restrict unwanted interruptions in computer users' attention. The software (Attentional User Interface, as the team calls it) attempts to use statistical techniques to determine whether a particular item in the incoming information stream would be a desired interruption. The work is designed to counter the onslaught of information from the Internet.

Despite these worthwhile research efforts, however, we see no near-term solution to these problems. Computer scientists will continue to tell us that they are working on intelligent agents that will solve our e-mail overload problem, and we'll continue to find these solutions ineffective. Perhaps what we need are not utopian systems that would filter our attention for us, but rather tools that would let us become the protectors of our own attention. What if, for example, we had a little filtering button to click on every time we logged on to our e-mail? The button could have a highly restrictive setting, which would filter out all messages from unknown parties, all messages with multiple recipients, and all messages from "bozos"

Exploitation. As Jakob Nielsen, a Silicon Valley expert on software usability, put it in an article about the Microsoft work, "Most Internet entrepreneurs treat the users' attention as a third world country to be strip mined."

Source: John Markoff, "Microsoft Sees Software 'Agent' as Way to Avoid Distractions."

we don't like. Those messages wouldn't be deleted immediately, just saved for possible browsing later. Less restrictive settings would allow some or all of these types of messages for times when we feel we have the attention to deal with them. Such simple, user-driven tools are likely the best thing we'll get in e-mail attention protection in the short run. And in the long run, we're all either retired or dead, so what do we care?

Operator?

Devices for filtering out unwanted telephone calls have proliferated over the past couple of decades. First there was the telephone answering machine, which had call-screening capabilities just as valuable as the ability to record messages. Then came caller ID and various forms of call-blocking applications. The most recent and sophisticated variation on this theme is Privacy Manager, a service being marketed by local telephone companies. It works with your existing caller ID service to screen out calls from unknown numbers, out-of-area numbers, or numbers of pesky relatives you have specified in advance as being pesky. Just in case you want to find out whom you didn't have to talk to, the unwanted callers can leave a message that you can later elect to hear—or not. Callers you can identify as telemarketers can be delivered a curt message suggesting that their calls will not be answered until hell freezes over, so they might as well take your number off their list. It's a appealing idea, but again it requires some attention investment to be useful.

Small Screen

Given how much the average American watches television, technologies that could, say, reduce a thirty-minute sitcom to twenty-two commercial-free minutes would free up a lot of attention. With such a capability a TV viewer could watch more edifying television programs, or, for God's sake, read a few pages of a book. Of course, the ardent attention manager could have long ago recorded all his or her TV programs on a VCR, watched the tapes on a delayed-action basis, and fast-forwarded through every commercial. But that requires more planning and attention mania than most of us can manage.

Overheard. "To measure the man, measure his heart."

Malcolm Stevenson Forbes, <http://www.greaterhorizons.com/honesty.html>

A new device, however, threatens to bust the issue of television attention protection wide open. Called the personal television or the personal video recorder, the device stores television programming on a hard disk drive and receives daily TV programming information over a telephone connection. Two companies that offer these devices are TiVo and Replay Networks. Personal TV is both an attention-protecting technology in that it can skip commercials altogether, and an attention-structuring device in that it lets you decide in what order you should see what programs, rather than merely watching a network executive's idea about what you should be viewing. If you know your TV preferences sufficiently well, you can, for example, specify that you only want to see movies starring Adam Sandler, or news shows from Geraldo Rivera (this technology obviously doesn't improve tastes, but only allows them to be exercised more readily).

This new device could mark a revolutionary change in the attention (and financial) requirements of television. If viewers punch the "skip commercial" button too often, the advertising-based funding model for commercial television will break down, leaving subscription, pay-per-view, or advertising through product placement as funding alternatives. Of course, the television industry could co-opt the personal television technology and prevent the ability to skip commercials; the broadcast networks have already bought pieces of TiVo and Replay. And like other attention-protecting technologies, it requires that the users know and communicate what information they want, which itself requires attention. Thus far, most information consumers have been reluctant to make such wise attention investments.

Writer Michael Lewis, in a cover-page article in the *New York Times* Sunday magazine (perhaps the most attention ever given to an attention technology), argued that the most notable effects of personal TV may lie in the domain of attention measurement.

The devices can collect viewer preferences as excruciatingly detailed data, which TiVo and Replay will probably sell to TV networks and advertisers. This could revolutionize the TV advertising industry, Lewis argues. Since personal TV can store any program shown at any hour, it might break down the concept of prime time and allow more focused targeting of individual viewers.

Overheard. "The operative unit in TV ratings will no longer be the program but the moment. Advertisers and networks will know with weird accuracy who and what within each program best holds television viewers' attention."

Michael Lewis, "Boom Box"

Media Savvy

Similar trends toward personalization are emerging in other technological domains. In music, for example, consumers are increasingly able to customize the packages of music they listen to. Many consumers already download songs from the Internet using the MP3 protocol and storing them on a recordable CD, or saving them on a hard disk or portable music player. You can construct your own playlist, but you'd better know what you want and be willing to spend some attention on creating your personal music portfolio. The same general situation is becoming prevalent in radio. You can download your favorite radio programs (through Broadcast.com, for example) for listening when you feel like it. But if you are content to have your attention structured by a couple of local radio stations offering content in real time, you may not want to bother with streaming audio.

> Why read somebody else's collection of news when you can construct your own?

In the information industry, the trend for several years (e.g., from companies like NewsEdge) has been to allow customers to create their own customized newsletters or newspapers. Why read somebody else's collection of news when you can construct your own? Although companies like NewsEdge pose this sort of question, they may not like the answer that some people give. It takes some time to construct your own newspaper, and an editor (another human attention protector) is paid to think about what news you'll find important, and you're not.

The Trade-Off

We leave the world of attention-protecting technologies with a mixed message for you, our attentive reader. On the one hand, it's possible to employ technologies to filter and sift through information in most major media. This is good news from an attention management standpoint, and these technologies will undoubtedly proliferate rapidly. The bad news is that attention is necessary to make them work. It takes attention to determine your choices of information, to communicate to your chosen attention-protecting technology what you like and don't like, and to continually refine your choices as your information needs change. It will surely get easier to communicate the choices to the more sophisticated attention-protecting technologies of the future; maybe someday they'll be able to simply read our preferences directly from our brains. In advance of that capability, perhaps it's time to start thinking about what information you really like, and how much you want of it.

CHAPTER 6

THE HIDDEN PERSUADERS

LESSONS FROM THE ATTENTION INDUSTRIES

The power of attention is

no surprise to those who depend on it. The attention industries—advertising, movies, television, and publishing—are perhaps the best single place to learn about effective attention management. These industries have already encountered almost every issue that the ardent attention manager will come across, from an overall paucity of attention, to attention flows across content and channel, to attention measurement. Managers who understand the attention industries will be sought out for their expertise. For example, one reason that consumer-products executives have been able to move into other industries (John Sculley from Pepsi to Apple and William Campbell from Philip Morris to Citibank were two prominent movers in the 1990s) is that they understood how to capture consumer attention.

We will draw lessons from a few specific sectors of the attention industries, including movies, television, print media (book, newspaper, and magazine publishing), and advertising. This list does not include several other industries that vie for audience attention, including sports, live theater, education, even telecommunications. For every minute I'm talking with friends or relatives on the phone, I'm not watching television or reading the newspaper. You could even argue that work, vacations, and sleep are attention industries, because they all suck up attention—but don't worry, we won't. Nevertheless, all businesses that rely heavily on attention for their success should be some of the earliest adopters of attention industry lessons.

Before discussing each of these sectors, however, we will describe some important changes taking place in attention industries.

Consuming Attention

Veronis, Suhler & Associates (a New York-based media investment bank) predicts that by 2003, Americans will spend $878 billion on the products of the attention industries (print media, cable, home video, Hollywood movies, music, and advertising). This is a 44 percent increase from 1998, and will make attention the sixth largest industry in the United States, outranking food. By 2003, Americans will "consume" the products of the attention industries for an average of ten hours a day, thirty minutes more than in 1998. The size and growth of the industry is by itself powerful testimony to the importance of attention in business.

Zero-Sum Audience

Perhaps the greatest overall lesson from the attention industries is that we just don't have enough attention to go around. In the early days of the attention industries, managers in each sector probably believed that the sector's growth had no limits. Now, however, attention managers recognize that audience attention is limited and zero-sum. Gains in attention share for one medium can be made only at the expense of another. Much as this is bad news for the attention industries, it makes them a bellwether or leading indicator of the battle for attention that business and society are beginning to face more generally. Ken Sacharin, media director of The Media Edge and author of *Attention!*, bemoans the many setbacks that marketers and advertisers have faced in the 1990s.[1] Marketers and advertisers have long been studying and managing attention and have developed a sophisticated

---

Stay Tuned. Imagine a film so engrossing that it saps all the attention out of the viewer, leaving its victim in a zombie-like trance of contentment. In his edgy novel *Infinite Jest*, David Foster Wallace conjures a world in which entertainment is so abundant, and attention so scarce, that advertisers have to leave the confines of television and print and instead buy *time*—literally. Welcome to "Subsidized Time," in which you may be born in "The Year of the Purdue Wonderchicken" and graduate from college in "The Year of the Depends Adult Undergarments." One talented young filmmaker stumbles upon a way to transcend the attention problem and inadvertently unleashes "The Entertainment" on viewers, sucking up all their attention, along with their willpower, their freedom, and their selfhood. The next time you click onto the Sundance Channel, view with caution.

understanding of it. Yet, Sacharin notes, the erosion of tried-and-true marketing and advertising methods is undeniable: Coupon redemption rates, ad copy scores, and TV ad effectiveness are all way down (the last of these has declined 70 percent). Web banner ads never really had a chance. With so much competition for attention share, is it any surprise?

If managers and professionals can understand how one information medium has gained strength at the expense of another, they can probably determine how to steal or preserve attention from competing firms or initiatives within their own organizations. The most common shift in attention has been from print media to electronic—from books, magazines, and newspapers to cable and satellite TV, videos, video games, and the Web. Declines in newspaper reading have been especially pronounced. Paid circulation of U.S. newspapers is down more than 10 percent from its 1984 peak, even as the population continues to increase. In general, the newspapers requiring the most attention to be digested (and not coincidentally, those supplying the most and highest-quality information), such as the *Wall Street Journal*, *New York Times*, and *Washington Post*, have a declining circulation, whereas easier-to-attend-to papers such as *USA Today* have had long upward trends in circulation.[2]

> The most common shift has been from print media to electronic—from books, magazines, and newspapers to cable and satellite TV, video games, and the Web.

The attention no longer paid to newspapers, however, is not automatically going to other print media. A study of reading habits in the 1990s suggests that Americans are reading less. Younger people, in particular, exhibited precipitous declines in reading. For example, 36 percent of males between eighteen and thirty-four said they read for at least thirty minutes a day in 1992; by 1999 the percentage had dropped to 22 percent (can the Harry Potter books reverse this trend?). Perhaps their attention simply needed a rest; the activity that increased most during the period was sleep. Another survey found that the percentage of Americans who had not read a book in the past year rose from 8 percent in 1978 to 16 percent in 1990.[3] Of course, this decline in reading didn't stop U.S. publishers from releasing ten thousand more books in 1998 than they did in 1993.

Spotlight on Next Generation Network. Next Generation Network is ushering in new-economy advertising in the form of electronic billboards. These Internet-enabled video screens are now showing up in public places where people are likely to be bored and idle. "Say you're standing in line to buy a newspaper," says CEO Thomas Pugliese. "You can look at our screen or look at the back of the head of the guy standing in front of you. It's not a tough call."

Source: Erika Germer, "Attention, Please," *Fast Company*, June 2000, 86.

Although attention to electronic media has been increasing, not all electronic sectors have grown. Network television is a particular casualty of the past few decades. The top-rated network show in 1983 (the final episode of *M*A*S*H*) drew 106 million viewers; the top-rated show in 1993 (the closing episode of *Cheers*) was watched by 81 million viewers; the top-rated show in 1998 (the final *Seinfeld* show) pulled in only 76 million fans. During this period the number of television-equipped households grew by 16 million.[4] With many other competitors for audience attention, network television has been unable to maintain its hold on audiences. The overall amount of television consumed by U.S. viewers, however, has remained stable—an astounding 3½ hours per day for the average viewer.

Crossing Over

Even television, however, won't hold sway forever in the battle for attention. Today, of course, its strongest competition comes from the Internet. Although some observers argue for different attention categories for these media—passive attention for TV, active attention for Internet use—there is evidence of small declines in television consumption for heavy Web users. Further, as interactive digital television becomes more like the Internet, and streaming video makes the Internet more like TV, we will surely see increasing attention flows between these two media.

Technological crossovers are coming in the future, but content and advertising crossovers are here today. It's getting harder to specify a medium on which a particular type of content will be displayed. Feature films have long been on television as well as the big screen, but are also now available through video cassettes, DVDs, and increasingly the Internet. Newspaper content appears not only in broadsheets and tabloids, but also on the Internet and even on radio and television news programs. Television networks and cable channels also own Web sites and magazines, and they sell videos and soundtracks of their programs through newspapers, direct mail, and the Web.

The quest for attention has led managers of virtually every medium to seek viewers in other media

I'm from Hollywood

Do you want to hear the story of the Clinton-Lewinsky scandal one more time? Not likely, so why is the publishing world all atwitter over the new novel *American Rhapsody*? This latest oeuvre on the presidential shenanigans was penned by Joe Eszterhas, a writer most famous for his screenplay for *Basic Instinct*, in which Sharon Stone gets attention with her ice pick and her minimalist approach to undergarments.

How does Eszterhas get attention? First, his publishers strategically use the word "American" in his book's title to imply a serious heft to its racy subject; next, Eszterhas gives a slew of revealing interviews, like the one in *Salon*, in which he trots out his Hollywood credentials and makes confessions about his own sexual escapades with, you guessed it, Stone. What a killer instinct for self-promotion.

Source: Hendrik Hertzberg, "Basest Instincts," *New Yorker*, 31 July 2000, 23-24.

through advertising. Internet companies advertise their existence not only with Web banners, but also with spots on television, radio, newspapers, and billboards. The 2000 NFL Super Bowl was perhaps the high-water mark of Internet crossover advertising, in which sixteen e-commerce firms bought the most expensive commercial time available through the medium. Many spent several multiples of their annual revenues to try to get some attention. And according to Web site visits for the few days after the game, it worked, though later analyses have not been so positive. Consumer-goods firms, normally the biggest buyers of television advertising, are reducing their purchases in that medium because aggressive dot-com firms with venture capital dollars to spend are driving the price too high. (This competition problem, however, is ebbing as dot-com fortunes are ebbing.)

> **The quest for attention has led managers of virtually every medium to seek viewers in other media through advertising.**

No attention market—internal or external to a firm—consists of a single medium. If you're a manager seeking attention for your ideas, a memo or an e-mail is just a starting point. Any information that matters should also be delivered via phone, video briefing, audio cassettes for commuting, a presentation, and perhaps even an interactive simulation. If it seems too much effort to communicate in this fashion, then perhaps your message wasn't that important anyway.

At the software firm Symantec, for example, managers discovered that key information went unnoticed by many employees. As with many large and growing firms, Symantec employees are distributed across a wide geographical area and can focus their attention on many potential topics. Despite the usual communications channels, CEO Gordon Eubanks felt that these options were not enough. The company adopted a multimedia approach, including many of the media described above, and even one more—weekend express mail deliveries to employees' homes. Symantec executives felt that the effectiveness of communication improved considerably after these measures were undertaken.

The Long and Winding (Green) Road. Plenty of theorists allege that our attention spans are shrinking—we are inundated with the rapid-fire sounds and images of MTV, and interactive Internet advertisements (can you hit that pesky gopher on the head with the mallet before he pops back into his hole?). If the gloomy prognosticators are right, then our culture is being subjected to a perverse sadism at the hands of Hollywood. Check out the running time for some recent movies:

- *The Green Mile*: 180 minutes
- *The Talented Mr. Ripley*: 135 minutes
- *Magnolia*: 188 minutes
- *Titanic*: 194 minutes

Content Providers

The proliferation of media channels, all battling for viewers' attention, has led to huge increases in the premiums paid for attention-getting information content. Desperate channel owners are snapping up content sources—from the America Online acquisition of Time Warner to Rupert Murdoch's News Corporation acquisition of the Los Angeles Dodgers and several English football clubs. Prices for proven attention-getting content are escalating. Murdoch paid $300 million for the Dodgers, more than 1,200 times the cost to bring the Dodgers to Los Angeles from Brooklyn. Successful movie actors earn up to $50 million per picture, with directors and screenwriters not far behind. Sports stars, high-profile authors, and former U.S. presidents on the lecture circuit also earn millions. As long as audiences are willing to grant these stars their attention, the price of content will continue to soar.

Good content providers are equally important for internal attention markets within organizations. If you've got employees with something to say, or a unique and creative way of saying it, do whatever you can to hold onto them. They are your organization's best hope of getting attention from other employees, business partners, and customers in the marketplace. We're all information providers and content managers, and the best of us will reap substantial rewards in the attention economy.

Beyond the paucity of attention, the multimedia attention market, and the importance of attention-getting content, many lessons from the attention industries vary by specific media. For the remainder of this chapter, we'll discuss how movies, television, print media, and advertising get and keep the attention of their consumers.

ACTION! PRINCIPLE: Hollywood studio executives understand their audience before they make a play for their attention, and they manipulate setting, segmentation, and culture to hold onto it.

During the twentieth century, Hollywood became the most powerful attention factory the world had ever seen. The motion picture industry still attracts the attention of billions, setting trends, shaping culture, and

Start with the Fire. "You have only 30 seconds [in a TV commercial]. If you grab attention in the first frame with a visual surprise, you stand a better chance of holding the viewer. People screen out a lot of commercials because they open with something *dull*. . . . When you advertise fire-extinguishers, open with the fire."
Source: David Ogilvy, *Ogilvy on Advertising* (New York: Vintage Books, 1985), 111.

making an enormous amount of money on popular films. In darkened theaters all over the country, we sit like zombies, our attention totally focused on projected images and recorded sounds. When VCRs became common, some predicted that theaters would vanish for lack of interest. Not so. As the movie business proves, people actually like the captive-attention environment of the theater—as long as they are entertained. This bodes well for people who wish to manage attention, though it also shows how high the entertainment value of a message must be to capture people's focus.

Simulated Reality

Movies dominate our attention in part because of the setting in which they are viewed. The lights are low, the screen is all-consuming of the eye-ball, and the seats are comfy (except for some occasional stray chewing gum). The production values in good movies simulate reality—a domain that we have been bred to find attention getting. Well-known actors, most of whom are highly attractive, grab attention through familiarity and hero worship. In addition, attention-oriented directors know how to keep eyes and brains focused on the screen, with strong characterization, clear and compelling plots, and rapid cuts from one scene to another. Sex and violence, two reliable attention-getting themes, don't hurt either. The result: Hardly anyone ever leaves a movie, even during the preshow advertisements.

Open Mouths

It may be difficult to duplicate the movie-going experience to create rapt audiences for business information, but it's not impossible. First, get potential viewers away from other distractions—perhaps in a darkened auditorium. Make sure that your message tells a story, and employ high production values and jump cuts. Use music to emphasize key messages. If you can't use high-profile actors, let people see their own colleagues and themselves. Have you ever been to a business meeting in which the second day starts with a video made from Day One's highlights? You'll

Alternative Attention

Can't afford upward of $2 million for a thirty-second Super Bowl advertisement? Try some of these creative ways of attracting attention in these ad-saturated times:

1. Tattoo the bodies of your customers with your logo, as did Casa Sanchez restaurant in San Francisco (with their permission, of course).

2. Carve beach sand into your company's image using a service like Beach 'n Billboard of New Jersey.

3. Paint the next departing space shuttle; a Russian rocket recently lifted off bearing a Pizza Hut logo on its fuselage.

Source: Richard Tomkins, "It's an Ad Ad Ad Ad World," *Financial Times* (London), 21 July 2000.

see the same open-mouthed rapture as in the audience for a good movie—everyone's trying to spot themselves and their chums. We've even seen grown people cry over such rapidly produced flicks.

Movies are also highly segmented by age. If you happen to be the age for which the movie was created (most are created for fourteen-year-old boys, we suspect), you'll find it engrossing. If Adam Sandler is on the marquee or if the Farrelly brothers have directed, for example, many adults might want to invest their attention elsewhere. But the industry can also inform others about which themes, personalities, and products are appealing to certain age groups. Who, outside of the motion picture industry, would have guessed that the downright silly film *The Waterboy* would smash box-office records with its appeal to teenage boys? Who else knew that young girls would return over and over to the tragic love story *Titanic*, making it the biggest financial hit in history? Hollywood has to keep its finger on the pulse of generational attention trends. When marketing their offerings to different age groups, managers in all industries should pay attention to how the movies grab attention.

Although people who work in companies have a more homogeneous taste in attention, good attention managers can still exploit age-related differences. A firm may have as many as three or even four generations under its roof; targeting communications at each specific level may be helpful in getting attention, even if a manager has to make them all available to all audiences to avoid charges of discrimination.

Barometer

Moviemakers are great measurers of attention. Every successful studio executive is engrossed by the results of the first weekend's audience size. Formerly, directors and producers would have to wait several weeks to get projections of how a movie would do; now they get fairly accurate projections late on the Friday night of a film's release week. Even before that, studios employ measurement techniques to find out which versions of a movie will be most attention getting. Test screenings of various kinds abound. Directors often cut scenes that don't appeal to audiences or that stimulate only the urge to get popcorn.

High-Pressure Fronts. "It's the adverts that start to crank up my sense of claustrophobia. Now that I have begun to notice them, I cannot ignore them. . . . I count out a five-brands-a-second frequency on my walk down my street. . . . There is a storm of attention at major junctions. A hurricane of attention on Oxford Street, where most tourists trudge for their Saturday shopping. The attention weather passes over London, and leaves behind heaps of brands that gather in the lee of the streets. Empty wrappers, spent desires."

Source: Matthew De Abaitua, "Letter from London: Pay Attention," <http://www.hermenaut.com/a81.shtml>.

Intuition

Good moviemakers know when to stop with audience measurement and when to preserve the coherence of an artistic vision. This is why success in Hollywood is more a matter of attention management than attention manipulation. The best directors have an intuitive sense of what will get the audience's attention, and wise producers and studios know not to tinker too much with their intuitions. We've all seen movies in which the director was warned against an unhappy ending, but included it anyway—to box office success. Of course, the movie industry also offers lessons in negative attention. One need only read the Friday newspaper movie reviews to find examples of how weak plots, poorly developed characters, cynical manipulative tricks, and cheap production values can limit the attention a sophisticated moviegoer will give to the silver screen.

THE BOOB TUBE PRINCIPLE: TV grabs attention through short narratives, proper timing, solid characters, choice, and user friendliness.

Television is the most successful attention-getting technology in human history. For over half a century, humans have been sitting in their dens staring at these electronic boxes as though we've stumbled upon some kind of attention nirvana. War, sex, public executions, and perfidious politicians are all attention getting, but how do we find out about such things? Through the magic box, of course—for an average of 3 hours and 26 minutes per day per person in the United States, and 7½ hours per day per U.S. household.

Why this rapt attention? Part of TV's appeal is that it makes all the right biological moves. TV presents a cornucopia of things the human brain finds innately attention-worthy: color, movement, conversation, music, and lots of people going through extraordinary hardships or good fortune. It also panders to our biologically driven fascination with life-or-death issues. Love, sex, and the rearing of children are big sellers, as are scenes of disaster and death. Television programmers are happy to play to anything we like to

No New Program Ideas? No Hit Shows? No Problem!

The E! cable station thrives on chronic channel-surf syndrome. Although most of its viewers surf in for only a few minutes at a time, they do so loyally and frequently; and for the cable companies that include E! in their basic packages, small snatches of attention are sufficient. The few minutes that viewers spend gazing vacantly at low-production-cost or repackaged programming like movie trailers (provided free by the studios) or snippets of talk show highlights have catapulted the station's value from a few modest million to upward of $800 million.

Source: James Sterngold, "A Wasteland, and Proud of It," *New York Times*, 7 September 1998.

watch, because the primary use for their product is to get and hold attention (PBS programming notwithstanding). Although managers in other industries might not want to fully emulate TV moguls, all executives could benefit from analyzing the way television directs and redirects attention.

Short Stories

Television's staple is the serialized, short narrative. Stories like this have secured our attention since prehistoric humans first came out of the cave. But the most attention-getting television uses storytelling in a particularly engaging way. The stories are relatively short—a half hour or an hour—which means we don't have to commit too much attention. In the attention economy, it's rare that a multinight miniseries can succeed; too many contenders vie for that much sustained attention. Good TV programs are serialized, but the producers and directors make it relatively easy to join the story in midstream or to miss a few episodes. The programs (at least in the United States) always start on the hour or the half hour, so we know when to direct our attention screenward. This lesson from television was successfully adopted by the Web site Gamesville.com, part of the Lycos network. It always starts its new multiuser games at the top of every hour; each game lasts for seven minutes. Then after a three-minute commercial break, the game continues at ten, twenty, thirty, and so forth, minutes after the hour. Gamesville CEO Mark Hermann feels strongly that the short duration and predictability of the games' schedule is a major factor in Gamesville's high attention ratings.

> **All executives could benefit from analyzing the way television directs and redirects attention.**

Funnier, Younger, Prettier

Of course, some narratives are better than others. In the best television stories, characterization helps us identify with the protagonists and sympathize with their plights. These are not boring stories—a lot happens to the average television character, substantially more than to you or me. The

Even the Best of Us. "One might think that a man of genius could browse in the greatness of his own thoughts and dispense with the cheap applause of the mob which he despises. But actually he falls a victim to a more mighty herd instinct; his searching, his findings, and his call are inexorably meant for the crowd and must be heard."

Source: Carl Jung, quoted in Lewis D. Eigen and Jonathan D. Siegel, *The Manager's Book of Quotations* (New York: American Management Association, 1989), 372.

characters are generally funnier, younger, more attractive, and more fortunate than people in real life. And if the story itself doesn't get your attention, there are always the commercials, which prey on every human insecurity and vanity.

Television offers so many content choices, with such a wide range of styles and moods, that disenchanted viewers can switch products while remaining glued to the tube. This makes TV interesting to a huge and varied market. If you're male, the stereotype view is that you'll find just moving through the channels endlessly fascinating. According to the same formula, most women didn't get the gene that puts channel surfing on their attention-getting list.

Safely Hooked

Commercials have always been the fly in the attention ointment for network television. Sure, some commercials can be entertaining, but most of us use them as an excuse to divert our attention and change channels or head for the bathroom or refrigerator. But TV executives are getting smarter about commercials. In many prime-time periods now, there is no commercial break between one show and the next; commercials are clustered in the middle of the program. They get your attention safely hooked for the next one before turning to a word from their sponsor. And commercials themselves have become substantially shorter. Fifteen-second spots are not uncommon, and minute-long commercials, once the standard, are extremely rare and seem to go on for eons.

But commercials have one hugely beneficial effect on television's attention management. They force the medium to measure the attention it's getting on a regular, highly detailed basis. Had commercial TV never existed, Nielsen ratings and people meters may have been developed anyway just to measure the attention going to programming. The real driver, however, was clearly advertisers wanting to know how many eyeballs gave their spots rapt attention. As discussed in chapter 3, television audience measurement was the original attention-monitoring approach. Television producers are more than aware not only of the overall audience ratings for the previous week, but also of the particular age, gender, and income segments to which the show appeals. If ratings indicate a loss of attention, the show will pretty quickly get no attention at all, because it will cease to exist.

Television programmers can also measure attention to make the content more interesting to its intended audience. In *The Tipping Point*, for example, Malcolm Gladwell relates how the creators of *Sesame Street* measured children's eye movement to understand exactly what got the attention of the show's juvenile audience. At times some aspects of the program received too much attention; one segment featuring Oscar the Grouch, for example, attracted so much attention to Oscar that the children's eyes rarely saw the letters at the bottom of the screen. Gladwell also describes how the Nickelodeon show *Blue's Clues* was constructed to be even more attention getting for children than *Sesame Street*—in part because *Blue's Clues* benefited from more extensive attention measurement.[5]

Finally, TV also gets attention by reaching the peak of user friendliness. For the most part, television doesn't let complexity stand in the way of a good time. It's easy to set it up, turn it on, and find the channels you want (if not to record a program on your VCR, which is why few people do it). TV's simplicity applies both in terms of plug-and-play technology (although complex set-top boxes and interactive, digital, high-definition TV threaten this advantage), and also in terms of content. Television (in the United States, at least), seldom distracts its viewers with overly difficult, complex, or depressing information.

Fan-tasm

What occupies your back-of-the-mind attention when you watch a pitch sail over home plate on television? Princeton Video Image is betting on the spot behind the batter, and it is filling that spot with virtual ads. Computers generate and place these ghostly messages in the scenery alongside the main action on your television or PC screen. For example, the messages can be found lurking in the turf adjacent to a hairpin turn on the Indy 500 or emblazoned on the first-down line of an NCAA football game. Though they garner attention secondary to the main action, they can catch the eye with animation—an ad behind home plate, for example, can rotate to give the speed of a pitch.

Source: Amanda Beeler, "Virtual Ads Grab More Attention from Marketers," *Advertising Age*, 29 May 2000.

No matter what sort of information you're purveying over whatever medium, if you are a smart manager, you can adopt numerous lessons from the idiot box: Most importantly, tell a good story. Make it a long-running serial if you can—keep inventing new plot twists, but make them variations around a familiar theme. Make yourself or your representatives a well-defined character. Provide multiple content choices whenever possible. Measure how well your message is receiving attention. And don't let a new technology or a difficult message provide an excuse to tune out.

THE ROLL-THE-PRESSES PRINCIPLE: **Publishers focus on a particular audience, then use sex, power, and personality to expand it.**

With all the electronic media sprouting up in the 1980s and 1990s, publishing risked being left behind in the attention economy. As already noted, reading has declined, particularly among the young, and newspapers are not generally prospering. But a few bright stars still shine among the publishing firmament; some sectors of the industry are clearly doing better than others, and strong competitors exist in every sector.

In My Backyard

In publishing, one key vehicle for getting attention is to focus on a particular audience. City newspapers now tailor editions to particular (usually demographically attractive) suburban areas, and community newspapers are generally thriving. Special-interest magazines have prospered in the 1980s and 1990s, whereas the general-interest magazine is just about dead. Some magazines are even beginning to tailor ad and story mixes to particular readers' preferences or demographic profiles. We will certainly see more personalization over time as print media compete with the Web.

Learning Less

Another key to the success of print media is their loyalty to timeless attention-getting topics. As mentioned earlier, stories about presidential elections—the ever-popular appeal of tribal hierarchy—are appearing with greater frequency in leading newspapers. In 1991, a total of 392 stories on the 1992 presidential campaign were published between January and the end of August in the *Los Angeles Times*, *New York Times*, and *Washington Post*. During the same months in 1995, some 575 stories about the 1996 campaign appeared in the same papers. In the same months of 1999, there were 687 stories about the 2000 campaign. It's not that these stories are getting more detailed and issue oriented; in fact, they're getting less so. Many of us seem to be reading more about the race, but less about the horse. Of course, we're voting less too; perhaps driving to the polling place simply requires too much concerted attention, or citizens feel that their votes won't affect the tribal hierarchy. Perhaps the near tie in the 2000 presidential election will bring on greater attention to voting in the United States.

Move over, Big Brother

A new study of how the media affect voters confirms our claim that attention really does impel action. The Ohio State University study shows that people who read or watch news about politics are the most likely to pull the lever on election day. Although news coverage does focus the spotlight on issues that voters will consider most important, the media do not exert an Orwellian control over voter opinion about these issues. People who are already disposed follow the political process may use the media to educate themselves, but they form their own opinions.

Source: Tim Feran, "Are Voters Mere Dupes of the Media?" *Columbus Dispatch*, 7 September 2000.

Sex Sells

Another perennial attention getter is sex, of course. Print media—magazines in particular—have discovered this route to attention in a prominent way. Even once-staid women's magazines such as *Redbook* and *Ladies' Home Journal* now have sex-oriented articles and cover teasers. The revealing swimsuit issue, of course, always gooses *Sport's Illustrated*'s sales. *Maxim*, a new men's magazine, used sexually oriented content to increase its circulation dramatically.

Sex-oriented magazine advertisements have also become apparently more common. In 1983, according to a University of North Texas study, only 1 percent of magazine ads containing at least one man and one woman depicted or implied sexual intercourse. By 1993 the percentage had risen to 17 percent. "Provocatively" dressed females in ads increased from 28 percent to 40 percent; men in various states of undress increased from 11 percent to 18 percent.[6] This tendency has probably continued since the end of the study in the mid-1990s.

Monetary advancement is another popular theme. Virtually every newspaper's business section has added content on personal finance. "Hot Stocks to Buy" is always popular as a financial magazine topic. Personal finance books—e.g., *The Millionaire Mind*, *The Millionaire Next Door*—generally ride high in both business and general nonfiction best-seller lists.

Celebrity Memoir

Fast on the heels of Hollywood, print publishers have also begun to focus heavily on personalities as vehicles for attention. In magazines, the emphasis has been on the coverage of famous people; more new magazines belonged to this celebrity-oriented category than any other in 1999. One magazine group that's focused exclusively on this category has been spectacularly successful. The People Magazine Group, which includes *In Style* and *Teen People* in addition to the flagship *People*, has increased its circulation over 600 percent since its founding in the mid-1970s. Hey, it's important to know what George Clooney is up to!

Teen Attention

These advertising vehicles grab the most teen attention (numbers reflect percentage of possible 100 percent in each category):

• Ads on cable TV: 54 percent

• Ads in magazines: 53 percent

• Commercials on the radio: 50 percent

• Commercials on broadcast TV: 35 percent

• Commercials before the feature on rented videos: 28 percent

• Ads on billboards or scoreboards: 28 percent

• Ads in newspapers: 26 percent

• Ads through the mail: 20 percent

• Ads in school: 15 percent

• Ads or other promotions at sponsored events: 13 percent

• Ads on the Internet: 12 percent

Source: Teenage Research Unlimited Teenage Marketing & Lifestyle Study, <http://www.teenresearch.com/syndicated/indexsyndicated.html>.

Printing very personal information about people considered either celebrities or freaks has proven to sell well in the attention era. Publishers have risen to new heights (or sunk to new depths) in offering this kind of information to the reading public. Tabloid books that address sensational issues or personalities tend to grab attention. So do memoirs, some about famous people, some about ordinary folks who have some sort of unusual experience to report. Both tabloidism and memoir mania demonstrate that attention in our culture goes to stories of people—especially people experiencing rare or shocking events.

Book publishing, too, relies more than ever on the personalities of authors. The best-selling authors are most often those with familiar names whose personal lives have been heavily covered by the media. We know perhaps more than we need to, for example, about the lives of John Grisham, Stephen King, Danielle Steel, J. K. Rowling, and other celebrity authors. Publishers give these sorts of authors increasing advances because they are proven commodities; less-well-known authors find it increasingly difficult to appear in print.

Finally, sellers of print media have realized that print itself doesn't sell enough print. Smart retailers have found ways to broaden their attention-getting repertoires. In addition to seeing simple shelves, book buyers now find stores packed with color, music, the smell and taste of coffee, and soft chairs where they can relax and sample the merchandise. Retailers in other industries, as well as managers trying to influence their employees, can learn a lot from bookstores.

MADISON AVENUE PRINCIPLE: Advertisers stay ahead of info-glut by employing a wide array of techniques, from repetition to emotional appeals.

Managers hoping to capture and direct attention better can draw on the techniques of those who've been managing attention effectively for years—advertisers. Since it's generally agreed that advertising doesn't work unless someone pays attention to it, advertising agencies and advertising-oriented marketers in companies have long tried to get, keep, and measure attention. Some of the principles used by advertisers can easily be applied by other types of attention managers.

Attention before Truth. "The first thing one must do to succeed in advertising is to have the attention of the reader. That means to be interesting. The next thing is to stick to the truth, and that means rectifying whatever's wrong in the merchant's business. If the truth isn't tellable, fix it so it is. That is about all there is to it." (Nineteenth-century copywriter quoted in Stephen Fox, *The Mirror Makers: A History of American Advertising and Its Creators* (New York: William Morrow and Company, 1984), 28.

New, Improved, Free—and Often

To get and keep attention, advertisers emphasize frequency and repetition. They have always understood that the way to gain mind share is to keep reminding people of your basic message; one hundred separate one-page ads make a much greater impression than a single, hundred-page report. Of course, there's a fine line between using repetition to keep attention and using it to bore your audience, and good advertisers know when they're crossing it.

> There's a fine line between using repetition to keep attention and using it to bore your audience, and good advertisers know when they're crossing it.

Not all types of content benefit from repetition, however. Advertisers know that a good slogan can encapsulate their key message—and lodge it in people's heads for all time: Own a piece of the rock. Be all that you can be. Plop, plop, fizz, fizz, oh, what a relief it is. Give a hoot, don't pollute. In some firms, managers have caught on to the idea of giving major change initiatives catchy titles and slogans, as in Coca-Cola's Project Infinity (perhaps an unfortunate choice for an information systems project), MetLife's Project Mystic, Dell's Genesys, GE's famous Workout, and Motorola's Six Sigma. Our advice: Skip the tedious project mission statement and create a catchier and more concise encapsulation.

Abhor a Vacuum

Once the message has been developed, plaster it everywhere. Advertising abhors a vacuum. We see ads posted now where they never went before: on toll booth plazas, on grocery receipts—even in bathroom stalls. One firm touting a new customer service program found all kinds of unclaimed attention space around the firm. They plastered the message on the airline ticket jackets issued by corporate travel, on PC startup screens and mouse pads, on the backs of single-page memos, and more. These strategies, of course, will have to be refined in conjunction with an increase in filtering technologies and behaviors.

Effective advertisers also make use of multiple, complementary channels to get attention. Advertisers have gotten their media purchases down to a science; they hit their targets simultaneously through as many channels as

---

We've Known It for Years. "People are very sophisticated about advertising now. You have to entertain them. You have to present a product honestly and with a tremendous amount of pizzazz and flair, the way it's done in a James Bond movie. But you can't run the same ad over and over again. You have to change your approach constantly to keep on getting their attention."

Source: Mary Wells Lawrence, quoted in *Newsweek*, October 1966.

possible, rolling out shrink-wrapped buses, for example, to coincide with radio ads. Even e-commerce firms realize that they can't restrict their advertising to the Internet; their marketers also buy newspaper ads, billboards, and radio and TV spots, and mail out catalogs. Some Internet-oriented firms have gotten very creative in bringing their message to the public; one day in 2000, for example, one of us was able to go through Massachusetts Turnpike tollbooths for free, courtesy of Energy.com, which had posted a sign saying, "Your toll is free today, compliments of Energy.com." Smart managers will be similarly creative, taking advantage of every pre-existing communications vehicle in the firm (internal newsletters, training programs, intranets, etc.) and inventing others as necessary (free lunch in the corporate cafeteria on behalf of the big, new quality initiative?) to achieve saturation.

Advertisers also play on the attention-getting attributes of personalities by using a trusted spokesperson. One of the very first successful gambits in advertising was to seek the endorsement of a well-known personality. The technique, of course, lives on—witness the ubiquity of Michael Jordan. In electronic commerce, celebrity spokespeople are becoming common as well—William Shatner for Priceline.com, Whoopi Goldberg for Flooz.com, Tom Peters for Jobs.com, and so on.

In the organizational setting, finding a spokesperson often translates into gaining an executive champion for both internal and external messages. For example, when Carly Fiorina was named CEO of Hewlett-Packard, the company began to showcase her in both external advertisements and internal communications much more than it showcased her predecessor, Lew Platt—a capable manager, but not a very attention-getting one. It can also mean procuring the endorsement of a respected outsider—like a popular management guru. General Electric's Jack Welch has long made himself available to respected academics, who have significantly raised Welch's attention profile by writing books and articles about him.

Refreshing Fun

Selling benefits rather than features is truly Advertising 101: the need to appeal to the customers' needs and desires in their own terms. Michelin doesn't try to explain the chemical engineering of its rubber compounds

---

Overheard. "Marketing is a contest for people's attention."

Seth Godin, *Fast Company*

to buyers; it shows a safely cradled baby. Coca-Cola never mentions sugar, water, or carbon dioxide—just lots of fun and refreshment. Yet managers routinely fail on this point, not addressing the needs and desires of the people whose attention their project needs. Here is a notable exception: A manager proposing a radical change program went to his CEO with a mocked-up cover of *Fortune* magazine, dated two years in the future. The CEO's own smiling face was pictured next to a headline about the turnaround he had effected. The CEO bought into the initiative.

> **People want to work on the project on which everyone seems to be having fun—and they may pitch in out of pity for one portrayed as an underdog.**

The best ads engage our attention on an emotional level. Usually, they're crafted to evoke a positive response—like the Gap's high-energy ads featuring swing dancers. Sometimes, negative emotions are sought—as in the public-service ads that make cigarette smoking repellent at a visceral level, or the Benetton ads featuring death row prisoners. In management, the same thing goes. People want to work on the project on which everyone seems to be having fun—and they may pitch in out of pity for one portrayed as an underdog.

Finally, sophisticated advertisers micromarket to audiences: They target closely defined demographic categories with highly specific messages. Buy a package of size-one diapers at the supermarket, and the checkout register spits out a coupon for formula. In similar fashion, in one enterprise resource planning implementation project we know, the update delivered to top management is just as true as, but nothing like, the one sent to energize the configuration team.

Curtain Call

We live in a society in which a considerable fraction (more than a quarter, according to one estimate) of its gross domestic product is devoted to persuasion.[7] It's a culture suffused with media, entertainment, and commercial messages. The average American spends several hours a day watching television, reading newspapers and magazines, playing video games, going to plays or movies, and otherwise burning up attention. Given all our experience with the attention industries, you would think that we'd all be expert at applying their lessons to manage attention effectively in business.

Overheard. "Caution: Cape does not enable user to fly."

Batman costume warning label

But we're not. We assume that boring text, long columns of figures, and dry talking-head presentations will gather sufficient attention so that our targets will internalize our message and change their behavior. We apparently assume that business information is inherently interesting and we don't have to glamorize it. If we were using the same techniques to provide information in the attention industries, we'd go out of business.

We must think about some business information and messages as if they were a content, entertainment, or media business. It makes little sense to start from scratch in this pursuit when various industries have been addressing similar issues for decades. Of course, the lessons are there for everyone to draw from, and if everyone did so on an equal basis, there would still be insufficient attention to go around. As with most lessons, however, some students will be more astute and hardworking than others. They'll get the attention they deserve.

CHAPTER 7

EYEBALLS AND CYBER MALLS

Overshadowing Lansdowne

Street is Fenway Park's left-field wall—the Green Monster. On one side, ballplayers do their thing. On the other side, club kids, dancers, and the after-work crowd are out for loud music, a few drinks, and laughs. In this part of Boston, everyone's a player. One wonders if Dan Kastner had this in mind when he opened POPstick.com in the Lansdowne area last year. A quick survey of the POPstick office tells you little. Inside the front door sits a Baldwin baby-grand piano, reams of sheet music, a bass drum, amplifiers, fireplace fixtures. Behind dividing walls, headphoned workers sway to hidden beats. They stare at flashing screens, occasionally removing headphones to exchange a quick word or two. A Charles Mingus composition plays on a boom box for the benefit of anyone not sequestered in a headphoned listening room.

We wonder how much the decor is an extension of Dan's personality—what's there to inspire employee creativity, what's just clutter. As we talk, he rocks back and forth to the rhythm of Mingus's drummer. He's used to this sort of thing, unconsciously listening to a drummer while focusing on something else. Before making CEO he was a professional pianist and conservatory student. You can tell that Dan's bursting at the seams—with creativity and with business insight, but also with an overflow of "documents," client demands, and an impulse to set the priorities for each of his twenty employees himself.

If Dan's professional life has an underlying theme, it is just this—personalization. His product, customized media-rich interactive content, embodies it. So does his desire to hone his company's data-mining capability. A company's got to know its customers with greater precision than ever before. Down the road, he'd like to create a "wizard agent" to add instantly focused personalization to online purchases. "If I want to buy a bike from MountainBikes.com," he says, "I have to shuffle through page after page of useless information before I can find what I want. A wizard agent would start the personal dialogue immediately." He sorts though his calls and e-mail this way—those he knows, he responds to first. Most of the unsolicited material gets trashed. A three-foot pile of mass mailings sits by the back door. Next stop: dumpster. Mass anything is anathema to Dan. The trick, he tells us, is to do a bulk e-mailing and have it appear customized. Since the new driver of business is attention, you've got to get personal to get it.

Of all the business domains on which the attention lens can be focused, Dan's realm of electronic or Internet-based commerce is as close as you can get to an attention "pure play." Nowhere else are the economics of attention more prominently displayed. The need for attention is obvious, given the more than a couple billion Web pages and the inadequate attention to go around to focus on most of them. Designers of Web sites are often painfully conscious of the need to attract and retain attention. In e-commerce it's relatively easy to know whether you are getting attention—the attention market is a visible one. In short, companies that wish to sell their products and services over the Internet will live and die by the attention they receive.

Though the connection between attention and e-commerce may be obvious, the potential of attention management in this environment is

---

Chinese for Stickiness? Corcoran.com, a luxury homes real estate agent, consulted a *feng-shui* expe to evaluate its cyberspace in light of the Chinese tradition's physical-space design principles. The concl sions? The site's objects were not aligned to promote harmony—or e-commerce. Discordant elements included misaligned "dream" and "help" buttons.

Source: Matt Richtel, "Compressed Data: Finding the Alignment for E-Commerce Impact," *New York Times*, 17 April 2000.

largely unrealized. Certain aspects of the Internet are naturally attention getting—personalization and multimedia capabilities, for example—but firms' abilities to execute them are still limited. Although Web site designers strive to incorporate attention-getting design elements, there is little science to the process. The Web allows personalization of the informational desires of individual users—a key attention-getting tactic—but only the most sophisticated sites actually personalize their content. Despite the Web's powerful search technologies that can connect human attention with the information it desires, the searches are still highly imprecise, requiring an inordinate amount of attention to find the right information. And though Web technologies enable the monitoring of attention, all the measurement systems developed thus far are flawed. The current attention-related shortcomings of e-commerce are frustrating, but we can only expect them to improve over time.

MOLASSES PRINCIPLE: "Stickiness" is an important indicator of how much attention is being paid to an Internet site.

One of the most critical attention issues in electronic commerce is simply attracting it. The vast imbalance between Internet information and the eyeballs and brains to look at it means that most Web sites will not get much attention, and hence will probably not accomplish their objectives. How can Web sites succeed in this regard and attract the attention they need to survive? To attract eyeballs, you've got to be multifaceted. And because of the zero-sum nature of attention, not everybody can win. Gains in attention for some sites will be losses for others.

The good news is that the Internet attention problem has a name: *stickiness*. A sticky site lures Web surfers, holds them, and keeps them coming back for more (exhibit 7-1).

Exhibit 7-1: Sticky Qua Non: Tactics for Achieving Your Stickiness Objectives

Relevance
- Content that fulfills a need
- Appropriate scope
- Frequent updating
- Steady stream of benefits
- More of what customers love

Community
- Sense of ownership/belonging
- Co-creation
- Personalization and customization
- Flattery and recognition

Engagement
- Interactivity
- Competition
- Production values
- Entertainment
- Narrative

Convenience
- Quick downloads
- Intuitive navigation
- Bite-sized chunks of information
- Minimal distractions

To be sure, stickiness doesn't guarantee success. But sites that aren't sticky can't possibly succeed, as Time Warner discovered with its failed Pathfinder venture. Despite a vast amount of content, the site simply never attracted enough viewers or held them for very long.

Metrics

Stickiness is neither easily defined nor easily measured. Right now, for example, three commonly cited parameters measure stickiness: (1) the total time spent at a site, (2) the number of visits per person, and (3) the number of pages viewed per person. Although portal sites like Yahoo!, AOL.com, and att.net are sticky by all three measures, other sites may be sticky by one measure and not sticky by another. In fact, this variable stickiness is as it should be. Different measures of stickiness are appropriate under different circumstances, and companies need to determine which stickiness metric is consistent with their business objectives. For example, news and information sites can charge high advertising rates if the numbers show that they keep viewers on-site longer than their competitors. But for e-commerce sites trying to sell goods and services on the Internet, a high score by the time-spent metric may mean that customers can't easily find or buy what they want.

Though stickiness metrics may seem somewhat unremarkable, the very measurement of stickiness represents a revolution in commerce. When it comes right down to it, stickiness is a quantifiable indicator of attention in a Web context. Nonelectronic media and physical stores cannot assess attention nearly as easily. The shapers and players in the new economy recognize this vital link between attention and sales. That's why Web advertisers, Web-strategy firms, and business-to-business and business-to-customer companies all must consider stickiness alongside other core concerns such as securing venture financing or hiring talented employees.

Stickiness is critical, but how do you achieve it? The stickiest sites skillfully use four tactics, which can be broadly defined as *relevance, engagement, community,* and *convenience.* How many of the four tactics are necessary? Not one or two or three: The successful site will combine all four strategies to ensure stickiness.

What Actually Gets Attention on the Web?

According to the Media Metrix Top 50 lists from the summer of 2000, the following types of sites are most popular (for simplicity's sake, we'll blend the three distinctive metrics mentioned above):

- Portals and search sites to more information (AOL, Yahoo!, Netscape, Lycos, Excite, AltaVista, Xoom, GoTo)
- News-oriented sites (Time Warner, CNN, About.com, weather.com)
- Technology-oriented sites (Microsoft, CNET, ZDNet)
- Community sites (GeoCities, iVillage, Blue Mountain Arts)
- Auctions (eBay)
- Commodity information-based products (Amazon, Barnes & Noble)
- Pornography (Porncity.net)
- Travel (Travelocity, MapQuest, Expedia)

Relevance

The most important questions in Web site design deal with the audience and its needs: Which viewers do we want, and what do they want from us? In the aftermath of the mysterious crash of TWA flight 800, for example, the airline quickly redesigned its Web site to give prominence to updates on the investigation. The company recognized that visitors to its site—families of victims, the press, and others—were visiting because they had an urgent need for information. User needs drove the design of the site. This is a principle honored by all the stickiest sites on the Web. Preparing content in a person's native language is another way that relevance is achieved. SINA.com won accolades for providing the best Chinese language content for China, Hong Kong, Taiwan, and North America. Sticky sites deliver information, products, and services that have real relevance to users.

> Even on sites whose content is expected to remain unchanged, visitors crave novelty and want to know that the site is actively managed and the material not obsolete.

Some sites, AOL and Yahoo!, for example, achieve stickiness by maximizing breadth and depth. They are seeking to be relevant to the broadest possible audience. But some sticky sites define their audiences more narrowly and therefore are more selective about what they offer. @Brint.com, an e-business and knowledge management portal, targets business researchers by offering ample depth, but not so much that users are lost in the data stream. Similarly, collectors who visit the auction site eBay will almost certainly find several specimens of whatever they are searching for, but not so many that the task of plowing through them becomes overwhelming.

Things change quickly on the Web. User needs are not static. Information that is highly relevant today may be useless tomorrow. Frequent updates—even including near real-time changes in stock prices—are the key to sticky success for financial sites like MoneyCentral.msn.com, schwab.com, iii.co.uk, and Consors.de. Even on sites whose content is expected to remain unchanged, visitors crave novelty and want to know that the site is actively managed and the material not obsolete. Britannica's

---

Techno-Attentive Future. "Tomorrow's customers, competitors, and business partners, born and raised on digital technology in their homes, schools, and toys, will not only expect but demand commercial relationships that are technology enabled. Children who grew up playing with 64-bit networked video games won't simply reject text-based interfaces and suboptimal connection speeds, they will find them incomprehensible, like some form of hieroglyphics. And their attention spans for new goods and services are themselves expressed in Internet years—that is, they are about one-seventh as patient as adults."

Source: Larry Downes and Chunka Mui, *Unleashing the Killer App: Digital Strategies for Market Dominance* (Boston: Harvard Business School Press, 1998), 159.

editors accomplish this by constantly updating its home page with lists and reviews of the best Web sites, magazines, and books. Sites that promise a steady stream of benefits, such as the more-than-a-portal Italian ilsole24ore.com and Scandinavian SOL.no, create stickiness because each mouse click brings more news, service, and value than the last.

The stickiest sites are also authoritative—or at least claim to be, using time-honored techniques that establish their credentials with users. Amazon.com now boasts the "earth's biggest selection" of goods, Fast Search (www.alltheweb.com) the "world's biggest fastest search engine," and Hitsquad.com touts itself as "the world's biggest music software site." Meanwhile, 1-JOBS network (www.1-jobs.com) calls itself the "fastest-growing Internet recruiting service," and ECeurope.com claims it is the "largest B2B eMarketplace."

Sneaker.com uses online question-and-answer sessions with professional runners to position itself as an authoritative source. Computer and electronics vendor CNET.com creates an aura of credibility by bestowing a gold and red ribbon icon on certain vendors that marks them as "CNET Certified Merchants."

WebPagesThat Suck.com

In the mid-1990s, well before the principles of stickiness had been firmly established, everyone with *HTML for Dummies* and an Internet service provider (ISP) was putting up his or her own craftily designed Web pages. Noticing that many pages "sucked," Vincent Flanders set up a reference site for those looking "to learn good design by looking at bad design." Through links, chat rooms, and news-group buzz, the site received so much attention that Flanders was soon able to charge for advertising space, acquire paid public speaking engagements, and write a best-selling book.

Engagement

Relevance alone may not be enough to make a site sticky. With more than two billion pages on the Web, surfers can probably find relevance in more than one place. No subject is so specialized that it enjoys a monopoly; even a search for such an obscure subject as the ancient Anglo-Saxon epic poem *Beowulf* turns up several sites, some with audio files of original-language readings.

The stickiest sites also succeed in engaging their audience. The main tools of engagement are interactivity, competition, high production values, entertainment, and narrative.

Interactivity is a proven way to keep the attention of Web site visitors. Some measure of interactivity comes with the Web territory, of course, since visitors have to keep clicking the mouse to keep pages coming. But many sites have taken interactivity a step or two farther. Take the *Atlantic*

Monthly's "post and riposte" feature, for example. Readers can post their reactions to articles they have read on the site's message board (www.the atlantic.com) and can revisit the site periodically to see what other readers have to say—about the article as well as about their comments. All of that time online makes this a sticky site; similar comment-and-response features are used on other sites, including *Harvard Business Review* (www.hbsp.harvard.edu), CNN.com, and Epinions.com.

Competition is an especially sticky form of engagement and not just for sites whose main purpose is online gaming (although Gamesville.com and uproar.com, which both feature real-time cards, bingo, and trivia for cash winnings, are among the stickiest Web sites). Many nongaming sites now feature various forms of competition to encourage people to linger. Disney .com offers users several different games, and the UK's sports-oriented football365 features trivia quizzes and arcade-style games that cater to a sports fan's sense of competition.

Production values make their own statement, particularly in a visual age, in which images often trump words. Faced with a multitude of competing sites, visitors often discriminate on the basis of what they see. The British clothing vendor Racing Green, for example, goes to great lengths in designing its Web site to look and feel like a high-quality catalog. At the highest level of production quality, one may wonder whether technology begins to blur the line between commerce and entertainment. boo.com, a now-defunct casual-apparel site headquartered in London, entertained shoppers with virtual mannequins and rotating 360-degree views of clothing, so that even the backs of printed shirts were shown. As if that were not enough, Miss Boo, a three-dimensional, interactive, animated avatar, answered shopper questions and assisted with sizing. The story of boo.com may serve as a cautionary tale to those who don't properly harmonize stickiness with business objectives. Were the site designers trying to entertain visitors, or were they trying to sell clothing? Although the site may have kept visitors on for lengthy stays, it apparently didn't drive the visitor toward a sale often enough.

Narrative is an especially memorable way to present messages. Some sites get their narrative content from users, as in parent soup's publication of members' "birth stories." Few sites offer original narrative content, but

---

The "Look-at-Me" Market. Teens crave the attention of friends and other teens. Many have a greater comfort level with their PC than their parents do and turn to cyberspace for interaction and self-promotion. Teen-constructed, all-about-me Web sites are ubiquitous in cyberspace. Some advice: Forget about building a cyber-store-front. Dot-coms that want to make a legitimate play at the $150 billion teen market should position themselves as interaction or self-promotion enablers.

as bandwidth to homes and businesses increases, people may submit digitized video commentary and advice that will play like cinematic dramas scrolling across Web screens. Sites like DotComGuy, which allows visitors to view a person's real-life existence courtesy of e-commerce sponsors, may prove to be as sticky as daytime TV soap operas.

Community

Web designers use co-creation, customization, personalization, recognition, and flattery to give users a strong sense of belonging and ownership. The type of community that results gives visitors a sense of belonging and even ownership in a site that keeps them coming back.

Co-creation—in which users make a substantial investment of their own information to build the content of the site—is the main force behind the stickiness of investment sites like Fidelity's and Schwab's. Customers have to enter their own financial profile information and investment preferences to get full value from the sites—and then they're stuck. Internet calendars available on sites like When.com and AnyDay.com depend on co-creation; their stickiness is directly proportional to how much scheduling information the user has added to them. Co-creation is also the driving force for any site that makes heavy use of online discussion, such as the women's community site iVillage.com. Ratings sites such as Epinions.com and AllExperts.com, in which users supply their ratings of various products and services, are enormously successful at bringing raters back to the sites to provide more ratings and assess their status as raters.[1] Co-creation is also a key to the stickiness of Bluemountainarts.com, which allows a well-wisher to add a personal sentiment—as personal as one's own recorded voice—to an online greeting card. What do all these sites have in common? In every case, user-provided content makes them more useful and harder to abandon—in other words, reliably sticky.

Customization is a form of co-creation, but usually

Flycast

High-tech start-ups, and Internet companies especially, often have great stories about their founding: an idea and a few nights of midnight pizza, and—boom!—a multimillion-dollar company is born. For a while, the media embraced each new Net business with ardor; after all, every idea was a new one. But now, with a bumper crop of new companies popping up in every sector, companies are finding it difficult to get noticed. Here's Flycast Communications' (a Web-based advertising firm) get-itself-noticed strategy:

1. Admit that the in-house public relations (PR) department was not enough.

2. Hire Schwartz Communications, a PR firm that focuses on entrepreneurial companies.

3. Schwartz distinguishes Flycast from the industry crowd by emphasizing its specialized services.

4. Flycast thus creates a buzz in general Internet and financial publications, not just industry-specific rags.

Source: Peter Rojas, "Your Attention, Please: Flycast and Investor Broadcast Network Strive to Stand Out," *Red Herring*, October 1999, <http://www.redherring.com/mag/issue71S/news-pr.html>.

depends more on filtering and manipulation than on the addition of information by the user. For example, MyYahoo!.com allows sports, stock market, or weather buffs to put whatever news most interests them at the top of the page. In the business-to-business sector, Dell's Premier Pages site employs customization by letting corporate customers exclude information not relevant to their account.

Amazon.com is a good example of a site employing *personalization*—beginning with the cheery "Welcome John Smith" that greets Smith on sign-in. At a deeper level, the site targets previous customers individually by providing gift registry and matching solutions for friends and family. Follow-up e-mails concerning purchases from the company are also personalized. If they were not personalized, they would probably be deleted as junk e-mail. Preview Travel (now part of Travelocity) uses a similar approach to sell travel services, with personalized recommendations based on the customer's prior travel patterns.

Amazon.com's reliance on reader-submitted reviews is often touted as an example of co-creation. But the stickiness impact of this tactic may have more to do with the *flattery* and *recognition* of the reader doing the posting. Today, not just authors but reviewers as well get their own ratings on Amazon.

A sense of community can be a powerful stickiness builder and an effective marketing advantage. The sports fans who populate sites like NFL.com, NBA.com, and NHL.com show their commitment to a sort of community by wearing the team-logo merchandise and using the team-logo credit cards available through the site. A visit to the official Web site for UK's Manchester United would be a waste without a click to enjoy the shopping experience at the team's online "Megastore." Beansprout.com brings child-care vendors, physicians, and referral agencies to the screens of a virtual community of families.

Convenience

Surveys of Internet users suggest that faster access speeds would be the single most important factor driving increases in their usage. One implication of this finding is that multiple formats and complex technologies for playing sound and video over the Web may in fact have a real downside. Though they do help to draw attention to a site, they may frustrate

---

Overheard. "Attention is the hard currency of Cyber space."

Gerard Van der Leun and Thomas Mandel, *Rules of the Net*

visitors who quickly tire of waiting for sound and video to load when all they really want is rapid access to information. Many sites recognize this risk, and offer visitors an option to get the pages without the bells and whistles of flash technology.

Intuitive navigation helps make sites more convenient; so does delivery of content in digestible *chunks*. USATODAY.com, thanks to the company's long experience in print, is a model of the bite-size presentation. The UK-based consumer and home products vendor Argos forgoes banner ads in favor of graphics that quickly navigate a visitor to the store's products.

Unlike television and radio, which also strive to capture your attention, the Internet is not a passive medium. People must click and click to keep the content flowing. When it's just as much work for a user to stay with you as to leave you, the pressure is on to deliver. That's why stickiness matters—and why a successful retention strategy will involve some form of all four tactics (relevance, engagement, community, and convenience). Competitors are bound to be racing right now to make their sites more relevant, engaging, and easier to use, or to build a stronger sense of ownership and belonging between the user and the site. In a world in which attention is one of the scarcest resources and attention retention is the key to success, experience shows that these tactics work.

Hurdles

One difficulty that Internet users face is the high level of attention necessary to find the information desired. Although search technology is already quite capable and improving all the time, it's not generally up to the task. The problem is partially one of simple volume—no single search engine can find all the relevant sites. A study from NEC Research Institute found that no search engine could find more than 16 percent of the Web's pages.[2] The ambiguities of language and the lack of user training for Internet search techniques also add to the difficulty of—and the attention needed for—searching and finding Internet information.

Another problem requiring excessive attention is poor information design on the Web. Jared Spool, an expert in Internet usability, found that users of fifteen large commercial sites could only find information 42 percent of the time even though they were taken to the correct home page. A Zona Research study found that 62 percent of Web shoppers have given up looking for the items they wanted to buy online; 20 percent had given up more than three times in two months. Of the few information designers in the world, fewer still are skilled in Web design. It's safe to assume that the vast majority of sites have never been blessed by a professional information designer's attention.

Even when the design has some orientation, most Web site designers generally work more from matters of fad and fashion than from any serious understanding of human-computer interfaces. The fads involve either new technology-enabled "advances" in what is possible in site design, or mistaken impressions about what design attributes attract attention or

LITERALLY STICKY

Compare these two paragons of stickiness to your Web page. How does it stack up?

	GECKO	GUM
Description	Small tropical lizard	Used to freshen breath, also comes in industrial variety to adhere surfaces together in construction and manufacturing
Soundbyte	"Has stickiest feet in the universe"	"How do I get this out of my son's hair?'
Mechanism	Until recently puzzled scientists–thousands miniscule hairs, or *setae* on its feet can be angled when in contact with surfaces, even in a vacuum	Until recently also puzzled scientists–chemical or physical bonds cause adhesion between gum and surface.
Adhesive Force	Ten times greater than needed for body weight, 600 times greater than the simple frictional force between lizard skin and the surface	Ten thousand times stickier than theoretical models say it should be
Measurement Tool for Determining Adhesive Force	Microelectrical-mechanical	Probe pulled out of gum at a constant rate
Secret of Stick-cess	Setae operate at the molecular level, utilizing intramolecular stickiness, or van der Waals forces	The rough and wavy boundaries of the probe trap air bubbles between probe and the gum; these act as microscopic suction cups
Results of Stickiness	A Volvo-esque safety margin when running on hotel ceilings or fleeing predators	Modeling of the suction effect in industry research could lead to more temperature-sensitive and environmentally friendly adhesives

Sources: "Stickiness. Blame It on the Bubbles," *Economist*, 23 January 1999; "Climbing the Walls," *Economist*, 6 October 2000.

facilitate understandability. One such device was "frames," which split up a Web page into sections and may have briefly attracted attention, but often hindered readability. A large amount of white space, another Web design fad, proved ineffective at transmitting information; humans read faster with more, smaller words on a page (up to a point, of course).

Colors, which abound on many pages, are often deafening to user attention on the Web. According to the psychology of perception, many different colors and highlighting approaches simply "flood" the screen. If colors are used sparingly, a colored message will get the user's attention. Since our retinas have more red-sensitive cones than cones for any other color, red is especially suited to getting attention. Yet an informal survey of Web pages suggests that red is not particularly prevalent.

Some Web services firms, or eCIs (electronic commerce integrators), try to overcome these deficiencies from the ground up. They recognize that the very blueprint for the new economy must be redrawn, or "architected," along attention lines because the old business models no longer work in an attention economy.[3] Whereas the emphasis has traditionally been placed in areas in which firms can exercise full control—on their products or brand—Web services firms now advocate a customer-driven approach.

Understandably, a sense of anxiety might ensue for, say, a brand manager who doesn't discern the new attention-girded foundations of e-commerce. Because the emphasis is now squarely on knowing the customer, not managing the brand or product, Web services firms are finding means of securing some degree of control for their clients. Two attention issues are at work here, the second building upon the first. First, as companies create e-commerce strategies, they must attend to the right end of the business model equation—the online customer. Second, e-commerce strategy should attend to the complexities inherent in the "Know thy customer" model. Customers' needs, insights, buying habits, reactions to Web site design, demographics, complaints and kudos, and favorite and least favorite products rule the day. As a result of this new attention to the customer, Web services firms implement customer-monitoring software, such as Accrue, and build Web sites aimed at customer attention.

Some e-commerce integrator firms are actually reinventing job descriptions to underscore to clients the importance of managing virtual customer attention.

Netscape

Back in the dark ages, when "free" seemed counterintuitive, Marc Andreessen achieved first-mover advantage and drew unprecedented attention to the Netscape brand by giving away Web browser software. Many people were still so caught up in the rush of not paying, they hardly flinched when they later had to purchase Netscape's Web server software to support the "free" browser.

We're beginning to hear of job titles such as "structural designer" and "cognitive designer." Structural designers *build* both the Web site and the information architecture with the end user's attention in mind. Cognitive designers, on the other hand, *examine* the relationship between attention, behavior, and interface design. In both cases, it's the user experience—how the information architecture and design platforms invite attention—that rules.

It's not surprising, then, to hear about cognitive designers working in conjunction with focus groups and conducting usability tests. In this attention economy, the focus group takes on a distinctive character, whereby the flow of participant attention in a Web environment becomes the focal point.[4] While focus group research seeks to understand a Web customer's *attitude* toward a particular information or page design, the usability test seeks to determine the *behavior* of that customer. How long does he or she stay at a site? What seems to motivate desirable and undesirable behaviors by a customer? In both focus groups and usability tests, designers gauge attention by direct interaction—through pointed questions or observations—with the participants. Instead of drawing conclusions about customers using the impersonal tracking and metrics that we mentioned earlier, cognitive designers can make first-hand determinations before recommending specific strategies, products, or technologies to clients wishing to enhance their Web presence. The clear advantage here is that aspiring e-businesses can shift from a reactive to an anticipatory stance with regard to virtual customer attention patterns and needs.

> **Customers' needs, insights, buying habits, reactions to Web site design, demographics, complaints and kudos, and favorite and least favorite products rule the day.**

CONVERSION PRINCIPLE: Internet attention is only a starting point; online advertising must engage the viewer and lead to behavior change.

Many seeking attention on the Web get so caught up in the intricacies and the novelty of the medium that they fail to recognize their ultimate goal—to convert attention into cash. As Aristotle noted, "any successful endeavor starts with a keen attentiveness to the end-goal."

For someone to have seen your Web banner or interstitial (a full-page

---

Overheard. "Most ads on the Internet today are like handbills stapled on telephone poles: you walk by them, but you don't pay much attention to them. . . . The biggest gamble on the Internet is whether most Web sites will ever make real money by renting eyeballs to advertisers."

Peter Schwartz, "Scenarios"

message that loads in the ten or so seconds between Web pages on the user's screen) isn't enough. What really matters is that someone actually clicks on a banner or button, visits an advertiser, and ultimately buys products and services. In the short run, because measurement approaches aren't fully developed yet, you may get away with more rudimentary behaviors. If you can simply demonstrate that a lot of eyeballs have come to call or that an ad has received many "impressions," it may be enough. But monitoring of Web attention has already increased in sophistication over these simple metrics. In the beginning, it was simply *hits*, or requests for data. Later the key measure became page views, then *click-throughs*, or the percentage of viewers who respond to an online ad. More recent measures include the number of unique visitors to a site (i.e., the number of unique Internet addresses visiting) and a page's reach (the percentage of a sample that looks at a page in a given month). Forthcoming

INSIGHTS FROM THE CONVERSION PRINCIPLE

- *Eyeballs are much more valuable when you know to whom they belong.* If an anonymous eyeball is worth ten cents, a registered one is worth at least a dollar. If you know the actual person who has visited your site, you can start pursuing all those marketing clichés that everyone talks about: relationship marketing, one-to-one marketing, lifetime customer value, and so forth. A simple prerequisite of close customer relationships is knowing the customer. Of course, it's difficult to get people to register; basically you've got to offer something valuable in exchange. Intermediate levels of identification also offer value; an anonymous visitor with a cookie file, for example, is more valuable than one without.

- *Not all eyeballs are created equal.* The more valuable ones belong to those who actually buy, those belonging to bodies with fat wallets, and those with the target demographics sought by the sponsor. Print and television eyeball seekers have known this for decades, but the Web is just getting into it. Now, we don't really know yet which Web site design equates to which demographic group (the same way we know which demographic groups like tabloid versus broadsheet

newspapers), but we certainly know which products different groups like to buy, and how that relates to occupations, hobbies, and interests. We can thus expect that the eyeballs that visit golf- and tennis-oriented sites will probably be more valuable to advertisers than those that hang around stock-car-racing sites.

- *If you can't measure attention, you can't get paid for it.* As noted, the Internet has several attention metrics. But this can lead to some confusion. Through either sampling or server-based tools, we can measure whether someone has visited a site, whether the visitor clicked on anything (e.g., an advertisement), and how long the visitor stayed. Most sites don't use that relatively simple information very well to redesign or customize their sites. But wouldn't it be useful to know how the visitor felt about the content? Eventually, at least for a sample or focus group of viewers, we'll be able to evaluate feelings through brain-wave monitoring, galvanic skin response, heart rate, and the like. As described, these technologies are already being used to measure other kinds of attention, and they will increasingly be used in conjunction with the Web.

measures will assess user behavior (length of stay, repeat visits) and, most importantly, how many customers actually buy. Ad agencies for television and print ads are beginning to be compensated on the basis of performance—revenue or market share increases for products advertised—and the same trend will ultimately reach Internet advertising.

As Web-based advertising proliferates over time, managing and measuring the attention it receives will become even more important. Standard, well-accepted approaches will be developed for the measurement of attention and the actions that result from it. We'll almost always know exactly whose attention is going where. We will even develop some level of "science" about what attributes of Web advertisements attract and hold attention. Then, of course, everyone will adopt these attributes—which will create the need for continual creativity and innovation in Internet advertising.

> We will even develop some level of "science" about what attributes of Web advertisements attract and hold attention.

E-Commerce Attention Economics

The economics of attention are more transparent in e-commerce than in any other environment. Much, but not all, of the economics is mediated through Web-based advertising. From an attention standpoint, advertising is significant because it is the primary vehicle for turning attention into money. Many Web sites rely solely upon advertising to generate revenues, but there is more advertising than there are eyeballs to attend to it.

Internet advertising is not yet a huge economic force in itself. In 1999, an estimated $3 billion was spent on Web advertising. Although a small fraction of what is spent on TV and print advertising, Internet advertising expenditures in 1999 did pass outdoor (billboard) advertising in annual expenditures. Internet advertising is growing rapidly, but it nevertheless competes for attention with every other form of advertising and promotion of goods and services. These other outlets show no sign of diminishing. In 1998, for example, U.S. advertisers sent 87 billion pieces of direct mail, up 25 percent from five years earlier. In 1999, 15 billion catalogs were delivered to U.S. households—50 for each man, woman, and child. As one catalog company CEO put it, "There's definitely a sense of urgency about getting customers' attention."[5]

Despite its small size in the grand scheme of attention-getting devices, however, Internet advertising is disproportionately influential on the advertising industry and on anyone else interested in attention management. Whereas advertising has always been about the conversion of attention to money, the Internet is the first advertising vehicle we know of in which viewers of ads are paid directly for their attention. It is quite common for Web sites (e.g., clickrewards.com, cybergold.com, motivationnet.com) to give points or rewards for a viewer's clicking on advertisements. In the go-go days of e-commerce, Internet companies would supply free Internet access (e.g., NetZero), and even free computers (Free-PC.com, now merged with eMachines) to users who were willing to view screen ads. We can't recall anyone receiving free televisions for watching TV commercials.

Fifty Seconds

When an advertising firm wants to home in and successfully campaign for your attention on the virtual front, what is its best strategy? More specifically, what kinds of ads are likely to get attention on the Internet? This is a critical issue, because not all ads do get attention. In fact, attention levels fall off rapidly beyond a small set of advertisers. And even for the most successful banner ads, the average user clicks through at a rate of less than 0.5 percent. If users do click through, on average they hang around at a given page for less than a minute. If you want to bring visitors to your site and you've got some money to spend, you need to decide whether advertising on the Internet is worth the trouble. The following tactics below can help you make the Web advertising decision.

Multiple Media

Given that Internet users also frequent other information sources, it makes sense to employ multiple media to attract attention to a particular Internet offering. Internet companies are increasingly using television to pitch their sites. Print and even billboard ads point viewers to Web sites. Television networks (CNN, CNBC, the Weather Channel) produce content for the

Napster

Original business model—none, just get attention and worry about the details later. . . . Advertising revenue, membership fees, worry about that down the road—can always cash in on the attention. Or so went the thinking of Shawn Fanning, a nineteen-year-old Northeastern University student who designed a downloadable program called Napster that enables a PC to play and lend out digitized music files, or MP3s. Because Napster software converts hard drives into MP3 file servers, Fanning argued that receiving the Beatles' "Revolution" via Napster is conceptually the same as borrowing the physical CD from a friend. But Fanning began to change his mind when Bertelsmann, a large music publisher, took a substantial ownership position in Napster.

Web at the same time and frequently remind their viewers of their Web addresses. On the masthead of almost every major newspaper today is printed the URL (uniform resource locator, or in common language, the Web address) for its online version. The astute attention seeker will work across as many media fronts as possible, but will target specific contexts. Internet-using households, for example, tend to watch somewhat different television programs than those without Internet access.

The Rich Get Richer

In a listing of the top twenty-five advertisers for a month in 1999, the higher-ranking advertisements includes such Internet stalwarts as Microsoft, Amazon.com, Yahoo!, America Online, Netscape, AT&T, E*Trade, eBay, and Ameritrade. These firms already have strong Internet brands and can attract attention because of their size, breadth of offerings, and reputation. If you don't already have that kind of online recognition, banner ads may not have much effect.[6]

Rich Media Get Richer

Choose between conventional "picture" (called GIF) banners, or "richer" media involving moving images. At least one controlled study comparing three rich ads to three lean versions of the same ad has suggested that richer media get more attention. The ads were more likely to be noticed, had a higher click-through rate, and were more likely to lead to positive feelings about the company being advertised. The technologies used for rich media, however, sometimes require users to have previously downloaded special software. The study also found that rich media ads tailored to attract attention had more impact than those tailored to provide increased functionality (e.g., ordering a book directly from the ad banner).[7]

Participation Rules

In a study of a single month's rankings in 1999, the single most likely ad banner to be clicked on was one from First USA, a credit card company, and Microsoft. The ad allowed chess players to compete with the Russian chess expert Garry Kasparov. It's a sure bet that many who clicked on the banner didn't actually plot to get Kasparov's queen, but the prospect of doing so is certainly attention getting. A leading ad in November 2000 encouraged viewers to "Click on the 33 for a chance to win $31,000,000" (click on a numbered circle changing rapidly on the screen and be entered into a lottery) or "find the ball and win."

Exotic Products and Services Need Not Apply

Successful advertisers offer well-understood products and services; one might even call them commodities. The top ten ads in one month offered inducements for mortgages (GetSmart), cars (AutoWeb), charitable contributions (Red Cross), faster Internet service (Acceleration Software), credit cards (CapitalOne, eBay/First USA), gambling (Casino-on-Net), and cheap air travel (Lowestfare). You may have to be creative to succeed in Internet advertising, but the things you are selling apparently don't have to be.

Let Us Entertain You

Web sites that simply inform the viewer, but don't try to sell anything are difficult to use effectively from an advertising perspective. The biggest problem with such sites is that users don't hang around for long enough. It's difficult to build brand identification when an ad is viewed for only a few seconds. Some firms, however, now offer entertainment-oriented sites in which the primary purpose is to hold the viewer's attention over time while that person views advertising of various types. Mplayer.com, for example, offers games, chat, classrooms, and talk shows to viewers, all with the idea of securing their attention for advertising. The average user's session is about an hour. During that time, viewers might see banner ads, pop-up ads, or interstitial ads. Even the backs of cards in a solitaire game can have ads on them.

If You Don't Like the Rankings, Wait a Week

How different advertisers perform from week to week, from month to month, and certainly from year to year varies considerably. This suggests that Internet users click on ads that seem novel or interesting. If you're contemplating putting up a banner, don't buy it for the long run.

Be Creative

Creativity on the Internet involves the manipulation of multiple elements: the placement of the ad on the page, the text and graphics within the ad, and the choice of locations in which the ad is placed. Some research suggests that users tune out banner ads fairly quickly. This phenomenon is sometimes called sensory input filtering, and can only be countered by maneuvering the ad around several parts of the screen. Several companies, for example, are beginning to offer *interstitial ads* (as mentioned previously, full-page messages that load in the ten or so seconds between Web pages on the user's screen). The lack of anything else to look at on the screen was always one reason that television advertising was so successful. Why should the Internet be any different?

Counting Those Eyeballs

It's also relatively easy for advertisers to know whether their ads have received attention on the Internet. Nielsen NetRatings, one source for such monitoring, reports every month how many banner ad impressions, or viewings, occurred on the Internet. In one month during 2000, for example, 466,205 Microsoft banners were seen by (or, more accurately, appeared on the screens of) 43.8 percent of home Internet users in the United States. Though one might debate whether that number is large or small, good or bad, it is certainly precise. The data aren't perfectly accurate, based as they are on samples of Internet users, but they are better than anything received by advertisers at equivalent points in the history of any previous medium.

As mentioned earlier, monitoring and measuring attention on the Internet is a tricky game. One analyst reported that the Web magazine *Salon*'s site is viewed by either 1.2 million people per month, less than 500,000, or too few to count, depending on whether you believe the site owners, Media Metrix, or Nielsen, respectively.[8] Internet users in schools, at work, located outside the United States, or using America Online are often not counted. Server-based counters count pages requested, but can't verify that the page actually reached the screen before the viewer went to another site. Accurate metrics matter because Web sites charge for ads by the thousands of impressions viewed. If the metrics differ, the price of attention is uncertain. The Internet Advertising Bureau has begun to try

---

Attention Ratings Equals Value. Using sampling techniques, Web site ratings firms such as Media Metrix, Nielsen NetRatings, Net Value, and PC Data try to measure the relationship between attention and Web sites. A site's rating and its value are undeniably related. Ratings have long been considered the determining factor for many investors and for investment banking analysts before they set stock prices. Independent studies at five universities in the late 1990s confirm that ratings move dot-com stocks and affect valuations. The key question here—one yet to be fully answered—is how reliable are ratings? Another question, one germane to our discussion, is this: Do these firms make distinctions between the types of attention they are monitoring?

to standardize metrics, banner sizes, and other aspects of the medium. Before we can have a mature attention market for Internet advertising, these measurement problems will have to be solved.

Free Money?

Advertisers and other Internet players are now finding that the "free cash and prizes just for looking at our ad or Web site" tactic is becoming obsolete. While eyeballs are important, they must be converted into names and credit card numbers. GoTo.com represents an improvement over simple "cash for eyeballs" plays. GoTo.com is a search engine for which the business model is based entirely on the economics of attention; the only basis for finding and listing Web sites is the amount paid to GoTo.com. The GoTo site is also the most transparent attention market we've ever seen. Let's say, for example, that you want to search the Web for sellers of digital cameras. You enter that term into the search engine, and a number of sites, all of which have paid for being listed, appear on your screen. You're informed that if you click on a link to a particular seller of the cameras, the Web site will receive seventy-four cents from the company listed first, seventy-three for the second, down to twenty-nine for the last listed.

GoTo.com takes attention economics to a new level. It's similar to a small business getting a bigger display in the Yellow Pages if it pays more to the telephone company. What makes GoTo's model an improvement is that the company seeking customers only pays if viewers actually click on the link to its site—one step closer to converting eyeballs to Visa numbers.

Advertising and search aren't the only competitors in the e-commerce attention market. Web sites that sell products, such as Amazon.com, are sometimes paid to display products. Amazon places certain books or book reviews in prominent positions based on payments by publishers. Although some observers complained about this policy, it's no different from what happens in physical bookstores or grocery stores. In these environments, makers of products have long paid for prominent positioning within the store. It's only when we assume that e-commerce is a noncommercial environment that our expectations feel violated.

Linux

When Bill Gates says he doesn't feel threatened by a Windows rival, most industry analysts say one thing—Linux has really gotten Gates's attention. That's the point. Linux offers free "open-source" software, creating an enormous interactive community—one in which those who improve the code gain acclaim. Consider what his speaking and consulting fees will be when Linux's founder, Linus Torvalds, decides to cash in.

Click Off

Content on the Web will continue to proliferate for several years. We're still in the habit of thinking that every business and many individuals need a Web site. But if someone builds a Web site and nobody looks at it, it might as well not exist. Perhaps in the future it won't.

CHAPTER 8

COMMAND PERFORMANCE

Ever wonder what runs

through a chain-saw juggler's mind during a performance? Two saws in the air, one in each hand. Timing and hand-eye coordination are pitted against motorized razorlike teeth. It's the power of concentration against the power of steel and gasoline—risk management in the most literal form.

John Burns is a juggler of sorts. He runs five companies in five industries—trucking, minerals, nuts and bolts, railroads, and insurance. How does he allocate his leadership attention across so many information-intense areas (he reads over four thousand reports a year for the mineral business alone) with such success? First, John's been mining mountains of information his entire professional life. He started as a Wall Street analyst and started running the five companies twenty-five years ago. He draws a lot on his experience, and his primary attention management tool is something we can't teach you in this book—intuition. But how about the more formal leadership roles? Here, John also tries to keep it simple. Years back a friend gave him a three-pronged philosophy about where a leader's attention should go. John wrote it down and keeps it on his desk. It has helped keep him focused over the years. Starting at the end of the list, the third rule is "Plan for future profit improvement." The second is "Make improvements to the present plan." But it's the first rule that John shares with the chain-saw jugglers of the world: "Avoid disaster."

Some seasoned business leaders like John have long been using attention management tools, which constitute a large part of their success. Unfortunately, many leaders do not. What is to be learned? Since the end of World War II, thousands of books and articles have been written about leadership. But few have addressed the relationship between successful leadership and attention. We are not just talking about getting attention; we are also talking about managing and sustaining one's own attention and that of others to perpetuate a cause. Consider the great business leaders of this century—Ford, Watson, Morita, Barnevik, Welch, Gates—they have always captured attention (their own and yours) and used it to their ends. They make you feel good about following them.

But even these pillars of attention management would have a tough go in today's increasingly plugged-in world. The universe is available twenty-four hours a day at the click of a mouse, and there's more distracting information than we could ever absorb. Now, more than ever, leaders have to find innovative means of capturing and directing attention. With greater efficiency and creativity, leaders will need to secure the four elements of attention leadership:

- Focusing their own attention

- Attracting the right kind of attention to themselves

- Directing the attention of those who follow them

- Maintaining the attention of their customers and clients

DOWNSTREAM PRINCIPLE: **Attention flows downstream from leaders to workers to clients and customers.**

The first attribute of any attention leader is the ability to focus his or her *own* attention. This means recognizing where one's attention is directed and discerning if it is appropriately and effectively aimed. This recognition precedes any attempt to tell others where to put their attention. Each day, we focus on a set of particular items to the exclusion of others. But how aware are we of why we chose to attend to some items above others? Whereas followers might wander through their days oblivious to where their attention goes, effective leaders are perpetually aware of where their attention is directed.

> **Attention can work for or against us—and misguided attention often is more detrimental than no attention at all.**

Research conducted by Cathy Walt and Alastair Robertson at the Accenture Institute for Strategic Change suggests that leaders who are more self-aware are the most successful at directing the attention of others. This trait entails being conscious of the focus and depth of their attention at all times.

And like any skill, such self-awareness requires continued effort. Since we weren't offered an Attention Management 101 course in college, self-awareness typically is a skill we must refine on our own. Like most things, attention can work for or against us—and misguided attention often is more detrimental than no attention at all. Just as we make attention allocation choices every moment of every day, so do our employees *and* customers. To manage attention well, we must be self-aware and believe passionately that the issues we focus on are the most important ones for our own careers, our company, our employees, and our customers. This level of awareness comes to few of us instinctively.

Trickle-Down

Whether you recognize it or not, your field of attention, the set of concerns and goals that you focus on, impacts you *and* your employees. It has a discernible trickle-down effect. Employees throughout a company make decisions about what to pay attention to based on their *perception* of what their leaders pay attention to. Because leaders are busy people, their attention focus is deemed to be most important. Consequently, leaders have to be more careful about how they invest their attention, for themselves and for their subordinates.

Overheard. "Vision grabs. Initially it grabs the leader, and management of attention enables others also to get on the bandwagon."

Warren Bennis and Burt Nanus, *Leaders*

To measure attention distribution and perceptions, we administered the AttentionScape to the leadership of a small high-tech company, a firm with one office, where the employees interact daily. We took the average score of the three partners of the company, compared them to the average score of their employees, and found a direct correlation (.7) between what the leaders *said* they spend attention on and what their subordinates focused on. (In other words, 70 percent of subordinate attention was focused on the same issues—identical amounts and types—that the leaders focused on.)

In a larger company, the correlation between leaders' and their followers' attention is less profound, but still exists. We studied the leaders of a large, multinational, UK-based firm and found a .54 correlation between what the leaders spent attention on and what some of their followers focused on. Because the trickle-down effect is less prominent, managing attention in larger organizations can be more difficult. Consequently, leaders in larger organizations must work *harder* to make certain that attention translates into the type of action they expect. This goes far beyond memos and lip service.

Know Thyself

You can improve your own attention focus—and the impact it has on your employees—by following these steps:

1. Go public about where you spend your attention. By telling others about the items in your field of attention, you'll also become more self-aware.

2. Set attention goals for yourself. Know where you want to spend your future attention.

3. Get feedback from the people around you. Family, friends, and employees may have a better sense of how you spend your attention than you do.

Can't Fool 'Em

Employees are smart. With considerable accuracy, they can assess what their leaders actually pay attention to, regardless of what the leaders claim. We asked a three-partner team in the small high-tech firm to rate their own attention, then asked their employees to assess where they thought leadership "spent" its attention. The employees were accurate 80 percent of the time in gauging their bosses' AttentionScapes—yet they followed that lead only 70 percent of the time. They were more adept at predicting than following because they also had their own agendas.

Now remember, this was a highly productive and *small* company. In companies plagued by low morale or competitiveness problems, we'd expect the discrepancy to be much greater. In this particular case, the 10-percent discrepancy was probably a result of the employees' own attention chains competing with those of their bosses. Even if your employees don't always follow diligently, they want to know where your attention is focused. They want to understand what company leaders really pay attention to, in part so they can focus on the same things. Clearly, a manager's field of attention is at least a curiosity to those along the attention chain.

But how do you turn that curiosity into a productive following? How do you capture that extra 10 percent or, dare we dream, 20 percent of attention? Sometimes it is best to get explicit.

The Right Stuff

The second attribute of successful attention leaders is that they are *appropriate attention seekers*. They have risen through the organization by knowing how to get the right attention at the right time, and how to avoid inappropriate attention. Some of this may be a natural instinct. Some of it may be pure luck. But their ability to attract or divert attention from themselves (as the situation demands) is key in their rise and their ability to flourish on top.

Consider Nobuyuki Idei, CEO of Sony. His appointment as CEO surprised many. Idei surpassed at least fifteen executives more senior than himself to ascend to the CEO position. Considered a maverick and extremely international by Japanese standards—not necessarily assets in a society that covets conformity— Idei lived outside Japan for much of his career and speaks five languages. He created the French subsidiary of Sony in 1968 and spent a quarter of his career living in France and Switzerland. Idei attends rock concerts and, when he started as CEO, drove a Jaguar to work rather than being chauffeured. All in a land where the "nail that sticks up gets pounded down."

How did Idei get promoted past his colleagues in this group-consensus world? Part of the reason was his ability to attract—or divert—attention at the right time. According to staff members, Idei was "practically invisible" and never had a major success at Sony *until* he became CEO. Idei diverted attention away from his nontraditional management style by taking positions far from headquarters. Further, he carefully

Hank Greenberg of American International Group

Hank Greenberg directs the attention of his employees through clear communication. In his monthly division-head meetings, he forcefully criticizes poor performance, but he never personally denigrates employees. As AIG executive Joseph Boren explains, "He doesn't say, 'You must be the biggest dope I've ever seen,' but he might say, 'You're alarming me. You don't sound like you're in control.'" Cold? Perhaps. As Boren admits, it may be nice "to walk into a meeting and have everyone say, 'How are you today? Did you have a nice weekend?' But that's not the way our business works, and that's why our business is successful."

Source: Joseph B. Treaster, "Polar Opposites? Not Where It Counts," *New York Times*, 23 July 2000.

managed communications channels to accentuate the positives and minimize the negatives of his career. He was his own best attention publicist.

When he saw that his management acumen matched the needs of the firm, he came out of "hiding" and captured the attention of board members by making all the right moves after the entertainment arms of the firm (Columbia Music and Pictures) ran into trouble in the early 1990s. According to Sony executives, when then-CEO Ohga sought someone to manage the entertainment business, "Idei was the only one near the top of the firm who was interested in the entertainment businesses." Everyone else in Sony's upper management came from an electronics background and possessed little patience or interest in the new business—indeed, most were in favor of divesting these seemingly far-flung enterprises. Conversely, Idei readily expressed his belief in an "entertainment future" for Sony. And no one, it seemed, was better suited to bring electronics and entertainment together within Sony and make both businesses profitable. It all came about for Idei because of his ability, in addition to all else, to secure and manage appropriate attention.

> Boring and probably smart may get you to the top of an organization as a "good soldier," but these are not the qualities that keep you on top.

All too frequently, our inability to manage attention becomes our downfall. Consider the former CEO of a large U.S. electronics firm, described by a close aide as "kinda boring . . . but probably very smart." Boring and probably smart may get you to the top of an organization as a "good soldier," but these are not the qualities that keep you on top. Sometimes making it to the top is a simple matter of outlasting the rest. But remaining at the helm means capturing and molding the sustained attention of followers, board members, and customers. The aforementioned CEO lasted less than a year in the job.

Vanity Mirror

Leaders require followers who pay attention to their beliefs and actions. Without followers, the progression from self to captivating the attention of others gets interrupted. Self-awareness becomes simple vanity.

Formerly, leaders could rely solely on their positions in the organizational hierarchy to attract and direct attention, but that isn't the case today. Although the old methods of leadership—power and position—

Overheard. "I can't say I'm proud of everything I've done to motivate a kid, but if I think I've been wrong, or somebody told me I'm wrong, then I tried to find something else to motivate."

Source: Bobby Knight, quoted in "Knight Has Nothing 'To Apologize For.'"

are still effective at *getting* attention, they are decreasingly effective at *maintaining* attention. Consequently, as the organization's most important information consumers *and* producers, leaders must ensure that everything they "produce" gets out there and gets the attention of employees. Most subordinates will automatically follow their boss's lead. But positional authority alone will not *keep* the attention of employees.

Rick Younts, who formerly ran all of Asia and the Americas for Motorola Corporation, admitted that an e-mail from Motorola CEO Chris Galvin would get his attention. "I open it immediately to see if it was an absolutely critical issue," he said. But what he does with the e-mail after he reads it is his own decision. "No one decides where to put my attention but me. Chris may assume that I'll answer his e-mails first, but what I personally am interested in will get more of my attention than what anyone else is interested in. And I know that the people who work with me are doing the same thing. I can't force them to pay attention to anything."

> The key to directing attention is to accept that you can't *control* anyone's focus.

The key to directing attention is to accept that you can't *control* anyone's focus. True, you can control a lot of related things: how much time people spend at the office, where they sit, what they talk about, and so forth. You even can make people feel as if they *should* pay attention to something. But ultimately, people direct their own attention, based on their own attention chains (hence, the 10 percent discrepancy noted previously). Controlling one's own attention is the one freedom an individual will always possess, whether that person is a hostage, a slave, or a coworker sitting in the next cubicle.

Attention leaders influence behavior by creating a meaningful context for information—as mentioned previously, attention is awareness with meaning. As we've said, our whole culture is up to *here* with information. However, most of this raw material lacks meaningful context. Thus, selecting and contextualizing information—choosing what to focus on and how to focus on it—is essential to successful attention management.

A Bullish Management Style

When you're Michael Jordan, it may be difficult not to attract attention, but his hands-on management of the Washington Wizards leaves no questions about where his own attention is focused. After head coach Gar Heard was fired, Jordan said, "From this point forward, I'll be doing all the hiring and firing . . . it's on me now." Jordan has also made it clear that low-energy players are disposable and that he will be spending time on the court, running new players through one-on-one games and living up to his promise to leave his "imprints and footprints all over the organization."

Sources: Steve Wyche, "Jordan Brings His Game to the Wizards; NBA Legend Joins Front Office, Becomes Part Owner of Franchise," *Washington Post*, 20 January 2000; and Richard Justice, "For Now, Walker's in Charge; Hands-On Management Is Grabbing Attention," *Washington Post*, 1 February 2000.

Anything that disrupts your expectations or relates to something you find highly meaningful, Larry, will capture your attention. For example, right now you're probably either thinking, "Who the heck is Larry?" or "My God, they know my name!" Probably, the word "Larry" got your attention because it seemed jarringly out of context. As social primates, we've evolved with an innate propensity to focus on interpersonal relationships, and our attention goes to anything that shapes those relationships—such as addressing a particular person by name. If your name is Larry, you probably zoomed in on the word as soon as you turned to this page. Perception studies show that our own names are so important to us that we notice them before our brains have had time to *consciously* process any data at all. In fact, the more distracted we get, the *more* likely we are to search out data bits that have high context associations. The best leaders either give or tap into meaningful context for the issues they want their organizations to pay attention to. These leaders channel attention in the most appropriate ways—and that starts with their own personal attention.

> The best leaders either give or tap into meaningful context for the issues they want their organizations to pay attention to.

Don't Fuss

Great leaders create environments in which employees *want* to pay attention. To do so, leaders forge a balance between excitement and the pressure to focus attention. Also, they excel at recognizing and managing forces that divert attention. Good leaders realize that whenever they want to add a new attention item to their employees' agenda, they have to remove the requirement that the employee pay attention to another issue. If someone is already juggling as many items as he or she can handle, you don't chuck several more at the person without taking some of the existing issues off his or her hands. Additionally, great attention leaders are also skilled at *blocking* attention.

For example, John Browne, CEO of BP, realizing that attention resources were limited in his organization because of a series of mergers

---

On Why We Need Five Minutes of Wastebasket-Basketball. "Management tends to concern itself with full and continuous concentration on the work at hand . . . [but] disengaging from an involving task, one with which we are not quite finished, does not amount to abandoning it. Quite the contrary. While conscious focus shifts elsewhere, the subconscious keeps grinding away, considering anything that comes to it as grist for the mill."

Source: Jerry Hirschberg, *The Creative Priority: Driving Innovative Business in the Real World* (New York: HarperBusiness, 1998).

and acquisitions that the firm had completed, instructed his information systems managers to delete half of the information-technology applications in the firm's internal system. With oil prices fluctuating wildly and a couple of big organizations to integrate, he needed to free up some management attention.

At one of the Big Six (when there were still six) accounting firms, management instituted a policy that employees could not send broadcast mailings or e-mails during tax season. The firm wanted to keep employees focused on the books. As an attention leader, you need to help your followers prioritize their activities and make attentional trade-offs.

The recommendation of limiting e-mail goes against the grain for many managers, who fear the counterintuitive act of *taking away* responsibilities from subordinates. Some critics might argue that there are good reasons for everyone in a firm to have access to firmwide communications all year long. They'd fuss that some important information might be lost by limiting e-mail usage for four months of the year—and they would be absolutely right. But anyone with an in-box today knows how much time

LEADERSHIP 101: SEND OLD INITIATIVES INTO RETIREMENT

IN A CORPORATE SETTING, nothing confuses an attention chain like multiple internal programs competing for attention. Many people we speak with in companies complain of "initiative fatigue," and note that they just can't pay attention to all initiatives. Bain & Company's annual study of management tools and techniques shows that large corporations, on average, use between seven and eight management tools (reengineering, strategic positioning, etc.) at the same time. One professor friend of ours asked a group of senior participants in a Harvard Business School executive program how many initiatives were under way at that moment in their companies. The average was fifteen!

Aren't company leaders shooting themselves in the foot by introducing so many new programs at the same time? Yes and no. Psychological studies show that when a new object is introduced in an experimental subject's field of sight, the mind immediately pays attention to the new object. Business leaders understand that new programs and initiatives can actually shake a group of people out of corporate ennui and give them some excitement in the workplace—something to live for. The problem with this strategy is that all too often the older initiatives are not retired. It is a difficult decision to make—usually the old program (while feeling old to many in the organization) has not yet run its course or achieved the goals originally established for it. In most large companies, more troubling is that these prior initiatives usually have a group of champions who really want to see the program through to completion. By yanking one program in favor of another, the leadership of the old program is likely to feel cheated. These leadership groups were usually chosen in the first place because they are some of the more valuable employees—the last ones the company wants to alienate. So rather than weed out the old as they plant the new, corporate executives allow multiple initiatives to function simultaneously. Generally, that approach simply doesn't work.

and attention "clearing your mailbox" can take. Insisting that employees respond to *all* their mail and e-mail—but also keep their noses in their ledgers—sends a mixed message. Don't do it.

Fido on Prozac

Leaders must know how to create, or at least encourage, employee motivation. Novell CEO Eric Schmidt says that motivated employees will exhibit some dissatisfaction: "I would be unhappy if people weren't whining. I want them to want more. . . . The kind of mild dissatisfaction with what you have is a key prerequisite for success in this business."[1]

In his book *The Nudist on the Late Shift*, Po Bronson describes how leaders succeed in the rarefied atmosphere of Silicon Valley. According to Bronson, the constant tension between the security of a high-tech job (albeit a job with a company that could easily go bust tomorrow) and the high risk-to-reward ratio of "new economy" opportunities (stock options, day trading, initial public offerings) makes employees work like mood-enhanced dogs.[2]

The feeling of a high-stakes gamble has proven to be addictive in lab animals, as well as humans. Pigeons who know they're going to get a pellet every time they press a lever get bored and stop, but when the pellets come out every few pecks, spaced randomly, the pigeons will hammer away at the levers obsessively. Because of the way attention works in our brains, chancy, high-pressure tasks may motivate us more than certain, easy ones.

REAL-WORK PRINCIPLE: Misallocation of attention is the by-product of poor communication and faux work.

Leaders must work to shift the organization's attention from *faux work*, or the politics that consumes too much daily energy, to "real work." Fortunately, it is easier to move the focus from faux to real when the unit of analysis is attention rather than time. Faux

---

Real Work and Dis-ease

Al Preble, president of Cambridge Leadership Group, a leadership consultancy, suggests the following three steps to focus employee attention on real work:

1. *State a clear position.* Get the listener's attention up front. Don't "ease into" the point you're trying to make. If you can't find a way to be direct without being offensive, you won't last as a leader.

2. *Provide data to support your position.* Describe the thought process and evidence that led to your position. This keeps the listener focused on the whys of the issue, and prevents him or her from quickly dismissing your point of view.

3. *Ask to be confirmed or disconfirmed.* When you ask the listener to respond directly to your point of view, the conversation stays on topic. Over time, feedback sessions develop their own rhythm in which listeners have to pay attention to the positions and data, knowing they will be asked to respond directly to both.

work can take a lot of time. You can see that your employees are slaving away at a project. Their computer screens show the right data, their phone conversations are on the right topics, and they report that they are getting the work done. After all, they are measured and rewarded on time, and the time is definitely being spent on "work issues."

It may look as if they are actively engaged in real work—but the faux work has their attention. While employees talk on the phone, enter data, or sit in meetings, they are seething. Politics dominates their thinking. How many hours have you spent in meetings dominated by bureaucratic politics, verbal sparring, turf battles, and other pointless personnel tussles? How many employees are you paying to sit at their desks and brood over who got promoted above them, who's making more money, or who has the better office? Many executives pull a paycheck for doing this kind of thing hour after hour. They think of it as work, and in a sense they're right—it takes a lot of time, energy, and, of course, attention. Unfortunately, though, this kind of thing isn't real work, by which we mean constructive action that contributes directly to the firm's bottom line. It's faux work. Good leaders know how to shift attention (their own and their followers') from faux work to real work.

The situation becomes increasingly poignant if your company relies on your employees for innovation. One of the worst things that can happen is employees' replacing the back-of-mind attention that they used to devote to real work to faux work. Instead of figuring out how to make the doohickey work better, they calculate how they can *convince* the boss that it works better. The further away from the customer your employees feel, the more they perceive that they are wasting time and adding little value to the entire process. The situation opens the door for even more faux work.

Certainly, some degree of faux work is inevitable in a business climate in which most employees fear loss of face more than the loss of a major contract. There's no stopping the human tendency to brood over issues around social positioning. People will always fret about things they can't control—from Sally at the next desk to the plumbing at home. It's the joy

The Search for Meaning after College

Today's college graduates do not expect to have one job for life, but they do expect their job to give them opportunities to advance in their careers. To quell the faux work that can seep up through the cracks of the generation gap, managers must adapt to give young employees the attention they crave. When American Express set out to motivate its young employees, it initiated more frequent performance reviews, flexible work options, and opportunities to move laterally in the company to acquire more skills. The company thus provided a more meaningful, career-oriented context for the work.

Source: Meg Carter, "Inside Track: Young, Gifted, and Demanding Attention," *Financial Times* (London), 8 September 1999.

of employing humans—the only species that worries. Leaders can't eliminate all political machinations any more than they can eliminate the need for sleep or food. Certain things, however, can be done.

Clear communication will go a long way toward driving the faux out of work. You may be surprised at how the lack of clear communication perpetuates faux work. Too often, both leaders and coworkers operate under the following unspoken rules of communication: (1) minimize negative emotion; (2) maintain unilateral control; and (3) direct listeners to specific conclusions through leading questions; while (4) always appearing emotionally detached. Here's how it looks in practice:

> **BOSS:** Hey, Pat, good work on the SuperDuper account.
>
> **PAT:** Thanks!
>
> **BOSS** (chuckling): Next time, maybe you could get it finished *before* the deadline, huh?
>
> **PAT** (also chuckling): Maybe!

At the end of this conversation, the boss thinks that the clear message was, "You missed the deadline on the SuperDuper account, you twit!" But all Pat heard was, "You did a terrific job; the timing didn't matter all that much."

Indirect communication styles are great for perpetuating thousands of person-years of faux work, but they can mess up a lot of projects without adding one dollar to your bottom line. The standard communication devices in a typical company are actually attention obfuscators. Like the word *obfuscators*, they look good but may muddy your meaning instead of clarifying it. Trying to be "nice," making indirect demands and comments, and appearing unemotional are quick ways to confuse listeners and divert their attention from the substance of your discussion. Consequently, every conversation becomes a political game in which employees try to read between the lines to see what you *really* want. To lead effectively, you must create a corporate culture in which people get used to communicating clearly and directly. Here's an innovative solution: Tell them *exactly* what you want.

Overheard. "It seems to me that we too often focus on the inside aspects of the job of management, failing to give proper attention to the requirement for a good manager to maintain those relationships between his organization and the environment in which it must operate which permits it to move ahead and get things done."

Breene Kerr, *Giants in Management*

Contagion

Our experience is that a direct communication style is contagious, especially when initiated and modeled by a leader. Everybody around the leader begins to pick up on it and use it (your employees have probably adopted your current conversational format, good or bad). Sometimes they don't even know that they've changed their communication style—they see it working and imitate it almost subconsciously. When you hear your employees saying to each other, "Here's my position," "Here's why I think that way," or "What do you think?" you're well on your way to eliminating faux work. Even when you're not around, your subordinates will manage each other's attention toward real productivity.

OWNERSHIP PRINCIPLE: Since we pay the most attention to things that are ours, include employees in the decision process at every turn.

Leaders who manage to shift their employees from faux work to real work are also taking advantage of another attention principle. To the extent that real work is about production (and it usually is), when you manage to get your employees to be productive, you are helping them "own" the activities even more completely. As discussed in Chapter 7, co-creation has been used to make Web sites more sticky. For example, MyYahoo! has maintained a loyal following of users by encouraging them to set up their start-up page with specific information in which they are most interested. MyYahoo! users can alter the shape, order, and types of information on the page. Once a user has made these relatively simple alterations to the page, the changes are automatically saved. Whenever the user logs on, the page appears personalized.

Stickiness is better explained by co-creation than by any other concept. When an individual has created something, the person feels a natural sense of ownership and belonging. We are biologically predisposed to pay attention to our own products. To the extent that a leader can tap into the attention-keeping nature of co-creation, the leader's organization will be allotted more directed attention to the right kinds of issues.

One of the best examples is Texas Instruments, whose CEO back in 1994, Jerry Junkins, put a priority on defining a new vision and strategic plan. To ensure that it received the attention it deserved, he put not only his strategic leadership team on the hook for it, but also a broader group of vice presidents, senior vice presidents, and other high-potential people viewed as likely successors to senior management. The process didn't end there. Once the initial draft was produced, over two hundred more executives were invited to participate in shaping the plan. Management could have herded this second tier into a large room and asked for comments, but it didn't. Instead, the leaders orchestrated a series of five-day events for groups of twenty-five to thirty managers and revealed the strategic vision only after two full days of exploring competitive dynamics and explaining the process that produced it. At that point, the participants had the knowledge base and confidence to offer thoughtful criticisms and recommendations—which were readily incorporated into the final product.

> Even if you get 100 percent of your employees' attention directed in the right ways 100 percent of the time, your company will still fail if you can't secure and maintain your customers' attention.

More recently, we observed similarly positive results from co-creation when a new technology strategy was disseminated within the pharmaceutical division of Johnson & Johnson. More than a hundred executives were enlisted to *teach* the principles of a new strategy. Senior executives reasoned that at least those hundred teachers would buy in, in part because of the co-creation commitment they had made.

Even if you get 100 percent of your employees' attention directed in the right ways 100 percent of the time, your company will still fail if you can't secure and maintain your customers' attention. As an attention leader, you must position your firm's products and services in the minds of customers and maintain this attention to keep those customers coming back.

POSITIONING PRINCIPLE: Put the right type of attention where it can make the biggest difference for your organization.

As mentioned in chapter 2, leaders try to get different types of attention from their customers. Michelin, for example, uses aversive attention, reminding you that "there is a lot riding on your tires." Pirelli, on the other hand, uses attractive attention. The company sells a stylish, sleek, smooth tire, which you buy because it will look good on your car *and* make the Chevy go faster.

Some companies hope that their products are very much front-of-mind. Coca-Cola wants you to think "The Real Thing" every time you feel even the slightest thirst. Other firms hope to be back-of-mind all the time. Your local grocery store wants you to hum its radio jingle subconsciously every time you need toilet paper. The store doesn't care if you give it front-of-mind attention; it actually prefers the routinized back-of-mind attention that has you parking your car in its lot even though you didn't even intend to go to the supermarket.

Conversely, when you give attention to the IRS, it is almost invariably captive attention. Most IRS employees know only how to manage (or perhaps aggravate) your captive attention and have no clue about how to procure and maintain voluntary attention. Meanwhile, the attention you give to television sitcoms is completely voluntary.

Repositioning

As an attention leader, you need to manage not only the amount of attention but also the *type* of attention your customers give to you and, where possible, to your competitors. We worked with a high-tech service provider—call them TechnoWiz—to help the staff understand what kind of attention their customers gave to TechnoWiz versus their competitors. Exhibit 8-1 shows one customer's responses to the AttentionScape. (Recall from chapter 3 that an Attention-Scape is a three-parameter graph of a person's or a group's attention.)

In this graph, TechnoWiz is represented as the large, vivid green circle in the bottom left-hand corner of the chart. The size of the circle indicates that this customer was paying a lot of attention to TechnoWiz—very attractive, back-of-mind, captive attention. Not big news to TechnoWiz. It had been the main supplier to this customer for ten years; it enjoyed a positive relationship with the customer who routinely called TechnoWiz when it needed technology services. Everything seemed wonderful!

Exhibit 8-1: One Customer's Attention to TechnoWiz and Its Competitors

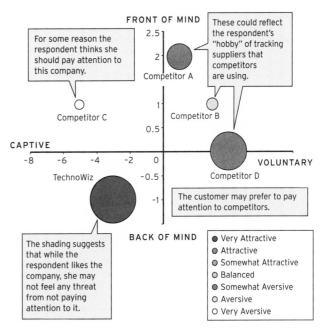

But TechnoWiz leaders were shocked to realize the type and amount of attention that their competitors received. Competitor D, for example, received a lot of attention in the chart—voluntary, slightly aversive, and front-of-mind attention! Competitors A, B, and C were also receiving voluntary attention, but less than Competitor D. We hypothesized that the customer was scanning for ways that other suppliers could better meet their needs.

We suggested that TechnoWiz add some aversive (if you don't pay attention to TechnoWiz, your business will suffer), voluntary (you *want* to pay attention to us), and front-of-mind" (we mix up the routine periodically to make the relationship interesting) attention in marketing and customer service. After all, that was the attention the competitors were receiving—so why not steal some of their thunder by eliciting the same attention from the customer? TechnoWiz made no adjustments, however. Two months after we administered the AttentionScape, the customer dumped TechnoWiz and started buying from Competitor D.

Stodgy

Leaders have many mechanisms by which they can manage customer attention. The marketing function is focused on this issue, under a number of different names: one-to-one marketing, customer relationship management, advertising awareness, focus groups. But attention to customers is the leader's responsibility, too: The leader's attention must flow smoothly and continuously from his or her own personal issues to those of employees and those of customers. Truly great leaders can focus attention at all these levels. Partly because they manage their personal attention so carefully (whether by design or by accident), those around them feel motivated to pay attention to similar issues, and ultimately customers buy into the same attention flow.

In the case of TechnoWiz, the attention flow was clearly inconsistent. Firm leadership was stodgy and old-world focused. The leadership team had very little sense of what was going on in the competitive marketplace because they were too busy worrying about securing their own positions inside the firm. This attitude spread throughout the organization—right through to the salespeople. Even when the customer said rather loudly

---

Overheard. "Anonymity and withdrawal are part of the CEO's inventory of power. The reverse of anonymity is visibility, which brings with it an expectation of accountability. If you want to operate without accountability, you make yourself difficult to reach."

Ralph Nader, quoted in Lewis D. Eigen and Jonathan D. Siegel, *The Manager's Book of Quotations*

and rather clearly, "I'm really thinking quite a lot about your competitors," the salespeople, their managers, and ultimately the top leadership of the firm were not prepared to pay attention to that feedback. Attention leadership in the firm was broken. Consequently, the customer's comments were lost, and ultimately, so too was the customer.

Bursting Through

In chapter 2, we explained that attention is "awareness tempered by meaning." A good leader knows how to attach meaning—important, powerful meaning—to the issues on which he or she would like coworkers and customers to focus their attention. The process starts with leaders who focus their own attention on meaningful issues. The meaning is communicated through the organization—via stories, incentives, and organizational designs—in such a way that the employees have no doubts that certain things matter more than others. This is how a corporate culture is born. And when that culture bursts through the organizational membrane to reach the external world, the customers know what the company stands for and how they are likely to be treated. But it all starts with the leader.

The logic, analysis, and personality necessary for attaching meaning to information to yield *attention* is one of the most powerful tools in personal, as well as corporate, management. It is what makes leaders great.

CHAPTER 9

FOCUSED CHOICES AND GLOBAL RESOURCES

Despite the proclamations

of some consultants and academic strategy gurus, business strategies are not God-given, but rather crafted by imperfect humans for use by other imperfect humans. Among the human imperfections that should be considered in such processes are both the human inability to focus attention on multiple subjects at once and humans' overall shortage of attention. Our attention-oriented view of strategy is an example of a behavioral approach, the goal of which is not to reveal the perfect strategy for an organization. Instead, the attention-oriented strategist strives only to pick something that works reasonably well within the current organizational and competitive environment. Furthermore, he or she pays attention to any signs that the current approach isn't working. An attention-informed behavioral approach considers that both the creators and the targets of strategy have limited attention. Astute businesspeople following this approach realize that even a better strategy and structure have no impact unless brought to the attention of strategists and the implementers of strategy.

BUSINESS-AS-UNUSUAL PRINCIPLE: Strategy begins when management or the CEO (or both) shift their attention away from business as usual.

Our favorite definition of business strategy is the one given by William Ocasio and mentioned in chapter 2: "[a] *pattern of organizational attention*, the distinct focus of time and effort by the company on a particular set of issues, problems, opportunities, and threats, and on a particular set of skills, routines, programs, projects and procedures."[1] Of course, companies don't have to do strategy. They may have no pattern at all to their organizational attention. We both have certainly worked with large, at least somewhat successful firms that lacked any explicit strategy. Such companies simply focus on daily operations—in some cases doing what they have always done—without devoting any attention to strategy or what they should be doing in the future. Therefore, to undertake strategy at all requires strategists to remove their attention from business as usual and focus it on how it might be better or at least different.

Abstractions

In *Institutionalizing Innovation*, scholar-consultant Mariann Jelinek describes strategy and management as activities in which the mental focus—in other words, the attention—of managers is pulled away from the specific tasks of work to abstractions of planning and strategy about how the work should be done. She explains that the act of strategizing itself, therefore, requires a redirection of attention: "[U]ntil what is routine is systematized and performance replicable without extensive management attention, management attention will necessarily focus on the routine."[2] If your organization doesn't have a strategy or hasn't gone through a strategic planning process in a while, you may have to redirect some attention to get it going.

You'll have to convince managers that their existing attention allocations are not adequate to plan for the future. The means for allocating attention to strategy are familiar and include the following:

Overheard. "On the bare stage of business, strategy is drama."

B. Joseph Pine II and James H. Gilmore, *The Experience Economy*

- Routinizing (or even outsourcing) meddlesome business problems that are preventing a strategic focus

- Bringing in an attention-getting speaker or consultant to shake up managers' minds

- Having a "strategic retreat" at which day-to-day business pressures are less visible

- Focusing managerial minds on threatening actions by competitors

OPTIONS PRINCIPLE: Business strategy is most fundamentally about focusing corporate attention on some options above others.

Once a firm has decided to focus its attention on strategy, it then has to focus it further to actually develop one. In a sense, formulating strategy is about calling attention to some aspects of the business and competitive environment and ignoring others—or referring to them as "mere tactics." It isn't always easy, however, to determine which aspects are worthy of strategic attention and which need tactical. If the Peloponnesian War was lost for the want of a nail, then perhaps strategists should worry about nails and other such tactical matters.

Any strategy involves choices—a statement with which few strategists would disagree. Managers must choose from a multitude of potentially valid alternatives which direction to take the business. Strategists may not realize that the choices are often about attention. To what strategic issues should we devote management attention? This is the question that firms are really asking when they craft strategy. Some strategy choices (phrased in attention-oriented terms) include the following:

- Should we focus our attention on market share or profitability?

- Should we focus our attention on growth within our existing business, or diversification?

- How much attention should we focus on traditional competitors versus new entrants?

- On what new technologies should we focus the organization's attention?

Overheard. "Rather than interpreting a strategy as a detailed long-term plan, it is more accurate and preferable to look at a strategy in terms of a portfolio of future options."

Cornelius A. de Kluyver, *Strategic Thinking: An Executive Perspective*

- Should we focus attention only on financial targets, or on operational ones as well?

- Can we ignore the prospect of changes in financial markets during our strategy, or do we have to focus attention on that, too?

- How about the political environment for our strategy: Does it need our attention?

POINT-OF-VIEW PRINCIPLE: Strategy is not just about choosing the right strategic option, but also about what point of view to take on strategy itself, who does the strategy, when it's done, and so forth.

Strategy also involves choices about what perspective to take on strategy itself and on your business. Though a business can view a strategy from many perspectives, it can't pay attention to all of them. Should your strategy be based on Michael Porter's five-forces model?[3] How about the core-competence notions of Gary Hamel and C. K. Prahalad or perhaps their later work on strategy as "stretch and leverage" or Hamel's even more recent work on strategy as revolution?[4] What about Adrian Slywotsky's value-migration notions?[5] One thing's for sure—you can't use all the strategy frameworks that compete for your attention. You must allocate your attention to one or perhaps two and ignore the others for the moment.

The traditional assumption was that strategy was formulated by senior executives and then disseminated to other parts of the organization. As we will discuss, this top-down communication of already-formulated strategy may still be a valid assumption in some organizations. However, current perspectives on strategy emphasize broader participation from the entire organization in setting strategy. In a company with many intelligent individuals, what are the chances that all the best ideas will come from a few senior executives? Consultant Gary Hamel argues that executives are perhaps the least likely to propose revolutionary new ideas, because their attention is fully allocated to the existing business:

> *The capacity to think creatively about strategy is distributed widely in an enterprise. It is impossible to predict exactly where a revolutionary*

Overheard. "As perspective, strategy looks *in*—inside the organization, indeed, inside the head of the collective strategists—but it also looks up—to the grand vision of the enterprise (that forest seen above the trees, or is it the clouds that are being perceived?!)."

Henry Mintzberg, *The Rise and Fall of Strategic Planning*

idea is forming; thus the net must be cast wide. In many of the companies I work with, hundreds and sometimes thousands of people get involved in crafting strategy. . . . In one company, the idea for a multi-million-dollar opportunity came from a twenty-something secretary. In another company, some of the best ideas about the organization's core competencies came from a forklift operator.[6]

Democratic Versions

If great strategic ideas are going to come from secretaries and forklift operators, those who are responsible for crafting strategy had better be paying attention to such folk. Of course, it's difficult to pay attention to everybody's ideas. Hamel suggests that certain classes of people are relatively likely to have revolutionary ideas. These groups include new employees, relatively young employees, and those who have close contact with customers (and the customers themselves). In any case, the more democratic versions of strategy suggest that managers must cast their attention nets widely if they want some nonconventional thinking.

> More democratic versions of strategy suggest that managers must cast their attention nets widely if they want some nonconventional thinking.

Another key issue relating strategy and attention is *when* the allocation of attention to strategy can end. Henry Mintzberg's appealing idea of emergent strategy essentially argues that managers should continue to pay attention after a strategy has been formulated.[7] The emergent-strategy idea erases the distinction between formulation and implementation from an attention standpoint; managers must continually attend to what's going on in the environment and to the results from strategic initiatives. The pace of business change in the Internet era provides powerful testimony for this ever-attentive approach to strategy.

Adjusting

Honda has often been cited as the poster child of good strategy formulation. Strategy consultants from Boston Consulting Group noted, for example,

---

Point of View and the Strat Guru. "A point of view must pass four tests: it must be credible, coherent, compelling, and commercial. . . . Many assume that only numbers talk. That's stupid. Only economists think we're perfectly rational. Beauty, joy, hope, justice, freedom, community—these are the enduring ideals that attract human beings to a cause. What is the ideal that makes your POV truly worthwhile?"

Gary Hamel, *Leading the Revolution* (Boston: Harvard Business School Press, 2000), 188, 190

that "Honda turned market preference around to the characteristics of its own products."[8] Consultant Richard Pascale and others, however, have noted that Honda was good not at formulating strategy, but rather at paying attention to the marketplace and adjusting its strategy.[9] When Honda's first large motorcycles in the United States leaked oil and had clutch problems, it fixed them rapidly. Moreover, after Honda managers noticed that small motorcycles were selling much better than large ones, the sale of small ones henceforth became their strategy. The company describes its strategy process as "trial and error." For that approach to succeed, however, attention must be paid to how well the trials are working, and to fixing the errors.

COMMUNICATION PRINCIPLE: Communicating strategy across multiple organizational channels is the key to getting attention for it and producing change.

Regardless of whether strategy is a one-time or continuous, emergent process, it must be communicated. James Brian Quinn points out that formal strategic planning processes accomplish "certain vital functions in coordinating strategies, including awareness building, consensus generating and commitment-affirming."[10] Certainly the "awareness building" in this statement has much to do with focusing individuals' attention on what is important in the strategic environment and what they must do to accomplish the strategy.

Some strategy and strategic decision-making processes formulate and communicate strategy at the same time, while engaging the attention of participants at a high level throughout. This is the appeal, for example, of scenarios, simulations, war games, and other strategic exercises. An engaging war game might attract substantially more managerial attention to issues of competitive strategy and the strengths and weaknesses of a firm relative to competitors than would a straightforward talking-head presentation, even if the CEO is the presenter. Arie de Geus, who managed the scenario planning process at Royal Dutch/Shell for many years, comments on the value of attention-getting strategic methods:

> The more in-depth the simulation, and the more that "play" triggers
> the imagination and learning, the more effective the decision-making

---

Overheard. "The more clearly a strategy is articulated the more deeply embedded it becomes, in both the habits of the organization and the habits of the people."

Henry Mintzberg, *The Rise and Fall of Strategic Planning*

process seems to be. . . . Decisions cannot be made in the old authoritarian manner. They need interaction, intuitive reflection, and the fostering of collaborative mental models. They need play. They need learning.[11]

One might also say that they need attention.

Mintzberg refers to research on how Air France developed its strategy, and points out several attention-getting activities to communicate and disseminate the strategy once developed:

a fifteen-page summary of "Le Plan" was circulated to each of the company's employees, 35,000 copies in all! This was supplemented by "a series of audio and visual documents, including a video discussion with the President," not to mention the several issues of the house magazine devoted to the plan and the 800 discussion meetings, averaging three hours and including 18,000 employees, which preceded all this documentation.[12]

THE SOFTER SIDE OF STRATEGY

IN THE EARLY 1990s, Sears acquired a new CEO, Arthur Martinez, the first outsider to head the company. He had a hundred-day plan to get the company kick-started; he sold off the Sears catalog, divested the financial services business, and closed 113 stores. Then in March 1993, he set an ambitious goal for the firm to quadruple margins and start gaining market share within two years. To do this, he introduced a strategic plan with five new priorities: customer focus, core business growth, cost reduction, responsiveness to local markets, and cultural renewal. Six months after this announcement, a survey of the firm showed that the priority most important to most employees in the organization was to protect the assets of the firm (not one of Martinez's five priorities). Protecting the assets of the firm had been the goal—almost a mantra—in the firm during the previous administration. It was a simple and straightforward message; employees grasped its meaning immediately and were accustomed to this perspective. Martinez found himself one-quarter of the way into his new plan, and most of his employees didn't realize there *was* a new plan.

Even one of Martinez's own change team members bravely confessed to confusion: "To be perfectly honest, I don't know what I'm supposed to be doing differently." This member was "aware" of the change goals, but the awareness had not yet been tempered by meaning to create attentional and behavioral change. With such confusion at the top, it is little wonder that the goals had not percolated down. Whether it was conscious or not, top executives at Sears changed their articulation of the new strategy—and with this change of articulation, the attention of employees also changed. Rather than academic-sounding goals (core business growth, customer focus, responsiveness to local markets, etc.), the new internal goals and external advertising became aligned under one battle cry: "The softer side of Sears." With this slogan, the firm captured the attention of both its employees and its customers, saying that the company would move toward new lines of soft goods in the stores (which involved cutting some traditional lines) and become increasingly accommodating (softer) toward its customers (who were mostly women). It was a brilliant and attention-getting campaign that reenergized employees and made customers feel much more comfortable than they had in a shopping environment in which employees were "protecting the assets of the firm."

Mintzberg goes on to comment that the exercise had more to do with communication per se—gaining commitment and understanding, overall consensus—than with attempting to create strategy. In our terms, the exercise was clearly one intended to get, and hold for a while, the attention of employees as a precondition of any behavioral changes that might be required of them. What may seem like communications overkill at Air France actually seems quite reasonable from an attention perspective.

Broadcasting and Scanning

But strategic communications isn't just about volume. Effectively getting strategic attention involves developing, and then broadcasting, a simple message that both gets attention and encapsulates many important ideas. Strategy also commonly involves scanning the competitive environment. Certainly not all aspects of the environment can be scanned or analyzed; strategists must decide to allocate their attention to certain aspects of it. Business academics Sumantra Ghoshal and Eleanor Westney, who analyzed three firms' efforts at competitive scanning in detail, report that one key aspect of such scanning is to redirect the organization's attention from some aspects of the environment to others. They refer to this purpose as

WELCH TAKES CHARGE

ONE OF THE BEST strategy communicators, of course, was General Electric's great CEO, Jack Welch. Shortly after becoming CEO in 1981, he announced to the senior management team that GE business units had to be first or second in market share by 1990, or they would no longer be part of GE. According to one account with close access to Welch, this seemingly simplistic goal incorporated several others:

The rule of No. 1 or No. 2 became the CEO's overarching strategy for solving all these [GE's business] problems. A business can be profitable without a No. 1 or No. 2 market share, of course, but Welch wanted a stable of champions. The huge revenues and fat profit margins that usually accompany leading shares would give GE the financial flexibility to dominate its markets.[a]

Welch also realized the power of financial performance targets in focusing organizational attention.

For example, Welch felt that GE had too many people, and given the company's culture that verged on lifetime employment, he had difficulty in getting attention for the idea of personnel cuts. To secure attention to the personnel issue, Welch relied on financial targets:

The idea of having a discussion about whether you should lay off 2000 people, or 3000, or 4000 is nonsense. You should be talking about how to deliver the results that a healthy business should deliver. It makes sense to talk about an earnings number. That number will force whatever head count or other changes the business needs.[b]

Source: a. Jack Welch, quoted in Noel M. Tichy and Stratford Sherman, *Control Your Destiny or Someone Else Will: How Jack Welch Is Making General Electric the World's Most Competitive Corporation* (New York: Doubleday Currency, 1993), 75.
b. Ibid., 77–78.

"sensitization," which involves challenging "the organization's existing assumptions about particular competitors, including in some cases changing the definition of the most significant competitor or of the most crucial dimensions of competition."[13] In other words, scanning is intended in part to change where the organization's attention should go in the future.

Scenarios, simulations, and other types of models commonly used in strategic planning are attention-focusing devices. They cannot model all the factors in the strategic environment, but only a few. As a result, they focus the participants' attention on some important factors as predictors or determinants of a company's function, and encourage them to ignore others. Attention-oriented managers should make sure to inquire whether the factors treated in such models are truly the most worthy of their attention.

> **Scanning is intended in part to change where the organization's attention should go in the future.**

Gathering Dust

The formal strategic plan in document form is also a vehicle, albeit an often ineffective one, for structuring attention. The creation of the document can focus attention on the key strategic decisions to be made: "We have to decide, so that we can write down our decision." This part of the process works reasonably well from an attention standpoint. Many plans, however, become shelfware, no longer attracting or keeping anyone's attention. A planning process that continually returns to the strategy documents would be more effective at focusing long-term attention on strategic issues.

Niche strategies are particularly attention oriented. They focus the organization's attention on a relatively small market or product segment. The phrase "stick to your knitting," popularized by Peters and Waterman in *In Search of Excellence*, is basically a command to keep your attention focused on the particular niche your company has chosen to defend.[14] Of course, a company's attention can be too focused. If customers or technology go elsewhere, an overly niche-oriented strategy can be disastrous. The key is to focus attention at the right level, so that it is not overly narrow or broad.

Strategy is largely about attention. Questions of strategy include how to focus attention on strategy versus daily operations, the strategic versus the tactical, the people who have strategic ideas, and how the world and your organization react to the strategy. Successful companies then use the principles of effective communication to focus attention on the strategy that's been developed. We should point out now, however, that a strategy that does a great job of focusing attention can still fail; attention may be focused on all the wrong things. If your strategy doesn't focus attention at all, however, its content won't make any difference. Neither the best nor the worst strategies will change organizations if no one pays any attention to them.

Going Global

Let's get more specific with an example of a key strategy issue that requires focused attention. One very important strategic concern for many managers is globalization. For example, the Baldrige Award Commission surveyed 300 U.S. CEOs in 1998 to find out which business issue weighed most heavily on their minds (see exhibit 9-1).

Not surprisingly, the ability to think globally was their top answer. This suggests that a precondition of successful global strategies is a set of managers who are able to think effectively about global issues.

Well-Traveled

So how do you get enough effective attention focused on issues of globalization? For one thing, you hire and promote people with the passion for global issues that is either inborn or shaped by very early experience. Does sending a home-grown executive out to travel the world increase his or her confidence toward globalization? Surprisingly, in a globalization attitudes survey of sixty-one executives, we found a statistically significant

Exhibit 9-1: Skills that CEOs Report They Need to Improve

	A Great Deal	Some	Not Much	None	Don't Know
The ability to think globally	72%	25%	2%	–	2%
The ability to execute strategies successfully	66	28	4	–	2
Flexibility in a changing world	63	31	4	*	2
The ability to develop appropriate strategies	60	34	4	–	1
The ability to rapidly redefine their business	54	35	8	1	2
The understanding of new technologies	52	38	8	*	2
The ability to work well with different stakeholders	50	41	7	1	1
The ability to create a learning organization	49	40	8	–	3
The ability to make the right bets about the future	43	40	13	1	3
The ability to be a visible, articulate, charismatic leader	41	39	17	1	2

Source: "The Nation's CEOs Look to the Future," a survey conducted for the Foundation for the Malcolm Baldrige National Quality Award, Study No. 818407, July 1998, <http://www.quality.nist.gov/ceo-rpt.htm>.

* indicates less than 0.5%.

negative correlation with the amount of international travel an executive does and *satisfaction* with his or her ability to think globally. Real encounters with the wide world opens people's eyes to the degree of complexity and the number of true challenges out there.

Adversary

Many of us fall into the cultural trap of believing that the way things are done in our native culture is the way business should be conducted everywhere in the world. Ethnocentricity—the belief that how things are done in Akron, Ohio, or Leeds, England, is both right and proper everywhere in the world—is one of the great enemies of global thinking. Adriana Stadecker, the former head of human resources at Invensys, a large UK-based industrial products company, put it this way:

> *Managers from both the U.S. and U.K. are bad at thinking they are not the center of the world. Ninety-eight percent of the managers have no clue how to be global. If anything, they think we are going to teach the rest of the world our way of doing things. There is a parallel between imperialism and most people's conceptualization of globalization.*[15]

Stadecker's use of the word "imperialism" is significant. In some ways, at least, imperialism with its assertion that "we know best, and we'll help you see the light and adopt our ways," remains a potent deterrent to true global attention and effective global strategies. Although such ethnocentrism is an attention-protecting mechanism in that it conserves the amount of attention we must give to the differences of a complex world, ethnocentrism may not be the best way to conduct commerce around the globe. Under an ethnocentric umbrella, we may survey the world, but not take in much, or take in only that which needs to be changed so that it is more like us.

Careful Aim

Although those in critical positions in global companies must have global orientation, not everyone needs a global orientation, as one manager stated:

> *It depends where you are in the company. Those who need global attention include the top management team, managing directors, and staff that deal with worldwide responsibilities. In our business, 20 percent*

of our customer base is global, and 80 percent is local. We want these 80 percent of the people to focus locally, using the power of the global corporation.[16]

BALANCE PRINCIPLE: Key strategy initiatives such as globalization involve a mix of activities and management attention.

To determine an appropriate globalization strategy, executives need to seek a balance between potential and ability. In other words, a company's strategy should balance *its potential to globalize activities* with *its ability to continually focus attention globally*. What do we mean by this? Let's consider this dynamic in light of the three different types of global strategy: complex global, optimized global, and applied global. These types represent the viable categories in the matrix shown in exhibit 9-2.

Exhibit 9-2: Global Attention and Activities Matrix

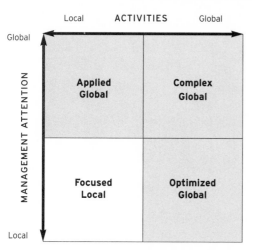

Complex Global

Complex global strategies are based on globalizing both activities and management attention. Although Ford may not be the ideal global firm, it has globalized more of its activities and top management has placed more of its attention on global issues than have most competitors in the automotive industry. Ford's big push began in 1993, when Alex Trotman was appointed chairman. The Scottish-born Trotman launched Ford 2000 the first year he took over as chairman. His objective was to create a single global engineering and manufacturing organization. In 1998, Trotman retired and was replaced as president and CEO by Jacques Nasser. Although Nasser had worked for Ford for over thirty years, he spent only six of those years in Detroit. Born in a mountain village in Lebanon and raised in Australia from the age of four, Nasser is the quintessential global leader. He has held key posts in Australia, Thailand, the Philippines, Venezuela, Mexico, Argentina, Brazil, and Europe; has a degree in international business; and speaks five languages. Other members of Ford's top management team

---

Overheard. "Managing effectively in this new borderless environment . . . means paying central attention to delivering value to customers—and to developing an equidistant view of who they are and what they want."
Kenichi Ohmae, "Managing in a Borderless World"

include worldwide design chief J. Mays, who came to Ford in late 1997 from Audi and Volkswagen. Another team member is Welshman Richard Parry-Jones, group vice president for product development and quality. Parry-Jones also spent most of his career in Europe. A fourth team member is James Padilla, group vice president for manufacturing. Padilla ran Ford's South American operations and was instrumental in turning around quality and productivity problems at Jaguar in the United Kingdom. A fifth member of the management team, Vaughn Koshkarian, vice president of public affairs, was most recently CEO of Ford Motor (China). The international composition of the top management team helps Ford keep global issues at the forefront.

On the activity dimension, Ford has operations in thirty-eight countries, where it manages 111 plants and 226,000 employees. In 1997, Ford generated $65.8 billion in foreign sales. Ford 2000 combined the company's North American and European units into a unified company, merged operations worldwide to create five global design and manufacturing centers covering all cars and trucks, and reduced procurement costs through global sourcing. Attempts at building a "global car," the adoption of non-U.S. designs for the U.S. market, and the national origin of the top executive team also suggest that Ford is more global in its attention than General Motors, Toyota, or BMW.

Optimized Global

Companies with optimized global strategies disperse activities worldwide, but headquarters managers pay little attention to ideas generated outside the home country or to international markets. They optimize decisions by

---

ATTENTION, GLOBAL TRAVELERS! (SOME FAVORITE MISTRANSLATIONS)

- "Is forbitten to steal hotel towels please. If you are not person to do such thing is please not to read notis." (In a Tokyo hotel)

- "To move the cabin, push button for wishing floor. If the cabin should enter more persons, each one should press a number of wishing floor. Driving is then going alphabetically by national order." (In a Belgrade hotel elevator)

- "Please leave your values at the front desk." (In a Paris hotel elevator)

- "Visitors are expected to complain at the office between the hours of 9 and 11 a.m. daily." (In an Athens hotel)

- "The flattening of underwear with pleasure is the job of the chambermaid." (In a Yugoslavian hotel)

- "It is not allow in the hotel room for guest participating in Illicit Arts, banging of firecrackers, gambling and wrestling." (In a Shenyang, China, hotel)

Source: <http://www.quoteland.com/quotes/leisure/translations.html>.

minimizing complexity, standardizing processes, and locating activities in such a way as to maximize internal efficiencies. General Motors is a good example of a company with an optimized global strategy. Although GM has positioned its operations throughout the world, its top management is mostly U.S.-centric in both experience and strategic outlook. The internationalization of GM's activities is very much in service of U.S. customers, U.S.-based operations, and the principally U.S.-based executive team and board of directors.

One reason that GM has been so successful through the years is the strength and independence of its international operations. GM employs almost 650,000 people on five continents and manages manufacturing, assembly, and component operations in fifty countries. From an activity viewpoint, the company is truly global. Yet, the company owes much of its success to the U.S.-centric mind-set of headquarters managers. Generally, the corporate officers in the United States just stay out of the way of the decision making in the foreign affiliates. Being globally optimized gives GM the global-scale economies and localized product life-cycle extensions of international activities without having to incur the costs of huge amounts of attention from headquarters. Furthermore, local managers are free to focus on customer needs in each market. For example, in Australia, the Holden facility is a major market player—it has considerable autonomy in product design, manufacture, and marketing. GM's top managers embrace this approach out of the belief that automobile customers are quite different around the world. Global cars designed to meet tough European and U.S. environmental standards don't sell particularly well in countries like Brazil or Indonesia. What's more, the rough roads in these countries aren't particularly well suited for cars engineered for the German autobahn and U.S. interstate highways.

Strategies to Monitor Change

Smooth adaptation to an organizational change like globalization will be increasingly necessary for a business's survival. Establishing a number of monitoring mechanisms will help ensure that attention is flowing to several strategies simultaneously:

1. *Engineering change:* Keep track of all related technological development.

2. *Benchmarking:* Maintain awareness of competitors.

3. *Customer relations:* Pay attention to the customer in all markets.

4. *Internal change:* Raise employee awareness of broad business issues.

Source: "Hyperion Guide to Business Analysis: Studying the Organization," *Independent* (London), 5 March 2000.

Global Teamwork. Many global companies turn to virtual management teams, linked on the company intranet, to ensure that adequate attention is directed to the relationship between home company policy and its impact on local markets. The key to making these teams effective, according to occupational psychologist Catherine Bailey, is to set agendas and decide on strategy as a team, but to leave the implementation of specific tasks to individuals who can do so locally. Nothing can replace the efficacy of face-to-face attention.

Source: Godfrey Golzen, "Trouble with Teamwork," *London Times*, 6 July 2000.

Applied Global

A company that only needs information or technology from around the globe has little reason to place its operations outside the headquarters country and is a good candidate for an applied global strategy. Applied global competitors actively seek out global learning opportunities—both product- and process-based. They then apply this knowledge to build world-class products or to offer world-class services out of the home country. In short, they globalize their attention, but not their activity.

Ferrari is a good example of an applied global competitor. Ferrari has located its critical activities in two centers in Italy—Modena and Maranello. There, the company employs nearly 1,900 people in R&D, design, production, and training. Ferrari has the advantage of not needing to do much in the way of advertising to perspective clients. Its clients typically wait for one or more years to take delivery of a Ferrari. To stay at the forefront of technology, Ferrari constantly searches the world for new product developments. It also sponsors a 350-person racing team composed of technical experts who travel the world. Not only does the team promote Ferrari automobiles, it observes, develops, and tests state-of-the-art technologies for inclusion in Ferrari production automobiles.

Benefits and Costs

Ford, General Motors, and Ferrari all have global strategies, but in different ways. Although a business can pursue a global strategy without globalizing its attention, the benefits of allocating attention along with activity are clear. Global attention

- allows companies to recognize the opportunities for greater internal efficiencies. Without global attention, many economies of scale would be lost.

- enables companies to recognize new market opportunities for their products and services.

Defining Moments. "Corporate managers have directed a great deal of attention to defining their businesses as a crucial step in strategy formulation. Theodore Levitt, in his classic 1960 article in the *Harvard Business Review*, argued strongly for avoiding the myopia of narrow, product-oriented industry definition. . . . As a result of these urgings, the proper definition of a company's industry or industries has become an endlessly debated subject."

Michael Porter, "How Competitive Forces Shape Strategy," in *Strategy: Seeking and Securing Competitive Advantage*, ed. Cynthia Montgomery and Michael Porter (Boston: Harvard Business School Press, 1991), 25.

- enables managers to recognize and exploit market differences in terms of the quality or price of inputs.

- enables companies to keep track of global competitors. In many markets, the real risk is getting blindsided by upstart competitors that appear out of nowhere with some innovative new product or service. Global companies minimize these surprises because top managers pay close attention to the global competitors as well as the competitiveness of key activities.

- provides companies with the opportunity to learn and import the best technologies around the world.

- affords companies access to the best management talent, irrespective of location.

Diminished Understanding

Strategic deliberations cannot simultaneously focus on global and domestic issues. As cultures are crossed and as distances increase, the ability to understand customers, governments, and markets *decreases*. Complex global and applied global strategies require huge amounts of management attention with associated opportunity costs.

There are direct costs associated with thinking globally about strategy. It starts with the hiring process. In many companies, managers take elaborate measures to hire people with global mind-sets. The Samsung Group, headquartered in Seoul, Korea, with mostly Korean employees and a completely Korean leadership team, is very cognizant of the need to globalize management attention. One initiative to achieve this goal started in 1997, when the corporation launched the Global Strategist Program. The program attempted to bring non-Korean MBA graduates from the United States and Europe into a variety of headquarters assignments as a way of injecting state-of-the-art Western management planning and competitive thinking. The initial group of about twenty-five individuals

---

Overheard. "Jet travel, photo-phones, television via satellite, electronic computers, worldwide news services all increase the range of factors to be considered and the speed of responses to events everywhere. And they add to the information explosion. One result is that strategic shifts must be more discerning and more frequent."
Boris Yavitz and William H. Newman, quoted in Lewis D. Eigen and Jonathan D. Siegel, *The Manager's Book of Quotations*

Overheard. "A good way to outline a strategy is to ask yourself: 'How and where am I going to commit my resources?' Your answer constitutes your strategy."
R. Henry Migliore, quoted in Lewis D. Eigen and Jonathan D. Siegel, *The Manager's Book of Quotations*

worked on two- to three-month-long projects with the goal of making their presence known in as many units of the firm as quickly as possible. These employees were seen less as an internal consulting team than as an international tactical commando unit ready to "parachute in" with powerful analysis and creative solutions.

Other global programs include formal training for more traditional employees. Companies like IBM, Sony, and DaimlerChrysler spend tens of millions of dollars every year on formal training programs designed to create globally competent managers. These and many other firms also use international assignments as mechanisms to develop global thinking. In many cases, these assignments represent more than $1 million in investment per employee. Research suggests that within a year of returning to their "native" company, as many as one-quarter of the managers leave their companies. One European equipment company, for example, sent twenty-four senior Chinese managers to a management training program in Switzerland. The twelve-week program designed to train Chinese managers in Western management thinking cost the company over $15,000 per employee. Within two years, twenty-three of the twenty-four employees left the company to take higher-paying jobs with competitors in China. Developing a pool of globally competent managers is enormously expensive and requires great commitment.

Complex global and applied global strategies require huge amounts of management attention with associated opportunity costs.

When combined, the attention and activities dimensions required to make major changes in globalization strategy are very time-consuming. It may take five or more years to reposition a company. There are no shortcuts when it comes to shifting activities and attention. Companies that will succeed in a more and more globally connected world in which management attention is a company's scarcest asset need to have a strategy for managing this asset across national boundaries. Deciding where you are as a company now, and where you need to be in terms of the mix of activities and attention, may be key determinants of future profitability and growth around the world.

CHAPTER 10

OFF THE ORG CHART

Business functions. Customer

types. Geographical regions. Product categories. All are important factors by which companies organize. But which should get more attention, and which less? Which deserve prominent boxes and lines on the org (organizational) chart? Organizational structure is the plan for—and the reality of—how power and responsibility are distributed across an organization. It's clearly the subject of great attention within organizations: who's moving up or on the decline, who will prevail in a disagreement, or who will come out on top in a reorganization or merger. Organizational structure reliably captures our attention because of some deep psychobiological urges. Since we are social animals, we focus attention on the hierarchy of humans in groups and on the strivings of our colleagues and competitors.

171

Because we are naturally oriented to structural information, organizational structure is also a powerful vehicle for focusing attention. The reason for creating a particular form of organizational structure is to focus attention on a particular aspect of the business. Structure is thus a potent tool for directing the attention of employees and external stakeholders. As with strategy, however, the attention-related aspects of structure have remained largely in the background of business thinking. In this chapter we'll bring them to the foreground and help executives use structure to send clear messages about where attention should go.

> **Structure is a potent tool for directing the attention of employees and external stakeholders.**

ORG CHART PRINCIPLE: Organizational structures focus attention on certain aspects of the business and ignore others.

Every organizational structure sends a message that some issues are more important than others. As noted in chapter 9, one way to help create a focus on customers is to organize around types of customers. A way to show employees, customers, and external observers that a company believes quality is important is to create a department for it and put someone in charge. Stan Davis and Paul Lawrence have focused heavily on organizational structure issues and the need for them: "One of the principal reasons people form organizations is to focus attention and energy on a selected goal."[1] Structure is not the only way to bring attention to a goal, but along with attention, it often pulls other means, including performance evaluation and compensation systems, organizational communications, and informal social networks. For individuals, the weight of an organizational title and a position in the organization chart are powerful forces directing attention toward a formally structured objective.

Many different ways of organizing are valid foci for attention, but of course there is only so much attention to go around. Therefore, firms must choose among them. Product-oriented structures deserve attention when a company makes multiple products, each with different customers and markets. Geographical structures deserve

Why Organizational Structure?

Concepts like organizational structure and span of control are originally military ideas. In traditional societies, large groups of people didn't come together with a common purpose except in churches and armies—structure was the main differentiator of the two. These structures were designed hierarchically (like pyramids) for a reason: The general at the top decided what the army was going to do and divided the task among his lieutenants, who pushed the thinking in finer and finer detail down to the individual soldiers. This structure was a way to marshal attention to a complex and difficult task—one job, one person.

attention when an organization must do business in various ways across its target geographical markets. Functional organizations focus attention on peoples' technical specialties—marketing, finance, manufacturing, etc.—when business problems are too large and complex to be addressed with a generalist approach. Some of these dimensions already receive much attention, that is, the attention synapses for them are well developed. One reason that functional structures are so persistent, for example, is that business education curricula generally follow a functional structure. Students take courses in functions, major in functions, and then are predisposed to devote attention to functions.

The Big M

But it's a complex business world out there, and organizations are frequently tempted to try to divide organizational attention across multiple dimensions. The so-called M-form structure (so called because the charts describing this structure look an M), for example, divides the organization's attention simultaneously across business units and functions, although an individual's attention can be largely focused on a function within his or her particular unit.

At other times firms are willing to divide individual attention across dimensions. One reason that many organizations choose to organize around multiple functions at once—in other words, they create a matrix—is attention.

Of course, once a matrix is formed, another attention issue comes to the fore: the ability to process a high level of communications and information. When a firm simultaneously diversifies both its products or services and its markets, however, the resulting complexity brings a much greater need for coordination, communication, and what academics call "information-processing requirements." We call it attention. And since people have only so much attention to spend, too much may get devoted to internal organizational issues.

Another problem of matrix organizations involves the allocation of individual attention to the management hierarchy. This is often referred to as the two-boss problem: Which boss should an employee attend to at any

---

A Matrix without Keanu? Stanley Davis and Paul Lawrence, who (to our knowledge) wrote the only book on matrix organizations, explain it this way: "It is no accident that the matrix first came into widespread use in the aerospace industry. To survive and prosper in the aerospace industry, any firm needs to focus intensive *attention* [italics added] *both* [italics in original] on complex technical issues and on the unique project requirements of the customer."

Source: Stanley M. Davis and Paul R. Lawrence, *Matrix* (Reading, MA: Addison-Wesley, 1977), 13.

given moment? Perhaps based on our psychobiological natures, we tend to think in terms of having one superior to whom we must pay attention in our work lives. Even when we're assigned two, innate predispositions and existing relationships may prevent both bosses—and both dimensions of organizational structure that they represent—from getting equal attention.

Even if the organizational structure has only one dimension, if it's new or different from what went on in the past, a manager must take concerted action to draw attention to the new dimension. If a firm is switching from, for example, products to geographies, it may take a while before managers stop looking at product category sales reports. Salespeople with well-developed attention synapses for a particular product may find it difficult to push other products with equal attention. In short, our attention to different aspects of organizational structure does not turn on a dime.

Process Management

We'll illustrate this discussion of organizational structure as an attention-focusing device with one specific example: process management. It involves an attempt by firms to carve out attention from other aspects of organizational structure to focus on a "new"—but essentially familiar—resource. Process management involves not only organizational structures, but also nonstructural mechanisms that have been put in place to draw sustained attention to the relevant goals and objectives.

Process management is one approach to an organizational structure that needs attention. Business processes, the activities by which work gets done in an organization, typically cut across other dimensions of structure such as functions and business units. It's generally believed that focusing on processes is a good thing when a company is trying to improve efficiency, reduce cycle time, and improve customer service. To make process management work, however, managers and employees must devote some attention to the concept. Some observers of process management have suggested that firms should adopt process management as the primary or even only dimension of organizational structure, referring to the "process-centered" organization, or the "horizontal" organization.[2]

From an attention management standpoint, however, this is a naïve view. It suggests that it is easy to transfer all the organization's attention to this new (to many individuals) dimension of organizational structure and to abandon the previous dimensions. Where, however, is the proof that existing dimensions don't still require attention? What will happen when functional skills, geographical variations, and different markets for business unit products and services no longer receive attention? Some part of the organization's performance will probably suffer.

Tech Clubs

Some organizations moving to a process-oriented structure have concluded that they went too far in taking attention away from other dimensions. The Chrysler division of DaimlerChrysler, for example, made a significant shift toward process management in the early 1990s, when it moved toward cross-functional "platform teams" that managed the entire process of developing a new vehicle. Overall, these teams were a successful approach to new car development at Chrysler, leading to attractive new car designs and significant improvements in development cycle time.

On the down side, Chrysler managers realized that something was missing from the new structure. The functional organization that had nourished and propagated technical skills was no longer in place. Technical experts found themselves working not with others of their ilk, but with manufacturers, marketers, and financial experts on cross-functional issues. The result of the removal of attention from the functional dimension was the recurrence of quality problems that Chrysler had previously solved. Since the end of the 1990s and the start of the new century, the company has been attempting to return some attention to functional and technical knowledge by organizing so-called Tech Clubs, so that engineers in specific domains of car development can meet with each other and exchange ideas. This form of attention sharing might be called an undercover version of matrix management, because it gives only informal legitimacy to a second dimension of structure.

Assuming that process management is important, just how much attention should be devoted to it? The "horizontal organization" and "process centering" rhetoric suggests that all or almost all attention going to organizational structure should involve processes. A matrix-oriented structure that adds process management

A Focus on Processes

Some alternative means for focusing organizational attention on processes might include the following:

- Tying process management to information systems initiatives (commonly done, for example, in large enterprise systems initiatives, with some success)[a]

- Relying on senior executive exhortation (for example, Larry Bossidy, CEO of what was then AlliedSignal, spoke frequently about the horizontal organization at his firm, without ever eliminating non-process dimensions of its organizational structure)

- Evaluating and rewarding employees on the basis of process performance

a See Thomas H. Davenport, *Mission Critical: Realizing the Promise of Enterprise Systems* (Boston: Harvard Business School Press, 2000), 135–159.

to other dimensions suggests a roughly equal division of attention among them. And a "club" structure like Chrysler's gives a particular dimension somewhat less attention than parts of organizational structure that are embedded in the formal hierarchy. (In Chrysler's case, the club structure applied to functional expertise, but firms could also organize "process clubs.")

Furthermore, formal structure is not the only way to bring attention to a type of organization. Process management, for example, received considerable attention in many organizations in the late 1980s and early 1990s through linkages to corporate change programs such as total quality management (TQM) and reengineering. Now that these programs have become either embedded in companies (as in the case of TQM) or discredited because of misapplication and extravagant expectations (as in the case of reengineering), firms must generally find other ways to bring attention to process management.[3]

The Downstream

Of course, attention isn't the only prerequisite to success in process management. After process issues get attention, someone has to address them and take action to redesign processes, eliminate bottlenecks, measure performance in process terms, and so forth. However, one can be fairly certain that none of these actions will ever take place if attention isn't first redirected to processes.

One organization that faced the issue of how much attention it should draw to process management is a joint venture of two large oil companies. The venture was created to jointly pursue the "downstream," or refining and marketing business. Managers in this organization, which we will call Oiliance, felt that considerable improvement in key business processes was both possible and necessary. Many processes were not performing well, and the two venture partners had brought to Oiliance different ways of doing business. There was considerable variation in how processes were done across the organization. Oil and gas are commodities; hence firms must compete on the efficiency and effectiveness of their processes. Oiliance was losing out to the competition in some situations.

To bring about these changes, Oiliance created a Process Design department and staffed it with experts on process management from within and outside the company. The group was relatively small, however, and attracted little attention. Further, it spent considerable effort on activities that had only a small chance of getting attention: developing a process management methodology, for example. Just the word "methodology" suggests to most people that they should keep their attention as far away as possible.

158 Initiatives

The larger context within the organization was even more troublesome from an attention standpoint. Many other contenders vied for the organization's attention—new management with an unclear agenda, other dimensions of organizational structure (including function, business unit, and geography), and much general organizational tumult. One manager counted all the various business improvement initiatives under way and came up with 158! In spite of all these initiatives and a high price for oil, the company's financial performance was poor. In short, process management wasn't getting the attention it needed to survive and thrive.

A new CEO had just been brought in from one of the parent companies. He believed in a back-to-basics approach to management fundamentals, which included reducing the number of initiatives to three or four. His conclusion about process management was that it was important, but not something the company was ready for. Advising the head of the process management department to wait a year, he also suggested that the department perhaps combine process change efforts with some other needed programs that might need attention (e.g., a reconfiguration of the company's enterprise system). He also began to postpone some electronic commerce initiatives, commenting, "We don't have the attention to do all this stuff." In this case, attention-oriented discretion was the better part of valor.

THE URGE-TO-MERGE PRINCIPLE: If two companies aren't getting enough attention, try combining them.

According to Securities Data Company, from 1990 to 1998, the number of domestic mergers and acquisitions more than doubled, from 5,654 to 11,655. The dollar value of mergers and acquisitions (M&As) in the United

---

Don't Look Now. Unless managers pay attention to implementing a well-defined post-M&A structure, competitors may take advantage of employee ambivalence to lure talent away. When Deutsche Bank acquired Bankers Trust, it had to pay huge salary increases to retain talented employees from *both* companies.

Source: Alfred Rappaport and Mark L. Sirower, "Stock or Cash? The Trade-Offs for Buyers and Sellers in Mergers and Acquisitions," *Harvard Business Review* (November–December 1999): 147-158.

States in 1997 was at an all-time high of $919 billion. And that record was shattered in 1998, soaring to $1.675 trillion (an increase of 80 percent)!

Why the compounding interest in M&As? The lure of M&As is strong—strategic synergies, cost cutting with the elimination of overlapping functions, expansion into new markets, access to new channels, economies of scale, acquisition of intellectual property, and widening product offerings—or so it seems. On paper, M&As make sense. With pressures to go global, the deregulation of key industries, steep competition, and antsy stockholders, corporate combinations are a tempting way for companies to grow, to achieve tactical initiatives, to strengthen their competitive positions, and to infuse new people and ideas into their systems.

> Plenty of companies have added points to their share prices as they acquire or merge with other firms—and a lot of that has to do with attention.

The strongest pressures on CEOs today, however, are to raise the stock price, and that's the underlying reason for much M&A activity. Shareholders and corporate executives alike hope that stock prices rise when a merger is announced—and generally that is the case. In an automotive industry study conducted by our colleagues Alan Martin and Ulmar Riaz, companies categorized as high acquirers (averaging one acquisition annually between 1992 and 1997 or achieving a cumulative disclosed acquisition value above $600 million during the same years) substantially outperformed low acquirers, achieving an average annual total shareholder return of 10.2 percent compared to –5.1 percent for low acquirers.[4] Plenty of companies have added points to their share prices as they acquire or merge with other firms—and a lot of that has to do with attention.

Big Dog

A basic attention getter in the natural world is size: Big things get our attention to a much greater extent than do small things. It is the rule of the jungle. Have you ever seen a dog threatened or getting ready to fight? Besides some snarling, growling, and baring of teeth, what is the surest sign that the dog has lost its composure and is prepared to attack? It's that line of hair standing on end all the way down its back. What evolutionary good does a line of hair in the air do for a cur that says grrrrr? It simply makes the dog look bigger. The mechanism, in one form or another, exists in most animals—paleontologists speculate that the stegosaurus (you know, the one with the plates on its back) had increased blood flow to its plates, which probably turned them bright pink during times of conflict, making the animal look larger (and signaling its displeasure). Similarly, fish puff themselves up, and chances are that you naturally stand up taller when you anticipate an altercation. Why all this physical show prior to a battle? Attention, of course. In any competitive situation, the battling parties want to look as big as possible.

In the corporate world, there is no faster way to get big than to merge with another entity. Companies are generally more competitive and control more of the marketplace when they are large. "Big" equals "good and strong" in most of our business minds—after all, you'll never get into the Fortune 500 unless you are just plain big. CEOs and corporate boards like to get bigger through acquisition because it's a relatively easy way to increase the revenue, profit, and the piece of the attention pie. Is it any wonder that companies combine over and over and over again? They have huge incentive for doing it. Rapidly growing companies get the attention of the press, their customers, their competitors, and ultimately the stock markets.

With stock price the principal basis for executive bonuses, corporate leaders entertain such unions for millions of reasons. CEOs who lead an acquisition spree often are some of the best compensated of their class. Stephen Hilbert, as CEO of Conseco, acquired over forty companies through nineteen acquisitions during a sixteen-year period and turned Conseco into the largest publicly held life insurer in the United States. The buyouts started small, with the acquisition of Security National Life Insurance for $1 million in 1982. Fifteen years and billions of dollars later, the firm owned companies like Colonial Penn Group, Pioneer Financial, American Travellers Corporation, Life Partners Group, and Washington National Corporation. In 1987 Conseco completed its largest acquisition—the $ 7.2 billion purchase of Green Tree Financial Corporation, a consumer finance company. Hilbert recalls that when Conseco first started the buyout binge, "Nobody else was active. Everybody laughed at us." But no one was laughing in 1998, when Conseco shares were priced at $58. Between 1994 and 1998, Hilbert collected $356.7 million in salary, bonuses, and stock awards, which made him one of the highest-paid CEOs in the United States. Growth was definitely good both for the stock price and for Hilbert.

But was all of the attention engendered by this growth good? By April 2000, Hilbert explained that he didn't understand why the markets had not valued the potential of Conseco appropriately. The firm's stock price was in the doldrums at less than $7 a share; the company had lost more than $16 billion in shareholder value. Finally, Hilbert announced that he was leaving the firm. Maybe the attention was not worth all that much for Hilbert after all, right? Wrong! Hilbert walked away from the job with all of his savings, stock options, and an estimated $72 million golden parachute.

Complexity

Of course, just as complex matrix organizational structures can lead to attention problems, excessively complex mergers and acquisitions can wreak havoc with attention as well. In reality, the majority of M&As never realize their potential. Some end in outright failure. And we're not getting any better at mergers, either. The mergers of the 1990s seem no more successful than those of the 1970s. In fact, in the last few years the link between acquisition volume and performance in the automobile industry, at least, has been weakening. As mentioned previously, Martin and Riaz found that although acquisitions and mergers were good for shareholder value through 1997, the relationship actually turned negative in the last few years of the 1990s. High acquirers as a group underperformed low

PRESSURES OF MERGING

MARTIN AND RIAZ SUGGESTED that three attention-related issues were at stake in the late 1990s problems of auto industry mergers. First, acquisitions in the auto industry in the late 1990s were generally larger and more complex deals than earlier ones. The nature of M&As was changing, which put tremendous pressure on the integration process. Increasingly the deals were outside the company's core business, often crossing borders and involving international organizations, which introduced substantially different integration and attentional challenges. In these late-1990s M&As, the acquired company had often made a number of acquisitions through the decade in its own right—making these firms more complex than the single-business firms acquired in the early 1990s. All this complexity is much more difficult to deal with in terms of attention management.

Second, a basic assumption of many mergers was that value would be produced through head-count reductions. Of course, the fewer heads there were to manage the combined business, the less attention available. It's natural that an attention deficit would result. In many cases, these large and complex firms just didn't have enough people to pay attention to all the problems and issues that arise in a newly merged company.

Third, the acquisition market in general became so overheated in some industries at the end of the 1990s that management had insufficient resources to pay attention to one buyout before feeling forced to move on to the next one. Martin and Riaz found that successful consolidators usually pause after an acquisition, taking six to eighteen months to integrate their purchase, reduce costs, and locate synergies across the new units. But when companies are coming up for auction and customers are continually demanding more scale and scope, consolidators lack the luxury of long periods between acquisitions.

acquirers on several indicators, including median total shareholder returns, return on assets, and earnings before interest expense and taxes.

Eye on the Ball

It is no secret that the managers most able to devote appropriate and timely attention to a corporate combination through the *entire* process are those most able to succeed. And once successful, companies must have strategies to maintain appropriate attention. Perhaps at no other times can attention so easily wane as during the M&A process. M&As fail more often than not because although they make sense from a competitive and customer standpoint, once the merger or acquisition is announced, the attention of both upper management and employees immediately shifts to internal issues. In other words, attention formerly given to customers, suppliers, partners, and other stakeholders suddenly becomes redirected internally to such faux work questions as "Will I be fired?" "Will my product line be cut?" "Who will I report to?" and so on. The longer these issues remain unresolved, the more attention is consumed and the faster the strategic value created on paper prior to the merger disappears.

Executives spend so much time, energy, and even attention cutting the deal for the merger that when it's finally a done deal, they're exhausted, ready for a well-earned vacation. They didn't have time to plan for the aftermath of the merger *before* the aftermath—issues as vital, or more so, than the merger or acquisition itself. There was too much uncertainty to plan very specifically for the postmerger period before the linkage was officially approved. But by waiting, we may (and in the case of M&As often do) doom ourselves to failure. As much focus must be given to creating the ongoing relationship as is given to cutting the deal in the first place. In our merger-happy world, few business leaders manage attention—not only their own attention but that of everyone in the organization—in a merger or an acquisition.

The tale of Megahertz Corporation provides an excellent example of the importance of attention management. In 1994, Megahertz, a $50 million PC-card modem manufacturer based in Utah, contracted with Asia Pacific Ventures (APV) to find a suitable partner to expand its operations in Japan. Megahertz already had captured 50 percent of the American PC card modem market as a result of the popularity of the XJACK, a pop-out phone connector that eliminated the need to attach a separate adapter to connect to phone lines.

Megahertz had many suitors in Japan, including large and powerful companies with broad distribution relationships. With APV's guidance, Megahertz selected Integran KK of Tokyo, which made Integran its exclusive distributor for Japan. Megahertz's decision was very much based on a predeal evaluation of which company could pay its products the most attention. Megahertz deemed that the large Japanese trading houses would not be able to focus on the Megahertz product line, because of all the other companies they represented in Japan. Integran, on the other hand, was presented as a scrappy reseller of modem products that could drop its current product lines in favor of the Megahertz brand.

Domo Arigato, Mr. Roboto

Much of Megahertz's success in Japan boiled down to attention management. Megahertz and its Japanese partner had the "attention thing" figured

FOCUSED ON UNO THING

AFTER THE UNION of Megahertz and Integran, certain attention-based dynamics helped bolster the success of the partnership. These included the following:

1. Megahertz experienced lackluster results in Europe, causing it to terminate all operations there, thus allowing international managers to give full attention to Japan. This also allowed Integran to get the attention of Megahertz's engineering and software groups to make necessary localization changes.

2. Because of some other partnership deals at Integran, little management attention had been given to the division that would work with Megahertz in the period preceding the Megahertz deal. By the time Megahertz came along, however, Mark Uno, vice president of the division, had become more committed and adamant about the need to give all his attention to the division and Megahertz. The president of Integran acquiesced, giving Uno complete freedom to manage his group. To most observers, Uno's intense focus (with total disregard to his personal needs and health) was the primary success factor to the Integran/Megahertz efforts in Japan.

3. Igor Best-Devereux, the manager of Megahertz's Asia-Pacific marketing group, recognized Uno's undivided attention to the success of the Megahertz products in Japan and gave him as much freedom as possible to achieve success—more freedom, actually, than that typically allotted to independent organizations under corporate policy.

4. Finally, an effective middleman ("marriage counselor") kept the relationship running smoothly despite language and cultural barriers. Integran and Megahertz decided from the beginning of the relationship to retain a United States–based external contractor, JapanWorks, to aid with translation and cultural interface. A small firm founded by bilingual engineers, the company ensured that communication was accurate and swift. In the days before universal use of e-mail, the JapanWorks team would receive fax messages from Japan in the middle of the night, translate the messages into English, and forward them to the Megahertz team. The translators would then follow up by phone to work out any potential problems. Even in an era of e-mail, this model of cross-border relationship management is not a bad one.

out. Then Megahertz caught the attention of US Robotics (USR)—a competitor—to such a degree that Megahertz was acquired and found itself a subsidiary of USR.

The USR takeover of Megahertz was good for both the acquirer and the acquiree. The relationship proved quite successful partly because USR was willing to let Megahertz continue to function independently—not distracting attention from managing its business. And there was good reason for this tactic.

Despite its domestic success, USR had limited operations in Asia. Mark Uno met with USR's international vice president before the completion of the merger to let him know that Integran clearly was the best partner for Japan. John McCartney, president and CEO of USR, could readily see that Integran's efforts with the Megahertz products had been more successful than USR's own efforts in Japan. Integran was awarded a contract to continue as the Asian distributor for the combined USR organization. The quick decision to leave all Asia-Pacific operations in the hands of the original Megahertz team was essential for two reasons: First, because the strategy was broadcast early, the Asia-Pacific team members were able to keep their attention on their work rather than speculate on their personal futures. Second, the decision created a centralized model with the Megahertz team members responsible for the distribution and sale of all USR/Megahertz products, thus enabling them to completely focus attention on the international arena.

Again, proper attention management reaped great rewards. The laissez-faire attitude toward acquisition was a common strategy for USR—the company did the same thing with Palm Computing and had considerable success in allowing the Palm Division to remain largely autonomous.

Compare this story with what happened when 3Com acquired USR in 1997. In this case, 3Com was less clear about its postmerger strategies, delaying decisions for several months after the merger was complete. Additionally, once decisions were made, the international strategy went from a centralized model, in which the team could pay full attention to international sales and support, to a distributed model, in which product managers were forced to allocate their attention between domestic and international markets. Since the domestic market produced a majority of revenues, the managers naturally focused most of their attention there, leaving local in-country offices to fend for themselves. Sales of modem products in Japan began to suffer.

Nobody Does It Better

The relationship between attention and merger success is not unique to Megahertz. Cisco Systems, among the most successful companies of the 1990s, has made a science out of corporate acquisitions. The firm continually surprises analysts with higher-than-expected earnings. Cisco financials for the late nineties are presented here:

	FY 99 (31/7/99)	**FY 98** (25/7/98)	**FY 97** (26/7/97)
Revenue	$12.1 billion	$8.5 billion	$6.4 billion
Net Income	$2.1 billion	$1.4 billion	$1.0 billion

Surprisingly, Cisco has catapulted itself to the forefront of the networking industry (competing against industry giants Northern Telecom and Lucent Technologies) largely through successful acquisitions. Cisco has accomplished this not just once or twice, but *forty-two times* from 1994 to 2000. Cisco's ability to identify, buy, and integrate companies successfully into its corporate structure has been a key source of competitive advantage. How has Cisco managed to successfully integrate so many companies in so short a time? Although there is no simple answer, a large part of it has to do with unique procedures and practices aimed at successful integration and retaining the company's most important newly attained asset: *employee attention.*

Cisco has a no-layoffs policy. This is surprising given the conventional wisdom of right-sizing and cutting waste through the elimination of duplicate functions. Bucking convention, Cisco keeps its acquired companies intact. The organization may not be as lean, but fears of layoffs and random organizational change do not hamper productivity. The attention of employees is preserved, allowing them to focus on expanding the business. All other human resource, organizational, and strategic issues are dealt with swiftly by Cisco's integration team of eleven individuals, led by Mimi Gigoux, whose sole job is to facilitate the process of newly acquired company integration.

Furthermore, after each acquisition, question and answer sessions are held with small groups, and customized meetings are held for sales, management, and engineering teams to discuss division-specific issues. The entire orientation process takes a scant thirty days. By the time it is completed, employees in the newly acquired company know clearly what their job is, to whom they report, what their benefits are, what their strategic role is within Cisco Systems, and anything else they care to know to become a fully functioning unit of the company. If further questions arise, they know whom to call or where to go to find the answers.

In short, Cisco has developed a system of concentrating attention on new companies immediately after the acquisition—but the attention doesn't get in the way of business. The parent company continues to do what it does best, while the new kid on the block does its own thing. Cisco retains a basic faith that sooner or later, the two will learn to play well together. With proper M&A attention management in action, attention remains focused on doing business.

THE DIVESTITURE PRINCIPLE: If there's not enough attention to go around, spin off or outsource something.

As noted, large and complex organizations sometimes run short of attention. They just don't have enough management focus to run the collection of businesses and business activities that have been acquired or grown up over time. In such situations, the answer is often a spin-off or some form of outsourcing alliance.

A far rarer corporate occurrence than the merger or acquisition is the spin-off. The urge-to-merge principle works against divestitures; nevertheless, given what we've said about keeping management attention on the right activities, it should not be surprising that spin-offs can have very positive bottom-line results. Having less to consider means that more attention is focused on the remaining elements.

Granting independence to operations under the corporate umbrella, however, is extremely counterintuitive to many CEOs, especially those steeped in the lore of vertical integration. In essence, it forces the CEO to confess that "a portion of the business would be run better if it were not under my control." Particularly for those who measure success by how many employees they control and how much revenue they produce, a spin-off can be a humbling experience. However, a study by Rick Escherich of J.P. Morgan shows that the typical spin-off between 1995 and 1997 actually outperformed the market by 2.6 percentage points. (Some spin-off successes include AT&T's spin-off of Lucent Technologies, and

---

Go Figure . . . With modern organizations extremely complicated, we've developed sophisticated organizational structures to deal with the diverse environments in which we work. Scholars have spent much time and effort developing models of organizational structure and arguing why one form is better than another. Is it any wonder that concepts like the centerless organization and empowerment have found favor among academics—those who most crave autonomy?

PepsiCo's spin-off of Tricon, its fast-food businesses. Sears also spun off noncore businesses as a key part of its turnaround.) In slower-economic-growth environments (like that of the early 1990s in the United States), spin-offs did even better. Typically, a layer of management is eliminated and corporate red tape reduced, thus allowing new management to focus more attention on making the spun-off business succeed. By essentially splitting a corporation into two or more autonomous entities, employee attention is enhanced, not hampered. Yet another reason for this success is that executives in these spin-offs who had never been eligible for stock options are eligible now. They now pay more voluntary attention to the stock price of the unit, as their fortunes are more directly tied to those of the shareholders.

The market success of a spin-off is arguably even more attention based than the managerial success of such a firm. Because a spun-off firm usually has a narrow strategic focus, its value is clearer to analysts and investors. The business model is usually easier to understand and attend to; hence the market values of both the original company and the spin-off may both go up.

Internet Alliances Are Here to Stay

In the supercharged environment of Internet businesses, survival depends on speed and the ability to evolve. If a business wants to broaden its consumer offerings, to add some technology, or to make its site stickier, the new trend is to skip messy mergers and instead form alliances. The attention of each collaborating company remains on its own area of expertise, whereas it profits from the expertise of its partners. Some recent strategic alliances follow:

- Amazon.com + drugstore.com + WineShopper.com

- Phone.com + MyWay.com + two hundred companies to design Web content to be viewed on handheld devices like wireless phones

- Ticketmaster Online + Active.com (a service that helps find sporting events)

Outsourcing Alliances

Corporations need to be able to attend to those things they do best and most profitably while allowing other related entities to pay attention to other necessary parts of their business activities. One Accenture study found that eight out of ten executives interviewed believed that alliances would become the prime vehicle for corporate growth. In a world obsessed with speed, an outsourcing alliance is a much faster way to achieve corporate goals than internal growth. By allying with (but not having to buy and digest) a firm that already does something you need to do quite well, you can hurry your core processes along.

Focusing attention on core processes—and handing over those that aren't core—is really what any good alliance is about. Once you understand what those core activities are, then you can decide whether to keep the noncore ones in house or to outsource them, freeing up management attention for the things that really matter to a business. Nonequity alliances that result in broad networks of interrelated firms are one of the hottest management techniques around. Just about every firm is trying to use brick-and-mortar and Internet-based alliances to improve bottom-line and shareholder value. And, in fact, some pretty good evidence shows that alliances and outsourcing are adding value to the firms that engage in them. A 1998 Booz·Allen & Hamilton study on alliances showed that about 35 percent of the revenue of the revenue of the top one thousand firms is expected to come from alliances. Companies like Cable & Wireless use alliances so much that they've adopt a slogan: "The firm is dead—long live the federation."

Any company process, customer interface, or market relationship becomes more effective through the careful channeling of attention.

Many outsourcing alliances find themselves created along natural *value chain* divisions. A supplier alliance partner makes the materials for your product, you assemble it, and then sell it through a variety of retail alliance partners. Each partner does what it does best—and one company alone isn't responsible for maintaining complicated, vertically integrated activities. The airline Star Alliance is an example of a *geographic* split of an alliance: United Airlines handles the United States, Air Canada does Canada, Lufthansa does continental Europe, Thai Air does Southeast Asia, and so on. Each airline can focus on its geography and handle the customer relations, airport relations, fuel purchasing, baggage handling, and other activities in its part of the world. The airlines don't get distracted by what is going on halfway around the world because they have alliance partners to protect that part of their attention. They can cut back on staff, aircraft maintenance, and customer relations in other parts of the world and bulk up in the geographies that they know best.

Can the success or failure of organizational restructurings, mergers, acquisitions, or outsourcing alliances be solely attributed to attention? We are not that naïve. But we would argue that because employee, executive, and shareholder attention is a scarce resource, attention is a decisive factor. Broad organizational boundaries naturally channel attention in specific ways. Any company process, customer interface, or market relationship becomes more effective through the careful channeling of attention. Leaders who understand the relationship between organizational structure and attention will be much more effective users of this particular lever of business change.

CHAPTER 11

"YOU'VE GOT (LOTS AND LOTS OF) MAIL"

MANAGING INFORMATION, KNOWLEDGE, AND ATTENTION

Bill Coleman is a finance

executive at one of the world's largest pharmaceutical firms. He travels weeks at a time for work—to places as varied as China, the Philippines, Belgium, and Australia. His expertise is fraud investigation, which requires him to wade through an ocean of data (the usual fare of balance sheets, profit and loss statements, general ledgers) each year, overcoming language barriers and divergent accounting practices. With preparations for a trip to Japan under way and a stack of books to show for it—local and federal Japanese tax codes, one on U.S. records for the Generally Accepted Accounting Principles (GAAP), an English-Japanese business dictionary— Bill also faces challenges at headquarters.

His company is going through a megamerger, and many of his subordinates aren't sure if he'll be their boss afterward.

Neither is Bill. They drop into his office nine or ten times a day, often confiding their fears for the future and seeking advice—or just trading jokes. The midtown Manhattan traffic noise, a clamor of cab honks and sirens, distracts him more than it once did, but the blinking neon "Liquor" sign outside his window, speakerphone conversations held nearby, and gurgling coffee machines distract him even more. Everyone in the office listens to Web radio lately, but he doesn't want to be the jerk to tell the staff to turn it off.

Sure, the essential tasks of Bill's job involve information: discovering hidden information, ensuring it's managed with integrity, and broadcasting it to higher-ups with clarity. But, as we're trying to show, things aren't as simple as they should be. We believe that his admission that he is most productive before 9:00 A.M. or after 5:30 P.M.—outside normal business hours—is indicative of a growing pathology in business today.

Scapegoats

Who is to blame for this pathology? At one point, we could probably have pointed to the information systems or the information technology (IT) function within organizations, and their leaders, the chief information officers, whose jobs have sometimes become synonymous with the mindless pumping out of more information. But even if IT people were the favorite scapegoats in the past, today's imbalance between information and attention has become everybody's problem: Everybody is an information and knowledge provider, pushing out information and knowledge in both electronic and paper formats. Coleman, like almost all of today's executives, sends e-mails, gives presentations, writes memos, contributes lessons learned, and chimes in on a discussion database. Like so many others, he is a consumer of all this content as well.

Everyone must figure out how to allocate his or her scarce attention amid a multitude of contenders. Of course, if you are a senior executive charged with effectively using the entire organization's resources or an information or knowledge manager, you know this problem intimately.

A Message in All These Messages

Let's assume that the average message takes a minute to process (probably more for telephone messages, the highest-frequency category, and less for e-mail, the second highest). That means the average U.S. office worker is spending almost half the day in message-related activity. This estimate is consistent with unpublished studies from Ferris Research and Lotus Research on e-mail usage, which found that average white collar workers can typically spend two hours per day on e-mail alone. Is this too much? Maybe our jobs have just become primarily a matter of exchanging messages. It certainly leaves less time for face-to-face interaction (remember "Management by Wandering Around"?), a form of messaging not included in the study. But nostalgia for a good hallway conversation isn't likely to interest hard-nosed senior executives in doing anything about information overload and the resulting attention deficit it causes.

Two Hundred Messages

Attention wasn't always a problem for everyone. Not so long ago if your business involved heating, beating, and bending metal or some other physical product, the production and consumption of information was an ancillary issue. Today, however, if you're in a service business or if your workers are mostly knowledge workers (and this very likely means you), then the processing of information is what your people do for a living. The production of information and knowledge and the effective allocation of attention is all they've got to offer. If their attention isn't focused on important information or if they are wasting their attention on things that don't matter to the business, then you are in trouble.

We all know to what extent e-mails are multiplying. An IDC study estimates that we receive 10 billion non-spam (not unwanted advertising) messages per day worldwide, increasing to 35 billion in 2005.[1] Moreover, paper usage in business (in the United States, anyway, according to the American Forest and Paper Association) went up a third during the 1990s—to about 1.6 trillion pages per year. Despite these astounding numbers, one isn't sure just how to react or on what basis to get senior executives to react. One dimension on which to evaluate this phenomenon, of course, is time consumed.

Chronic Information Syndrome

How about info-stress as a reason to act on overload problems? The Pitney Bowes study described in chapter 1 found that 60 percent of workers feel overwhelmed by the amount of information they receive. Another 1996 study of 1,300 managers around the world by Reuters Business Information was even more alarmist on the issue. Entitled "Dying for Information," the Reuters study suggests the rise of an "information fatigue syndrome," which is detected by the presence of the following symptoms:

- An inability to make decisions or cope in other ways

- Irritability and anger

- Pain in the stomach and muscles

Putting Knowledge to Work. "Knowledge management systems do not develop spontaneously or in a vacuum. They emerge out of the context and history of the organization, and their impact is conditioned by the subjective perceptions of employees whose experience is governed by that history. This draws attention, firstly, to the role of management in developing and linking these constituent elements and, secondly, to the role of key organizational processes and mechanisms in shaping the way they interact with each other."

Source: Shan L. Pan and Harry L. Scarbrough, "Knowledge Management in Practice: An Exploratory Case Study," *Technology Analysis & Strategic Management* 11, no. 3 (September 1999), <http://www.tandf.co.uk/journals/>.

- Frequent feelings of helplessness, listlessness, and lethargy

- Inability to sleep at night, waking at night with a sense of panic

- Loss of energy and enthusiasm for hobbies or leisure activities

The Reuters study found that 43 percent of managers believed that important decisions are delayed and the ability to make decisions is affected by too much information.[2] In another Reuters study about so-called information addiction, 55 percent of respondents worried about making poor decisions in spite of all the information at their disposal.[3]

Because both of us are doctors of social science, not medicine, we can't make a pronouncement on whether the excess of information has reached the point of inclusion in medical textbooks. If most people are like us, however, then they certainly feel stressed by the amount of information coming their way.

Without so much information bombarding us every day, we could perhaps find time to deliberate, or rely on our own intuition, before making important decisions. Further, it's unlikely that any project can get the concerted, long-term attention it needs if everyone is so busy responding to incoming e-mails and flashing voice-mail lights.

Just passively giving our attention to the information that arrives on our desktops and doorstops may also suboptimize our allocation of attention. A more conscious information strategy would assess what information is truly important to the organization's success and then ensure that it reached the right people's attention. Peter Drucker has argued for years that organizations would be well advised to pay more attention to external matters—market trends, customers, noncustomers, and so on—than internal. Yet what typically gets forwarded to us is the easy-to-find internal financial and operational information. Without a conscious plan for where attention should be directed, it's unlikely that members of an organization would go to the trouble to find the information that truly matters.

The Bobo in Its Natural Habitat

Move over, power-suited Yuppies, the Bobos are invading, according to David Brooks's new book on this emerging class, *Bobos in Paradise*. Sporting khakis and golf shirts, these bourgeois bohemians (get it?) drive their gargantuan sports utility vehicles to the office, where they work with a vengeance. Constantly on the receiving end of information, Bobos have no problem checking their e-mail before bed or during family vacation; work is their creative expression, their calling. Yet despite their free choice to pour attention into work twenty-four hours a day, many admit to performing "a perpetual balancing act" between their jobs and their selfhood.

Overheard. "More than ever, to deliver business results, you need people to . . . focus their attention on what you think is important. Yet choice overload is creating an opposing force. Self-preservation demands that we tune out a lot of what comes at us. This means that every project, every request, comes down to bartering for people's . . . attention."

Bill Jensen, *Simplicity*

Brain Expansion

What strategies can address the attention deficit? Let us quickly address some strategies that won't work. One idea is to increase the overall supply of attention, which requires that you hire more people, each with a fresh supply of attention. Or, you might try to find a means of expanding the ability of individual brains to pay attention. Obviously, the notion of increasing the head count is never a popular one, and the idea of increasing brain cells, though more appealing, is still in the realm of science fiction. (Someday, perhaps, you'll "learn to multitask in six easy lessons," but we know of no such nostrum today, and wouldn't trust it if it existed.)

DISTRIBUTIVE PRINCIPLE: Determine where attention is currently allocated and ensure that the right information is heard.

If attention can't be significantly increased, then organizations will have to find more effective ways to allocate it toward the information and knowledge that matters. Effective leaders must assess where attention is going, ensure that the information is attention getting, limit the intrusion of unnecessary information and knowledge, and try to prevent distractions.

Assessing Allocation

Perhaps the first step in better allocating attention is knowing where it is going today. We've described the AttentionScape in some detail in chapter 3, and ideally you'd employ it or some other measurement tool to understand what employees are attending to. But if that isn't possible, you might use several other, less formal means of understanding where today's attention is going. For several of these steps, you may need the complicity of your technology managers:

- Analyze Web site traffic to understand how much time is spent on non-work-related sites. Researchers have found that more than half of all visits to sports, personal finance, and even pornography sites are made from work during work hours; a Vault.com survey suggested that 90 percent of employees admit to viewing non-work-related sites during the average workday.

Overheard. "Every person seems to have a limited capacity to assimilate information, and if it is presented to him too rapidly and without adequate repetition, this capacity will be exceeded and communication will break down."

R. Duncan Luce, ed., *Developments in Mathematical Psychology*

- Observe or visit discussion-oriented intranet sites within your company to see what people are talking about.

- Employ software programs to analyze the content of e-mail messages at an aggregate level (we do not recommend that executives actually read other people's e-mails).

- Ask some employees whom you trust to tell you the truth about what people are talking about and focusing their attention on.

- If you want to see whether a particular information channel is being attended to, offer a prize to someone who responds to a message embedded deeply within the channel (e.g., if we practiced what we preach, we'd offer you $50 for e-mailing us and letting us know you read this sentence. However, we don't).

- Hang around the coffee machine or water cooler yourself.

These methods will help identify not only the work-oriented topics to which people in the organization are attending, but also the attention problem areas for your company—attention sinks involving outside distractions, faux work (as described in chapter 9), and information channels that are receiving no attention. You probably won't resolve all these problems, since it's effectively impossible to control what subjects people pay attention to. An assessment will nevertheless begin to suggest steps that you might take to correction attention imbalances.

As the Flower Grows . . .

"Although communities of practice are fundamentally informal and self-organizing, they benefit from cultivation. Like gardens, they respond to attention that respects their nature. You can't tug on a cornstalk to make it grow faster or taller, and you shouldn't yank a marigold out of the ground to see if it has roots. You can, however, till the soil, pull out weeds, add water during dry spells, and ensure that your plants have the proper nutrients. And while you may welcome the wildflowers that bloom without any cultivation, you may get even more satisfaction from those vegetables and flowers you started from seed."

Source: Etienne C. Wenger and William M. Snyder, "Communities of Practice: The Organizational Frontier," *Harvard Business Review* (January–February 2000): 143.

Read MY Message

If you are going to bother crafting a message to send to someone, wouldn't it be nice to actually get the person's attention? But knowing what qualities bring attention to a particular message is hard to sort out. We did a bit of research to assess this question: We asked over sixty individuals to rate some one hundred messages on their attention-getting qualities. We encouraged research participants to think of a message—in any medium—that had been particularly attention getting over the past day. Then we asked each person to describe the message, so that we might relate its attributes to the high level of attention it attracted. Exhibit 11-1 lists the factors we asked participants to rate for their attention-getting message, incorporating attributes of the message source, the context of the message, the content, and the situation of the recipient.

Factors Considered in Explaining Attention-Getting Messages

Which messages do you think were the most attention getting? The factor most related to the attention received by an informational message was personalization. When the recipients of information viewed it as having been created for them alone, they were likely to attend to it. Yet how often do we get messages created with a large group in mind? This research suggests that personalization is worth the effort. What it does not reveal is whether machine-made personalization—what might be called mass customization of information—gets attention as well as the human variety. We doubt that it does, however.

The second most important factor was whether the message provoked emotion in the recipient. We all know of circumstances in which we go first to messages that will make us happy—or even to those that will anger us. This finding is consistent with the approach to measurement we described in chapter 2 that both attractive and aversive stimuli get attention. Another important quality of attention-getting messages is their source—that they come from trustworthy or respected senders; this factor was even more important to our sample than whether the sender was influential or charismatic. When it comes to content, respondents say that concise messages are better than those that engage the senses (i.e., are visually appealing) or are unique. So if you want to get attention, send personalized, short messages from a trusted source that bring forth emotion in the recipient. That shouldn't be too difficult, should it?

Exhibit 11-1: Factors Considered in Explaining Attention-Getting Messages

The message source was . . .
 1. trustworthy or respected.
 2. influential or powerful (i.e., socially or politically or both).
 3. charismatic or appealing.

The message context was . . .
 4. personalized (i.e., directed to and about me).
 5. about a group I belong to or have interest in.
 6. related to a question or an issue I was concerned about.

The message's content was . . .
 7. concise, direct, or story-like in structure.
 8. engaging to my senses (i.e., eye, ear, touch).
 9. new, unusual, or unique.

The recipient was . . .
10. emotionally moved by the message (e.g., angry, pleased).
11. able to consider the message's implications or consequences.
12. convinced the message was important to my work or life.

PLUG PRINCIPLE: Set limits through policy and technology on the amount and distribution of information.

Another way to direct more attention to what matters is to reduce the amount that doesn't matter. Few firms have yet attempted to limit the volume of information that circulates within them, although as volumes continue to grow, this will surely come to pass.

How would this be accomplished? Information policies might discourage employees from sending nonessential information—jokes, sports pool scores, and the like. As noted in chapter 9, one accounting firm tried to limit nonessential communications during tax season. Some organizations have halfhearted policies suggesting that large distribution lists for e-mails be minimized (good advice, perhaps, in view of the importance of personalization). Firms with extensive knowledge repositories are beginning to pare back content to only the most valuable examples of lessons learned, sample proposals, and marketing presentations.

Free Access

In the future, firms will probably need more institutionalized approaches to limit the amount of information and knowledge that bombards their employees. One classic means of doing this is to charge information providers for the amount of content they send to consumers. Most media have done this from the beginning—what would television be like, for example, if advertisers weren't charged for access to viewers? Yet inside most companies and on the Internet, access to information recipients is free. If I want to send an e-mail to everyone in the company (thus absorbing a small fraction of a large group's attention), I can do so without charge or (probably) penalty. If I spam a large Internet mailing list, it costs me nothing (except the respect of others on the list and the wrath of militant antispammers of the world). In the future, however, this free access to employees' attention will inevitably change, as the costs of employee attention—whether bids come from internal markets (other employees, divisions) or external markets (advertisers, vendors)—are acknowledged. Indeed, content may still be free, but attention will not.

This economic approach is controversial because it involves determining

---

Overheard. "The amount of data available to them [marketing managers] is increasing at a pace that will defy their capacity to assimilate it. . . . Methods will have to developed to assimilate billions of numbers a day."

Andrew J. Parsons, quoted in Lewis D. Eigen and Jonathan D. Siegel, *The Manager's Book of Quotations*

access to information media not only by positional authority but also by perceived relevance. Under such a policy, senior executives would have greater ability to send e-mail or Intranet discussion postings than would lower-level employees. To some degree this is already the case; many corporate policies already specify, for example, that only senior vice presidents and their superiors are entitled to send broadcast e-mail messages to all employees. Even at Cisco Systems, an organization known for its flat organizational structure and widespread access to information, only certain groups of employees are allowed to post information on the company's intranet. The company cites both security and information overload as reasons.[4]

To be sure, access has always been an issue. With other forms of media, too, senior executives have controlled access to corporatewide memos, broadcast TV networks (in companies that had them), widespread voice mail messages, and so forth. Even corporate intranets are controlled through corporate initiatives— not viewed as free-for-alls or public spaces but as official company sites, reserved for company business. In the future as in the past, those in charge of setting corporate agendas—and allocating attention—will ultimately control the flow of information.

If business executives want to play this role in earnest, however, they need to invest a lot more effort. Through meetings and at other gatherings of coworkers, they could create strategy about what information truly matters to the business. They would have to develop policies about who was proficient to pontificate on what topics to whom. The business would need mechanisms for filtering out irrelevant or useless information. Of course, the executives would have to be careful not to make people feel stifled and unable to accomplish essential communications. Today we simply don't know much about how employees would react to sparing their attention, since few organizations have made any effort to do so.

Cultural Attention

"While productivity and efficiencies have been the initial focus of most knowledge management efforts, building deeper customer relationships and increasing the speed of innovation are the ultimate goals. And as e-business continues to change the way companies operate, issues involving leadership, motivation, and culture will gain senior management's attention."

Source: Brian Hackett, "Sharing Knowledge Can Prove Profitable," *USA Today Magazine* 129, no. 2663 (1 August 2000), 15.

Filter Chip

We've focused on policy solutions to attention deficit because we think it's the shortest and most pragmatic route to change. As argued in chapter 5, technology is too often seen as a means for managing information, but certain kinds of technology do more harm than good. Many firms have abandoned push technology, in part because of the inordinate amount of attention it consumed. Nevertheless, push technology can be used for other purposes, such as the automated distribution of work-related information. BackWeb's "Polite Push" technology, according to advertisements, automates the "delivery of critical information" to personnel, even issuing "multimedia graphical alerts" to say that an important piece of information has arrived. Such an approach is theoretically good, but not unless you can ensure that the right people are determining what information is important (back to policy, in other words).

Of course, the primary route to technology-based attention protection has always been the filter, or agent. Although filters work at least in principle, these technologies rarely seem to make it out of the lab and into our daily information environments. Popular e-mail systems such as Microsoft's Outlook have rudimentary filtering features, but they require the users to specify either senders or subjects that are to be deleted or dispatched to a particular folder without the message's being viewed. Most users don't have the ability—or at least the desire—to generalize about or predict such categories. And senders of useless messages and spam seem to endlessly refine their abilities to craft subject lines that resist easy deletion: "The information you said you wanted," or "Where were you at dinner last night?"

As a result, most technologies for attention protection and information filtering remain a vision (or a specter, depending on your point of view). We've all read about such tools since the early 1980s, but they have yet to affect our lives. In a 1999 *Wall Street Journal* supplement on information overload (the article itself is an indicator of the growing prominence of the topic), academics and scientists spoke of computers as "little slaves," "kind, intuitive butlers," and "activist software" that understand and meet information needs.[5] Unfortunately, our information environments will

Those Who Ask the Right Questions Should Get Attention

In management, few things are as dangerous as a comprehensive, accurate answer to the wrong question. This is pseudoknowledge. It easily misleads management into erroneous actions. Pseudoknowledge has mushroomed with the advent of computers, which have made available masses of data that answer questions managers found too costly to ask before. In too many instances, however, the data are collected but not used, because they answer irrelevant questions.

Source: Dale Zand, *Information, Organization, and Power* (New York: McGraw-Hill, 1981), 10.

Overheard. "A new study from Cal Berkeley's School of Information Management and Systems, *How Much Information?*, measures how much digital information the average American engages today. One data point: 610 billion e-mails are sent each year in America alone."

"Measuring the Bits," <http://www.goodexperience.com>

probably grow in volume and complexity of information types over time, probably faster than the ability of software and hardware to subdue the information.

Perhaps a better approach is to display information in a manner that both attracts attention and requires less of it to be understandable. This is the focus of several existing products available in the market-place. TheBrain (we didn't make this up), for example, a soft-ware product for knowledge display, formats information as a graphic representation of relationships between different pieces of content. It allows a user to navigate rapidly through a complex Web site or another complex online information environment. Another variation on this theme is offered by Inxight Software, a spin-off from the Xerox Palo Alto Research Center. Such tools require an investment in formatting the information visually in the first place, but the investment is worth it for information that will be viewed often or by many people.

> If your knowledge category has substantial competition, a "less is more" strategy works best.

Managing Knowledge Flow

One of the few quantitative studies on how attention relates to information was conducted by Morten Hansen and Martine Haas of Harvard Business School.[6] They analyzed how much attention was given to a set of online documents in a consulting firm's knowledge repository. The study found that a steady flow of small amounts of knowledge is one of the most important factors in determining how much attention a given online doc-ument receives. Specifically, Hansen and Haas discovered that the lower the volume of knowledge a particular group of knowledge producers pro-duces, the more likely each document is to receive attention. If the category of knowledge (indicated by the keywords used to categorize it) was crowded with many documents, each document was less likely to be viewed. The researchers also found that knowledge-producing groups that were very selective in what they released to the firm's repository got more attention in crowded topic areas. Furthermore, regular releases of just a few documents yielded more attention than releases of large batches. In other words, if your knowledge category has substantial competition, a "less is more" strategy works best. If the category is not crowded, releas-ing more documents makes sense.

Distraction Shields

By now we're familiar with the use of technology to get and keep attention. The other side of this coin involves protecting against the distractions that technology can bring. Again, we're of two minds on this issue; we wouldn't want our own attention controlled or our ability to use technology substantially limited. On the other hand, if an organization is paying for its employees' attention—at least during work hours—it should have some say in where that attention goes.

Three forms of distractions absorb attention in contemporary organizations. One is, of course, the Internet and all it has wrought. One 1999 survey (by Greenfield Online) found that 9 percent of employees feel that their work performance has declined because they get distracted while using the Internet for business purposes and move off to investigate leisure time sites.[6] Although most of the Internet's effects are beneficial, the amount of irrelevant information to which employees (and managers, for that matter) are exposed is undeniably huge.

SIFTING THE WHEAT FROM THE CHAFF

THESE DAYS IT'S hard to tell what information is in fact work related. Consider the following list of e-mails one of us received in a day.

- FT.com Internet information from the *Financial Times*

- IT2Go.net newsletter (unrequested)

- Request for information from a Ph.D. student whom neither of us knows in architectural design management (about which we know nothing) in the Netherlands

- A "five-minute" online survey about Internet usage for McKinsey alumni (from someone we don't know and who apparently is not a McKinsey alumnus herself)

- A request from someone we don't know to endorse the Chinese Knowledge Management Union (it does exist!)

- A survey from somebody at our firm asking us to evaluate the "geographic services" we use

- An e-mail on "new additions to the e-Strategy library"

- Something called the "Hurwitz Trend Watch" (unsolicited)

- An e-mail with the heading "The package you sent me," which turned out to contain a link to "hot girl pictures" (note to boss: we know this isn't work related, and we didn't click on the link!)

These e-mails came in addition to the forty or fifty e-mails judged essential. Although all but one or two on the above list were quickly deleted (we won't say which ones, but we believe we observed our firm's policy on this matter), evaluating their relevance to work and then deleting them took our attention. When you consider that every employee must go through the same process of sorting and deleting, it's not hard to imagine the lost time and diverted attention such activities produce. With 68,000 employees, our firm likely pays out several million dollars each day for employees' time in digesting and sorting the inessential e-mail stream.

Although neither of us is an expert in e-mail behavior management, we would argue that firms must begin to filter out as much of the spam as possible before it hits employees' in-boxes. Of course, you cannot easily know whether an external message for another employee is legitimate without reading it (which would both violate privacy and defeat the purpose of filtering). We suggest instead, for example, that employees be warned about opening e-mails from people they don't know (for security and attention-protection reasons). Employees whose attention is deemed the most valuable should have help from secretaries or assistants in filtering the e-mail stream. Strict policies that forbid participation in list-serves and "push" communications may not be appropriate, but employees should be encouraged to take a less-is-more approach.

The Routine Route

Finally, the second great distraction is activities (otherwise known as nuisances, snafus, glitches, etc.) that require departures from the routine. Any time we have to focus our attention on breakdowns in normal organizational processes and procedures, we don't have it to address something else. To free up attention for necessarily unstructured phenomena (e.g., responding to competitor initiatives or customer demands), it makes sense to automate routines and codify structured processes as much as possible. Standardize your data, technologies, and ways of working whenever differences don't add real value. A broken or idiosyncratic internal budgeting process, for example, may soak up attention that would be better focused on innovation and creative product or service development.

Overpowering with PowerPoint?

No discussion of attention deficit would be complete without some mention of that supreme distraction—the Power-Point presentation. According to the *Wall Street Journal*, PowerPoint presentations have come under close scrutiny from none other than the U.S. Army. Its high-ranking officers have expressed concern that so-called PowerPoint Rangers are exploiting the capabilities of the package to produce attention-getting presentations. Several army commanders have suggested that basic text-and-bullet-point presentations are preferable to animated, clip-art-festooned presentations that suck up too much attention.

When it comes to PowerPoint presentations, employees should be encouraged to save attention for what matters—for example, getting the attention of the customer. We don't recommend banning the technology, however. Let's just hope that over-the-top, wipes-and-swipes-laden PowerPoint presentations go the way of triplicate carbon paper.

A Little Personal (Computer) Attention. According to Chuck Sieloff, an attention-oriented manager at HP, PCs are complex and time-consuming for individuals to manage, yet they deliver important capabilities. Rather than trying to get everyone to do a better job of managing their PCs, a small group of specialists has created a fully automated environment for distributing, installing, and configuring PC software over a shared network infrastructure. This so-called Common Operating Environment has been voluntarily adopted by over 100,000 PC users as a way of dramatically reducing the amount of time and attention they have to devote to maintaining their PCs. For the most part, they are delighted to remain ignorant of the underlying expertise needed to create that environment.

Source: Charles G. Sieloff, "Is Knowlege Draining Our Attention?" *Knowledge Management*, July 1999.

Technology itself can absorb a huge amount of attention. Our philosophy is that in the vast majority of situations, it's what you do with information technology that brings productivity and competitive advantage, not the attributes of the technology itself. From an attention management standpoint, then, it's important to make technology as common and as generic as possible. At Hewlett-Packard, for example, IT managers created a "common operating environment" that has standardized many aspects of the desktop computing environment.

Teacher Shortage

Education about the proper use and management of information and knowledge is a powerful but underutilized tool in fostering good attention allocation. If employees and managers don't know how to use technologies effectively and how to manage their own information and knowledge environments well, they will be less productive as knowledge workers—that is, less productive than they might be if they had better education on how to use technology. Unfortunately, too few role models exist in this regard. Few companies educate their workers on how to find, store, and use knowledge and information—yet what skills could be more useful in the current era?

Outsell, a research firm that studies information markets, published a quantitative study comparing the information-seeking habits and behaviors of end users of information.[8] The study found that respondents' information-gathering skills did not come from any formalized training:

- Only 18 percent of all respondents had ever received more than eight hours of training in searching, gathering, and evaluating information and sources.

- Over half had never received any formal training.

- Of the respondents who primarily use the Web for research, 66 percent had never received any training, whereas 35 percent of the users of commercial desktop information products had received no training.

Information users don't know what they don't know. Despite the low levels of training found in the Outsell survey, 96 percent of respondents considered themselves skilled or very adept at finding information. Yet we

---

Overheard. "Even knowledge has to be in the fashion, and where it is not, it is wise to affect ignorance."
Baltasar Gracian, *The Art of Worldly Wisdom*

suspect that any information professional could find obvious flaws in the respondents' searching behaviors.

In addition to teaching its staff how to search, the progressive organization would educate its users in determining what information and knowledge they truly need relative to their jobs. Education would also be provided on how to set up an effective information environment that encompasses e-mail, important information on the Internet and intranets, paper information, filing structures, and archiving techniques.

No Silver Bullet

In short, we feel that a business needs a multifaceted approach to prevent information and knowledge from overwhelming the amount of attention a person has to comprehend it. No single technology, policy, or approach will suffice. Managers who care about managing their organization's scarcest resource must employ assessment, attention-getting techniques, controls to limit the volume of information, protection against useless information, and education. As the amount of information and knowledge that flows through organizations continues to grow, creative new methods for allocating attention and even increasing it will no doubt develop. These new methods will be both bottom-up—developed by individuals to deal with their own avalanche of information—and top-down—directed by executives who worry that their organization's attention is being squandered.

Once an approach to the internal allocation of attention to information has been developed, a likely next topic could be how customers devote their attention to the information and knowledge we produce. Customers are bombarded with information and don't necessarily attend to ours or to the information we consider most important. How do we get their attention in the first place? Given their certain attention shortage, how do we get customers to allocate their attention to the key information about our products, services, and relationship? How can we help them to free up their attention so that more of it can be allocated to us? If we don't help them with their attention, chances are good that we'll suffer from the lack of it.

CHAPTER 12

FROM MYOPIA TO UTOPIA

As that famous Yankee

catcher put it, "Prediction is hard, especially about the future." Or, as science fiction writer William Gibson suggests, "The future is already here; it's just unevenly distributed." Whatever the case may be, in this chapter we'll cover a lot of ground and propose some predictions of our own. We will describe the effects of attention in many different environments and economic sectors. These include the impact of technology on attention, the role of nontechnical policies and customs in changing attention behaviors, the shape of life at work and at home, new relationships between marketers and customers, the nature of education in an attention-oriented society, and the nature of economics in the attention economy.

Tech Apace

Certainly, the technological progress that has engendered our society's attention deficit will continue apace. Digital technology will grow smaller, cheaper, and faster, and fewer technical barriers will exist between you and someone who wants to send information—rich, complex, multimedia information—your way. If you've got the attention to devote to watching a two-hour streaming video on your wrist-based personal computer, it will undoubtedly be possible. Getting information into digital form will also be easier, as voice and handwriting recognition mature and as scientists make progress on other input devices—perhaps even direct mental input.

Technology and information will be not only more powerful, but also more pervasive. Wireless devices will let people communicate at any time in any place—not just by voice and voice recognition, but through tiny keyboards as well. If you're willing to communicate, you'll be able to do so. Of course, even today we can see the implications of the wireless revolution. One man has already been caught sending e-mails on a handheld wireless device as his wife was giving birth in the maternity ward.[1] No doubt many more fathers have sent and received cell phone calls—and not just to waiting grandparents.

The anonymity once conferred upon individuals by mass society will not last much longer. Your identity and many details of your preferences and purchases will be available to anyone who wants to pay for them. Today's technologies are already capable of capturing and analyzing your

> One man has already been caught sending e-mails on a handheld wireless device as his wife was giving birth in the maternity ward.

Attention and Information Design. One way to help information and knowledge get and keep attention is through information design. This is an established—but still not well-known—field. Information design specifies how information is laid out on a page or screen. Designers of information manipulate such design elements as typography, color, graphic elements, white space, and page size and shape.

From an attention standpoint, information designs that work have two attributes. One, they're clear. Nothing about the design distracts the reader's attention or deters it from reaching an important message. While information design isn't a science, some principles or rules of thumb certainly ensure clarity: Don't use too many type fonts, for example, or do highlight key information in a box.

The other information design objective is to be attention getting. Some element of the design should stand out and grab the reader or viewer. Our publisher has worked with us on this book, for example, to add some distinctive design elements like geometric forms at the beginning of chapters, and color. Of course, the objective of being different can conflict with that of being clear—particularly to information design amateurs like us. We suggested many bizarre design elements to our editor and designer, who wisely judged them overly distracting.

It's beyond the ambitions of this book to address information design in detail, but the field has many experts. For the design of plain old text, we like the work of Richard Saul Wurman, *Information Anxiety 2001* (Indianapolis, IN: Que, 2000). For online information design, we're partial to Clement Mok, *Designing Business 2.0* (San Jose, CA: Adobe Press, 2001).

preferences—the only thing missing now is the infrastructure to enable various parties to share customer data. Just look at how many "cookies" have surreptitiously been installed in your Web browser files. With each of

ATTENTION-CONSCIOUS KNOWLEDGE MANAGEMENT

IN THE PAST FEW MONTHS, we've begun to notice several examples of knowledge management that is highly conscious of its audience's attention. Within our own firm, Accenture, for example, knowledge managers are attempting either to produce more attention-getting knowledge or to protect employee attention by eliminating unnecessary distributions of knowledge and information.

For example, the following excerpts from the first issue of *The Informant*—an online newsletter, edited by Laura Johnson, for Accenture's Strategy and Business Architecture practice—depict an editorial attitude and a writing style that are clearly attention-aware:

> *"I am the new way to go*
> *I am the way of the future."*
>
> *We live in a world of short attention span theater. This is the age of the soundbite, MTV, CNN Headline News, Cliffs Notes, instant gratification, and the Internet, where most users are willing to give less than ten seconds before moving on to something more interesting. We relish in drive through restaurants, drive through banks, drive through weddings. We pay our bills, plan vacations, buy movie tickets, and keep in touch with our families over the Internet. In short, we're in a hurry. . . .*
>
> *. . . What's the point of this diatribe? Well, I've been the editor of the Strategy KX Bulletin for over two years now, and sometimes, like with parachute pants and leisure suits, you just have to know when to say goodbye. It's not just about the KX anymore. To continue publishing a 10+ page newsletter would be self-indulgent and would ignore the changing needs of you, our readers. In short, the KX Bulletin is dead. It has ceased to be. It has expired and has gone to meet its maker. This is a late KX Bulletin. It is a stiff. This is an ex-KX Bulletin.*

> *our mission: to educate and inform you in the most entertaining way possible.*
>
> *Meet the Informant. Instead of one long newsletter once a month, you will receive a short, to-the-point communication every week. Everything you need to know, nothing you don't. What can you expect in the future? The same helpful tips, important announcements, and cool stuff you loved in the KX Bulletin, only broken down into weekly, bite-size bits of information designed to be absorbed in three minutes or less—the time you would spend smoking a cigarette, waiting in line for your decaf skinny cappuccino, or remembering where you left your car keys.*

Another example of attention-conscious knowledge management within Accenture is provided by the editors of *Flashpoint*, an online technology newsletter created by the firm's Center for Strategic Technology and Research (CSTaR). Rather than attempting to make a somewhat tired subject more attention-getting, the editors simply decided to kill the publication, as the following excerpt from the last issue describes (in an attention-getting fashion):

> *Dear FlashPoint subscriber,*
>
> *FlashPoint, long comatose, is being killed outright. We found that there are only six or seven basic lessons associated with the future of technology and its impact on business, culture, and individuals. As we came to realize that every freaking FP story was pounding home one of those lessons, over and over, redundantly, relentlessly, without pause or relief, with the subtlety of a jackhammer, FlashPoint became steadily more difficult to write. So we've stopped, and I apologize for any wailing and gnashing of teeth our decision might cause.*

these developments will come new demands on your attention and, yes, some relief from those demands afforded by other developments. Even as the bombardment continues, information will become more targeted and hence attention getting. Advertising and commercial messages—both targeted and broadcast—will be everywhere, in all interstices of life. They will go beyond the advertisements that already beckon us at lobby shops, gas pumps, convenience stores, airports, and suburban train stations. As the CEO of one provider of such equipment put it, "We look for places to put our [electronic] billboards that coincide with moments in the day when people have a few seconds to listen."[2]

Though technology has caused many past attention problems and will continue to create attention deficits, its future effects will also be more positive. Despite little progress thus far in attention production through agents, filters and "bots," some advances in this domain will occur over the first decade of the 2000s. The attention problem will draw a substantial degree of market interest to such technologies, and vendors will respond enthusiastically. These filters and agents will begin to free us from routine attention allocations and mundane information. As a result, we may even have more leisure time. Just as information technologies first had little effect on productivity but have now begun to show substantial productivity benefits, attention-protecting devices may soon begin to show value.

> People will use attention-protecting devices to "tune out"— to think, reflect, and consider the implications of all the information they have received.

In addition to leisure, people will use attention-protecting devices to "tune out"—to think, reflect, and consider the implications of all the information they have received. We'll need some relief from the continuing stream of valuable information and info-junk. Today we already face the danger that we can't put information in perspective because of a shortage of attention. Unless technology or policy brings us some relief, we run the risk of making many poor decisions.

Attention protection has its cost, however. Users of these technologies will have to spend more time tailoring their information environment preferences. They'll have to specify in detail what kind of news,

---

"Class, Dismissed." "The crisis of attention that will most likely continue in the future makes the content of school curriculums more important now than ever. The current emphasis on raising student scores on standardized, minimum competency tests alarms some education experts. While test scores of basic math and reading skills are improving in many schools, the schools are cutting instruction in creative writing, physical education, music and the arts, to focus on the tests."

Source: Richard Rothstein, "Lessons: Attention to Scores Comes at a Price," *New York Times*, 24 November 1999.

corporate information, and electronic communications they want to see, versus those they are willing to let a computer read and analyze. For people willing to work with agents and filters, the battle between devices that seek user attention and those that protect it will continue. The winners will be the individuals most willing to invest in their own information environments and use attention-filtering technologies to greatest advantage. For example, one of us recently telephoned Phil Anderson, a professor at the Tuck School of Business at Dartmouth. Phil wasn't in, but his voice mail message noted, "I listen and respond to voice mail messages in batches at 9 A.M., noon, and 5 P.M. If you leave a message before those times, I can most quickly get back to you." We were impressed by Phil's efficiency, and we expect to see a lot more of that sort of thing in the future.

> **Companies will no longer be proud of how extensive their knowledge portals are, but rather of how targeted an information environment they can create.**

One attention problem of the past is that electronic information has developed not in substitution for, but in addition to, previous paper-based information formats. In the future, we'll venture a prediction that paper use will be reduced (a hazardous prediction made many times previously, always incorrectly). This will lead to a greater focus on "pull" rather than "push" of information. Companies will no longer be proud of how extensive their knowledge portals are, but rather of how targeted an information environment they can create.

Technology will increasingly be used not only to get and protect attention, but also to monitor it. Attention-monitoring devices will be pervasive in any situation in which people must pay attention: driving, flying planes, and receiving important content. These devices will monitor brain waves, eye movements, and perhaps heart rates and galvanic skin response. Those who provide content—advertisers in particular—will be able to determine whether their message was viewed and acted upon. Viewers of advertising will move seamlessly from print, television, or radio to a Web site or call center that will tell them more about the product or service and happily take their order for it (via codes embedded in the ads). With this kind of technology, advertisers can easily determine what messages really get attention.

Ron Culberson, Management Funsultant

As learning, work and entertainment merge, getting employees' attention may require a stand-up comedian. Enter Ron Culberson, who says that workers who infuse some humor into their jobs are more productive, more flexible, and perceived by clients as more approachable. His suggestions for lightening up at the office? Send out memos laced with cartoons, or deliver a committee report to the tune of the *Gilligan's Island* theme song.

Source: Brian Krebs, "The Cheerman Reports to the Bored," *Washington Post*, 22 March 1999.

Policies, Manners, Mores

If our ability to manage attention is going to improve, what isn't addressed by technology will have to be addressed by new policies or the adoption of new manners and mores. Policies in organizations have thus far not dealt with attention to any significant degree, but if managers begin to realize the importance of attention, policies will begin to emerge. The following list provides an overview:

- Companies may have strictly defined policies for who can send information to employees and who can't. Wasting another employee's attention will be viewed as a corporate sin, and access to corporatewide e-mail addresses will be strictly limited.

- Organizations may specify a hierarchy of what kinds of information most deserve employee attention. Messages from the CEO may be first in the list, followed by communications from customers. Customer-facing personnel may be told that face-to-face customer interactions should take precedence over telephone calls or e-mail (a policy we'd appreciate when checking into a hotel, for example!).

- Executives of companies will probably suggest to employees how much of their off-hour attention should be devoted to work-related topics. At Hewlett-Packard, for example, managers have already encouraged employees not to devote significant attention to e-mail or voice mail on weekends except in extraordinary circumstances. At the opposite extreme, one CEO told executives that it was inappropriate for them to record an "on vacation" voice mail message, because they should always be checking their messages, even when on vacation!

- As a complement to the policy above, it may also become common for employers to instruct employees about the amount of attention an employee can devote to non-work-related topics while at work. Work time has been called "the new prime time" for advertisers on the Internet, reflecting the high level of current Web use at work and the broadband Internet connections of many corporations.[3] The sites that employees are allowed to browse and the amount of time they can spend on approved sites will probably become matters of

Overheard. "Effective managers live in the present—but concentrate on the future."
James L. Hayes, *Memos for Management*

policy. For example, some firms already have policies about the use of the Internet for personal matters while at work. However, we expect that just as firms will support moderate attention to work issues at home, most will also allow moderate attention to personal business at work.

- Firms will probably also make suggestions to their employees about the amount of attention they should devote to particular work issues or information. For example, executives will address head-on the level of attention that employees devote to rumors about mergers, acquisitions, divestitures, and restructurings. If executives monitor the allocation of employee attention and learn that an unhealthy amount is going to these topics, they will naturally attempt to refocus employee attention on more productive topics.

- Firms will establish "information-free zones" or times during which they will be free to concentrate on their work. Computer Associates, for example, several years ago established the time between 10 A.M. and 2 P.M. as a time free from phone calls and e-mail. Although today's employees might find such isolation difficult to imagine, firms will have to institute such policies to allow employees to get noncommunications work done. Some managers and employees probably feel that all their work is communications-intensive. This is a sign that the attention problem has progressed very far.

> Like a cell phone call during a concert, behaviors that unfairly consume the attention of others will be considered rude.

Not all change in behavior will result from explicit policy. In many cases, employees and individuals will begin to realize the appropriateness and inappropriateness of certain attention-related behaviors. Like a cell phone call during a concert, behaviors that unfairly consume the attention of others will be considered rude. For example, people will view the sending of blanket e-mails to large distribution lists as extremely inappropriate. Even if there is no policy against it, employees will not be tempted to send out a message to all employees seeking help in finding a lost wallet.

Although not considered rude, behaviors inappropriate to the attention economy may be viewed as ineffective or suboptimal from the perspective of good business acumen. Successful people already have today a sense of how much attention they need to nourish their own careers, and how to get it when necessary. They are certainly good at allocating their own attention where it needs to go. Perhaps some future researcher will establish that "attention intelligence" is just as important as emotional intelligence in getting ahead.

Everyday Life

Conscious management of attention won't be restricted to business and other types of formal organizations. In our personal lives we'll also be aware of the importance of attention and its relationship to living a successful life. One key issue, for example, will involve multitasking.

In the future we'll begin to realize that the ability to multitask and allocate simultaneous attention is highly limited. As a result, perhaps a few of us will realize the attention trade-offs if we talk on cell phones while driving, watch TV while doing homework, answer e-mail while on the telephone, and so forth. Insurance companies and state legislatures will impose penalties for accidents that occur when people drive with divided attention.

However, despite increasing concerns about the ability to multitask, people try to do it with increasing frequency. In the not-too-distant future, many people will find it almost inconceivable to do only one thing at a time. With so much practice, the ability to pay attention to multiple things at once may actually increase slightly, though not enough to outweigh the increased risks of multitasking.

It's even conceivable that psychological or pharmacological research could uncover techniques or technologies that could radically improve the brain's ability to multitask. Perhaps the part of the brain that currently constrains us to pay attention to only one stimulus at a time could have its capabilities upgraded. We wouldn't count on this, however; far more likely is that we'll have to come to grips with our multitasking limits.

Perhaps we could someday use chemical aids that

"Pay No Attention to That Man Behind the Curtain": The Great and Powerful Oz

If the barrage of information streaming at you every day makes you feel like you're not in Kansas anymore, take a few lessons from Oz. Look at some of the ways that attention overload interferes:

1. Distracted by a full chorus of Munchkins cajoling her to "follow the yellow brick road," Dorothy wastes time walking around in a giant spiral before the road finally straightens.

2. Hideous shrieks, flying monkeys, and threats of "I'll get you, my pretty," obfuscate a simple solution: The Wicked Witch dissolves in water.

3. The wizard addresses his subjects with smoke, amplifiers, and a model of a huge, green head: You will find all these attention-getting strategies missing from our chapter on leadership and attention.

help us tune out the avalanche of information that will undoubtedly swell over us in the future. Just as some researchers and clinicians argue that Prozac makes even the mentally healthy into better, more confident personalities, drugs might help people deal with normal attention deficits. Ritalin, the drug often prescribed for dealing with attention deficit hyperactivity disorder, might, for example, play a role in enhancing mental focus for healthy but overloaded individuals. Perhaps we'll all take a Ritalin tablet with our morning coffee when we arrive at work.

We expect substantial generational differences in how individuals attempt to manage their attention in everyday life. Younger generations will want to have their attention stimulated much of the time. In classrooms, meetings, conferences, and other occasions in which attention was previously directed to a speaker or to colleagues, younger employees will simultaneously be surfing the Web, reviewing e-mails, sending instant messages, and even playing games. This behavior is currently viewed as impolite, but it will probably come to be viewed as normal. Individuals who adopt it, however, will have to accept the consequences of this multitasking.

For younger generations, the boundary between attention-getting infotainment environments at home and captive-attention, boring information at work will disintegrate. Business information content will have to incorporate aspects of entertainment. We already see differences today in the type of information to which different generations respond. Older workers and managers are content to receive black-and-white text; younger workers are far more likely to be tempted by graphically sumptuous information.

Giving It Away

In the future, huge amounts of marketing attention will be paid to understanding how to get attention. In the past, attention was taken for granted, and goods and services were considered valuable. In the future, many goods and services will be given away for free in exchange for a few seconds or minutes of the user's attention. Web sites, TV channels and programs, and other content sources that can reliably capture attention will be considered a highly valuable resource. The concept of paying large amounts of money to buy eyeballs will become commonplace. When the Web portal Excite paid $780 million for Blue Mountain Arts, a very sticky

Overheard. "Us sing and dance, make faces and give flower bouquets, trying to be loved. You ever notice that trees do everything to git attention we do, except walk?"
Alice Walker, *The Color Purple*

site that gave away free e-mail greeting cards, observers were astounded at how much could be paid simply for a source of eyeballs. They won't be astounded in the future.

Competing in attention markets will become a primary concern of brand management and marketing. In the latter half of the twentieth century, firms employed mass media—television, radio, and print advertising, for example—to extract a tiny fragment of attention from a large market. Mass media are now being replaced with a much broader selection of media and communications channels, each with its own narrow customer segment. The goal of Web-based advertising or even highly targeted direct mail is to extract a much higher degree of attention from a narrowly defined market. As the attention of consumers becomes ever scarcer, they will respond most favorably to commercial messages that were created specifically for them and that embody their own specific needs and situations. Thus we can expect to see increasing personalization in marketing of the future.

Marketers will increasingly attempt to create "industrialized intimacy" with their customers, attempting to make them believe that they are receiving personalized attention.[4] You'll be told that you're receiving offers tailored to your interests and purchase patterns. Your demographic profile will be well understood by the organizations with which you do business, and you'll be marketed to on that basis. You'll receive communications that use your name and purport to know your desires. Will all this personalized attention get your attention?

Yes, but only if the attempts are well executed and truly personal. Although personalized products, services, and communications are more worthy of consumers' attention, most consumers have some very sensitive antennae with regard to whether attention is truly personalized. Are you touched, for example, when you receive a direct mail piece with your name (even assuming it's spelled correctly) in the salutation? Even when attention seems personalized at first, we quickly become inured to false personalization.

For example, one of us once received a clipping about a public speaking course in a hand-addressed envelope. On the clipping was a Post-it note with the handwritten message, "Thomas—try this, it really works!" At first I was taken aback. "Oh no—someone

The Personal Touch

A study of Detroit hardware stores shows that the mom-and-pop is alive and well. The reason, according to loyal customers, is the personalized service they get as soon as they walk through the door, often greeted by name. As more goods and service providers clamor for consumers' attention, a real, human connection may decide who gets their attention and their business.

Source: Marge Colborn, "Hardware Stores Succeed with Service," *Detroit News*, 15 January 2000.

has seen me give a presentation, didn't like it much, and has kindly sent me this anonymous tip." But my suspicions were aroused by the use of the name "Thomas." No one calls me "Thomas." I then received similar mailings about once a month, although from then on I immediately discarded them.

For personalized marketing to get attention, it will have to include both human intimacy and industrialized intimacy. Computer-based loyalty programs and analysis of electronic transactions must be used to identify those customers who warrant individual attention from real people. The combination of human and technical approaches can make attention-getting personalization both affordable and effective.

Business Life

The years to come will see changes in the workaday lives of businesspeople, driven primarily by ever more capable attention technologies. Judging by the effects of the technologies developed thus far, this won't streamline your information load, but will increase it. If you feel overwhelmed now, just wait a few years. To cope with all this information, various trends will arise (or continue).

First of all, more information will require more delegation. Expect to see personal assistants whose primary job is to sift through information and eliminate unnecessary drains on high-powered knowledge workers' attention (perhaps we will call them "secretaries"). Firms may also employ technology specialists to keep their company's executives in touch with the latest attention-getting and attention-protecting innovations. Whole teams of people may be assigned to communicate attention to others on your behalf.

> More information will require more delegation.

An industry will develop around helping organizations and people manage attention. Consultants will make their livings helping organizations produce attention-getting information and knowledge—internal communications, external Web sites, and multimedia marketing messages. Senior executives will hire attention management experts to help them develop processes for dealing with the vast streams of information thrown at them. Although for years consultants have addressed both time management and organizing and filing systems, only recently have there been consultants for helping with electronic information.[5] It will undoubtedly be a few more years before they turn their attention to straightening out the mental clutter of attention deficits.

Increasingly, managerial success will rely on the ability to ignore or at least filter the vast stream of information that hits the desk, ears, and eyeballs. The ability to prioritize information, to focus and reflect on it, and to exclude extraneous data will be at least as important as acquiring it. If you focus on refining these skills, you'll be more successful, whatever your job. In the future, executives who have attention management skills will outperform others in almost every business situation. The attention economy has just begun. It will be years before every old dog in business learns the new tricks necessary to succeed in this environment.

> The ability to prioritize information, to focus and reflect on it, and to exclude extraneous data will be at least as important as acquiring it.

Because the attention of knowledge workers is the most valuable commodity that a future organization will have, considerable effort will be devoted to ensuring that attention is properly allocated. In the best organizations, this will primarily be a matter of trust and mutual respect between employee and employer. In the worst organizations, it will undoubtedly take the form of "attention surveillance" and violations of privacy. Already, many firms are examining employees' e-mail, Web usage, and computer-based activity in general—in part to ensure that employees' attention is being devoted to work-related topics. Much against the desires of pilots, airlines are considering putting video cameras in cockpits to record, among other things, where the pilots' attention is going.[6]

We suspect that this attention-monitoring will be intolerable to many employees, which may result in a generalized backlash to this use of attention technologies in the workplace. We hope that leaders of organizations will discuss the importance of attention with their employees and achieve high levels of attentiveness without the use of invasive technologies.

Domestic Front

In the attention economy, pressures that strain intimate relationships and traditional family roles will continue to increase. The attention economy has already transformed the way we live at home. A high-volume-information household sends and receives 240 messages per week across multiple media

---

Overheard. "As the dimensions of the tree are not always regulated by the size of the seed, so the consequences of things are not always proportionate to the apparent magnitude of those events that have produced them."

Charles Caleb Colton, *Lacon*

at home.[7] The typical parent's attention is far more distracted by work than it was ten years ago, and children are overwhelmed with attention grabbers as well (think of the attention-draining capacity of computer games, Internet chat rooms, and MTV). Technology will continue to weaken the barrier that separates home life from the intrusions of the outside world. Those who don't like this will try to find ways of defending their homes from attention technologies—but it's going to be an uphill battle.

As mentioned, attention technologies can help solve the very problems they create. That's as true in the home as it is in the office. Increasingly, attention technologies will be adapted to strengthen family relationships and other interpersonal connections. Spouses, parents, children, siblings, and friends will use a variety of gadgets to stay connected wherever they are. Future generations will wonder why we laughed at a scene in the movie *Clueless* in which two rich Beverly Hills High students chat on their cell phones as they walk through the halls between classes. In the future, this will be the rule, not the outlandish exception.

> Increasingly, attention technologies will be adapted to strengthen family relationships and other interpersonal connections.

Work will continue to make its way into home life; increasing numbers of workers will work at least sometimes from home. On the surface, this will mean that more attention can be devoted to family members. Even so, as work permeates free time, people will continue a present trend toward purchasing care for dependents. Attention to children and others who need care will be bought and sold more and more often, rather than being provided by family members, whose attention is already strained to the breaking point.

Education

Education is a dismal backwater in attention management. We had many years of education, and we weren't paying attention much of the time. You weren't either—we saw you nodding off, writing notes to Melissa, and shooting spitballs at Miss Poindexter, your tiresome third-grade teacher. In the attention economy, education may change dramatically.

In a world in which educators are oriented to attention management, teachers would be specifically trained to get and keep students' attention. (Both of us have taught at college and graduate-school levels, and neither of us received any such training. In fact, one of the main informal requirements of advanced education seems to be an almost superhuman ability to create and endure boredom.) In an attention utopia, dry lectures and textbooks would be replaced by more entertaining educational experiences—often technologically facilitated. The traditional one-way, passive teaching style would give way to interactive lessons, with students as involved as teachers. The material taught in schools would be relevant to the students' actual lives—much of the knowledge imparted in today's system is about as germane to students' real-world experience as skiing is to fish. Finally, the pace of education will turn to briefer, more varied learning experiences, instead of the drawn-out lectures that numb the brains of today's students. This trend of brevity is already taking place within corporate education environments. For example, managers at Dell's online corporate university say that ten minutes is about the maximum attention span for a worker seeking online training. For this reason, the company limits its intranet-based training modules to that length.

> The pace of education will turn to briefer, more varied learning experiences, instead of the drawn-out lectures that numb the brains of today's students.

In education as in other areas of life, attention technologies would play a vital role in improving quality and attentiveness. For example, a classroom might be outfitted with a panel of lights at the teacher's workstation, one light corresponding to each student's seat. If a student is paying attention, brain wave monitors note this, and the student's light is green. If the student's attention lags, the light goes red. When the teacher notes a red light, rather than rapping the student's knuckles with a ruler, he or she engages the student's attention by asking a question, focusing his or her voice in the student's direction, waving the arms wildly, or whatever. After the class has given thirty minutes of mostly green lights, the teacher calls for a fifteen-minute "attention break," during which the students make informal conversation.

If this prediction seems outlandish, realize that at least one company's electronic classroom of the future is planning a form of attention monitoring. ProfessorQ, a start-up firm, has received a patent on a video monitoring device that "is constantly patrolling for drooping eyes and nodding heads." The company's system also monitors attention by assessing response time to questions posed by a computer. If the system notes an inattentive pupil, "It can yell at you and say, 'Wake up!' Or it can suddenly play a piece of music or change the screen display," according to the inventor.[8]

Overheard. "The best way to predict the future is to invent it."

Alan Kay, *Creating Excellence*

One virtually certain feature of attention-economy education is that education will become more specialized. The proliferation of knowledge and information has already reached such an extreme that even though schools and students are including more data in the educational process than ever before, this constitutes a narrower and narrower percentage of available knowledge. Since human attention is not infinitely expandable, and knowledge is, specialization can only increase.

Economic Life

In the different domains of life described above, we've shown how certain facets of human existence—at least in advanced information societies—might be affected by the surfeit of information relative to attention. But these are only a few building blocks of an economy that will undoubtedly be transformed in multiple different respects. How we make our livings, connect buyers and sellers, and produce desirable products and services will all be affected by attention.

In the past, the key limiting factor in economic success was access—first access to means of production, and eventually access to markets and customers. With the advent of the Internet, the access problem has virtually disappeared. For only a few dollars per month, a small company can put up a Web site and offer products all around the world. As a result of this ease, some observers have heralded the rise of "friction-free commerce."

In the future, however, the friction is a matter of the human mind. Anybody can put up a Web site, but not everybody can attract attention to it. The limiting factor in the economy of the future will be the number of eyeballs one can draw to an ad or a Web page, and the number of brain cells the mind is willing to devote to it. Firms will think nothing of paying much more to attract attention than the cost of the product or service itself. The hit movie *The Blair Witch Project*, for example, cost only $350,000 to make, but was the beneficiary of more than $11 million in marketing expenditures. Ultimately, the best intermediate measure of a business idea—short, that is, of the amount of money that it makes—will be the amount of attention it can attract. Virtually every activity within sophisticated economies will be mediated by the variable of attention.

For example, as more people realize the centrality of attention in the new economy, attention measurement will be everywhere. Every performer,

---

Overheard. "Give me insight into today and you may have the antique and future worlds."
Ralph Waldo Emerson, "The American Scholar"

author, sports star, and politician will be painfully aware of his or her position on the universal attention index. People who are proven to attract a lot of attention will draw gigabucks in salary—and if you want their attention, you'll have to pay through the nose for it. Even sending e-mail will cost more if the intended recipient is rich, powerful, or famous. (Yes, as we've described earlier, your account will be debited every time you click "send." You can't expect to get attention for nothing.)

People—and companies—simply won't be able to get attention without paying for it. As we've discussed, e-commerce companies are already beginning to pay users for their attention. Similarly, small companies effectively buy the attention of Wall Street analysts by trading low-priced stock for research reports.[9] In the future, buying attention will become an accepted part of doing business, particularly with regard to media. In a world with over five hundred TV channels and a trillion Web pages, simple entertainment or information will no longer be enough to get one's attention on the television or the Internet. Some people may earn a living simply by watching commercials all day (and in our opinion, they will have earned every penny). Of course, high-quality-content providers will have to pay less for attention; the better *Seinfeld* reruns may get by for free.

In the past, to determine what deserved attention, our economy generally relied on third-party judgments by journalists, news producers, and corporate communications directors. In the future, the products, services, or information judged worthy of your attention may be those for which the providers paid the most. Already, search engines such as AltaVista can exchange favorable placement in search results for a fee. Why does a particular book get prominent treatment on Amazon.com? Probably because the author or publisher paid a fee to Amazon. What this means, of course, is that the rich (in terms of both money and attention) will continue to get richer. Although not a new trend, it is one that is accentuated by the attention economy.

In the past, we generally viewed information as something worth paying for. To get a magazine subscription, for example, you had to pay for it. Already, however, you can get a large assortment of free "trade press" publications that provide free content in exchange for your valuable eyeballs. In the future, we'll not just give it away; we'll have to pay for people to receive our information. Today, for example, if you want to go to a conference at which products and services from information technology vendors are

---

Overheard. "A speculator is a man who observes the future, and acts before it occurs."
Bernard Baruch, quoted in <http://www.bemorecreative.com/one/59.htm>

displayed and discussed, you typically have to pay something. In the future, the conference organizers will pay you to come. We heard about something similar to this. If you're a chief information officer with the ability to buy lots of hardware, software, and communications equipment, you can go on a free cruise. The downside is that the vendors get to go along with you, and your attention is somewhat captive while on the ship.

Of course, trading your attention for free goods and services is a devil's bargain. If attention is the scarcest good, people will ultimately realize that they should not trade it away lightly. We believe that knowledge workers will eventually realize the value of their attention, and anyone who wants it will have to pay a high price.

The trend of more information competing for less attention can't go on forever. Ultimately, people will begin to withdraw from the stress of an attention-devouring world, and information providers will begin to focus on quality, not quantity. For those who don't need to pay attention in order to make a living, the world will become much quieter. The rich will be able to live in attention-conservation zones, and ordinary folks will save up to vacation in environments in which their attention can be devoted solely to loved ones, bodily processes, and a few carefully chosen attention stimuli. In the end, the greatest prize for being able to capture attention will be the freedom to avoid it.

> Trading your attention for free goods and services is a devil's bargain.

NOTES

Chapter 1: A New Perspective on Business

1. Fifteenth-century information quoted from Joel Achenbach, "The Too-Much-Information Age: Today's Data Glut Jams Libraries and Lives, but Is Anyone Getting Any Wiser?," *Washington Post*, 12 March 1999.

2. Magazine Publishers of America, *The Magazine Handbook* (New York: Magazine Publishers of America, 1999), <http://www.magazine.org/resources/downloads/MPA_Handbook_99.pdf>.

3. Catalog figures are from Jonathan B. Weinbach, "Mail Order Madness," *Wall Street Journal*, 19 November 1999; direct-mail figures are from Stuart Elliott, "You've Got Mail, Indeed," *New York Times*, 25 October 1999.

4. U.S. Department of Commerce, *The Emerging Digital Economy* (Washington, DC: Government Printing Office, April 1998), <http://www.ecommerce.gov/emerging.htm>.

5. University of Illinois study referenced in weekly "e-brief" from Outsell, an information provider market research firm, in Burlingame, CA, 25 February 2000.

6. "Decline in New Product Introductions," *Frozen Foods* Digest 13, no. 1 (1997): 8.

7. Institute for the Future, "Workplace Communications in the 21st-Century Workplace," study conducted for Pitney Bowes, May 1998.

8. Drug Enforcement Administration, testimony before the Committee on Education and the Workforce, Subcommittee on Early Childhood, Youth and Families, 106th Cong., 2d sess., 16 May 2000, <http://www.usdoj.gov/dea/pubs/cngrtest/ct051600.htm>.

9. Donald A. Redemeier and Robert J. Tibshirani, "Association Between Cellular-Telephone Calls and Motor Vehicle Collisions," *New England Journal of Medicine* (13 February 1997): 453.

10. "TV Viewing in Internet Households," Nielsen Media Research study of Internet use and television watching, <http://www.nielsenmedia.com>. John Markoff, "A Newer, Lonelier Crowd Emerges in Internet Study," *New York Times*, 16 February 2000, describes a Stanford University study directed by Norman Nie at the Institute for the Quantitative Study of Society.

11. American Academy of Child and Adolescent Psychiatry, "Children and Watching TV," April 1996, <http://www.aacap.org/publications/facts fam/tv.htm>.

12. Michael J. Wolf, *The Entertainment Economy* (New York: Times Books, 1999).

13. Pew Research Center for the People and the Press, untitled sidebar in *Brill's Content*, December 1999, 135.

14. Herbert Simon, "Designing Organizations for an Information-Rich World," in Donald M. Lamberton, ed., *The Economics of Communication and Information* (Cheltenham, England: Edward Elgar, 1997).

Chapter 2: Attention, the Story So Far

1. O. S. Munsell, *Psychology*, or, *The Science of Mind* (New York: D. Appleton and Co., 1871), 11.

2. William James, *The Principles of Psychology* (New York: H. Holt and Company, 1890).

3. Jane Dutton, "Understanding Strategic Agenda Building and Its Implications for Managing Change," in *Managing Ambiguity and Change*, ed. Louis R. Pondy, Richard J. Bola, and Howard Thomas (Chichester, England: Wiley, 1988), 127–144.

4. James March, *A Primer on Decision Making: How Decisions Happen* (New York: Free Press, 1994); Herbert Simon, *Administrative Behavior: A Study of Decision-Making Processes in Administrative Organizations* (New York: Macmillan, 1957).

5. W. Schneider and R. M. Shiffrin, "Controlled and Automatic Human Information Processing: I. Detection, Search, and Attention," *Psychological Review* 84, no. 2 (1997): 1–66.

6. Mihaly Csikszentmihalyi, *Flow: The Psychology of Optimal Experience* (New York: Harper & Row, 1990).

7. W. B. Pillsbury, *Attention* (New York: Arno Press, 1973), 12.

8. March, *A Primer on Decision-Making*; and Simon, *Administrative Behavior.*

9. William Ocasio, "Towards an Attention-Based View of the Firm," *Strategic Management Journal* 18, S1 (1997): 188. Emphasis added.

10. Graham Allison, *Essence of Decision: Explaining the Cuban Missile Crisis* (Boston: Little, Brown and Company, 1971), 174.

11. D. J. Teece, G. Pisano, and A. Shuen, "Dynamic Capabilities and Strategic Management," *Strategic Management Journal* 18, no. 7 (1997): 509–533.

12. E. Hutchins, *Cognition in the Wild* (Cambridge: MIT Press, 1995); and Simon, *Administrative Behavior.*

Chapter 3: Doing a Number on You

1. Ronald A. Rensink, "The Need for Attention to See Change," project description, <http://www.cbr.com/~rensink/flicker/flickDescr.html>.

Chapter 4: From Amoebas to Apes

1. Abraham Maslow, *Motivation and Personality*, 3d ed. (New York: Harper & Row, 1987).

2. E. O. Wilson, *Sociobiology* (Cambridge: Belknap Press of Harvard University Press, 1975).

3. Charles Derber, *The Pursuit of Attention: Power and Ego in Everyday Life*, 2d ed. (New York: Oxford University Press, 2000).

4. Charlotte Joko Beck, *Nothing Special: Living Zen* (San Francisco: Harper San Francisco, 1993), 41.

5. Beck, *Nothing Special.*

6. Ellen J. Langer, *Mindfulness* (Reading, MA: Addison-Wesley, 1989).

Chapter 5: Luddites Beware

1. Roger C. Schank, *Tell Me a Story: A New Look at Real and Artificial Memory* (New York: Scribner, 1990).

2. Roger C. Schank and Chip Cleary, *Engines for Education* (Hillsdale, NJ: L. Erlbaum Associates, 1995).

Chapter 6: The Hidden Persuaders

1. Ken Sacharin, *Attention! How to Interrupt, Yell, Whisper, and Touch Consumers* (New York: John Wiley and Sons, 2000).

2. Felicity Barringer, "Paid Newspaper Circulation in U.S. Continues to Decline," *New York Times*, 3 November 1998.

3. Doreen Carvajal, "In Search of Readers, Publishers Consider Age," *New York Times*, 12 July 1999.

4. Network television figures from Michael J. Wolf, "The Battle for Your Attention," *Strategy and Business* (first quarter 1999): 30.

5. Malcolm Gladwell, *The Tipping Point: How Little Things Can Make a Big Difference* (Boston: Little, Brown, 2000).

6. Tom Reichert et al., "Beefcake or Cheescake? No Matter How You Slice It, Sexual Explicitness in Advertising Continues to Increase," *Journalism & Mass Communication Quarterly* 76, no. 1 (1999): 7–20.

7. Deidre N. McCloskey, *Knowledge and Persuasion in Economics* (Cambridge, England: Cambridge University Press, 1994).

Chapter 7: Eyeballs and Cyber Malls

1. For a discussion of ratings sites and their popularity, see Mark Frauenfelder, "Revenge of the Know-It-Alls," *Wired*, July 2000, 144–158.

2. Steve Lawrence and Lee Giles, "Accessibility of Information on the Web," *Nature* 400, no. 6740 (1999): 107–109.

3. Joel P. Friedman and Toni C. Langlinais, "Best Intentions: A Business Model for the New Economy," *Outlook Magazine* (January 1999), <http://www.accenture.com>.

4. Jared M. Spool, Tara Scanlon, Will Schroeder, Carolyn Snyder, and Terri DeAngelo, *Web Site Usability: A Designer's Guide* (San Francisco: Morgan Kaufmann Publishers, 1999).

5. Marc Braunstein, "Mail Order Madness," *Wall Street Journal*, 19 November 2000.

6. Nielsen//Net Ratings study, January 2000, <http://www.nielsen-netratings.com>.

7. Millward Brown Interactive, "Advertising Effectiveness Research: The Wired Digital Rich Media Study," January 1999, <http://www.mbinteractive.com/resources/reports/wired_rich_media.html>.

8. Peter Kafka, "Unaccountable," *Forbes* (3 May 1999), <http://www.forbes.com/global/1999/0503/0209086a.html>.

Chapter 8: Command Performance

1. Heather Green, "The Curious Culture of Silicon Valley," *Business Week*, 9 August 1999.

2. Po Bronson, *The Nudist on the Late Shift* (New York: Random House, 1999).

Chapter 9: Focused Choices and Global Resources

1. Ocasio, "Towards an Attention-Based View of the Firm," 188.

2. Mariann Jelinek, *Institutionalizing Innovation: A Study of Organizational Learning Systems* (New York: Praeger, 1979), 138–139.

3. Michael E. Porter, *Competitive Strategy: Techniques for Analyzing Industries and Competitors* (New York: Free Press, 1980).

4. C. K. Prahalad and Gary Hamel, "The Core Competence of the Corporation," *Harvard Business Review* (May–June 1990): 79–90; Gary Hamel and C. K. Prahalad, "Strategy as Stretch and Leverage," *Harvard Business Review* (March–April 1993): 75–84; and Gary Hamel, "Strategy as Revolution," *Harvard Business Review* (July–August 1996): 69–82.

5. Adrian J. Slywotzky, *Value Migration: How to Think Several Moves Ahead of the Competition* (Boston: Harvard Business School Press, 1996).

6. Gary Hamel, "Strategy as Revolution," *Harvard Business Review* (July–August 1996), reprinted in *Seeing Differently*, ed. J. S. Brown (Boston: Harvard Business School Press, 1997), p. 29.

7. Henry Mintzberg, *The Rise and Fall of Strategic Planning: Reconceiving Roles for Planning, Plans, Planners* (New York: Free Press, 1994).

8. Thomas M. Hout, Michael E. Porter, and Eileen Rudden, "How Global Companies Win Out," *Harvard Business Review* (September–October 1982): 102.

9. R. T. Pascale, H. Mintzberg, M. Goold, and R. Rumelt, "The Honda Effect Revisited," *California Management Review* 39, no. 4 (1996): 78–117.

10. James B. Quinn, *Strategies for Change: Logical Incrementalism* (Homewood, IL: Irwin, 1980), 140.

11. Arie de Geus, *The Living Company* (Boston: Harvard Business School Press, 1997), 73.

12. Mintzberg, *Rise and Fall*, 352–353.

13. Sumantra Ghoshal and Eleanor Westney, cited in Mintzberg, *Rise and Fall*, 374.

14. Thomas J. Peters and Robert H. Waterman, Jr., *In Search of Excellence: Lessons from America's Best-Run Companies* (New York: Harper & Row, 1982).

15. Adriana Stadecker, interview by author.

16. Interview by author.

Chapter 10: Off the Org Chart

1. Stanley M. Davis and Paul Lawrence, *Matrix* (Reading, MA: Addison-Wesley, 1977), 11.

2. The concept of process centering comes from Michael Hammer, *Beyond Reengineering: How the Process-Centered Organization Is Changing Our Work and Our Lives* (New York: HarperBusiness, 1996). The horizontal organization is discussed in Frank Ostroff, *The Horizontal Organization* (New York: Oxford University Press, 1999).

3. For a discussion of the problems of reengineering, see Thomas H. Davenport, "The Fad That Forgot People," *Fast Company*, November 1995, 70–74.

4. Alan Martin and Ulmar Riaz, "When Speed + Size = Danger," <http://www.ac.com/ideas/Outlook/pov/pov_speed.html>.

Chapter 11: "You've Got (Lots and Lots of) Mail

1. Mark Levitt, *Email Usage Forecast and Analysis, 2000–2005* (Framingham, MA: International Data Corporation, 2000).

2. Ed Vulliamy, "If You Don't Have Time to Take in All the Information in This Report, You Could Be Suffering from a Bout of Information Fatigue Syndrome," *Guardian*, 15 October 1996.

3. Michael Cunningham, "Glued to the Screen," *Irish Times*, 18 December 1997.

4. Cisco Systems example mentioned in Andrea Petersen, "A Fine Line," *Wall Street Journal* supplement on information overload, 21 June 1999, R8.

5. Ibid.

6. Morten T. Hansen and Martine R. Haas, "Competing for Attention in Knowledge Markets: The Case of Electronic Document Dissemination in a Management Consulting Company," *Administrative Science Quarterly* (forthcoming); also available as a Harvard Business School Working Paper, 2000.

7. "Cyberslacking at Work Continues to Threaten Productivity," Greenfield Online "QuickTake" survey conducted for JSB SurfCONTROL, press release, 6 March 2000.

8. Outsell, Inc., *The End User Speaks: Attitudes and Behaviors Toward Commercial Desktop Services and the Open Web* (Burlingame, CA: Outsell, Inc., June 2000).

Chapter 12: From Myopia to Utopia

1. Andrea Petersen, "Messaging Miss Manners," *Wall Street Journal*, 26 April 2000.

2. Quote from Thomas Pugliese in Erika Germer, "Attention, Please," *Fast Company*, June 2000, 86.

3. Marissa Gluck, "Workplace Targeting: Connecting with Consumers During the New Prime Time," *Online Advertising Report* 3 (May 2000), Jupiter Research, <http://www.jup.com/home.jsp>.

4. See, for example, Peter Kolesar, Garrett Van Ryzin, and Wayne Cutler, "Creating Customer Value Through Industrialized Intimacy," *Strategy and Business* (3rd quarter 1998).

5. Julia Lawlor, "Hired Organizers Can Create Order out of Computer Chaos," *New York Times*, 15 April 1999.

6. William M. Carley, "Talk of Video Cameras in Jet Cockpits Makes Pilots Fly into a Rage," *Wall Street Journal*, 7 April 2000.

7. Pitney Bowes study of household messaging, reprinted in *Wired*, April 2000, 92.

8. Teresa Riordan, "Patents," *New York Times*, 27 March 2000.

9. Charles Gasparino, "Hired Help: Starved for Attention, Small Companies Buy Wall Street Coverage," *Wall Street Journal Europe*, 14 July 1999.

INDEX

ABOUT THE AUTHORS

Thomas H. Davenport is the Director of the Accenture Institute for Strategic Change, a research center in Cambridge, Massachusetts. He is also a Visiting Professor at the Tuck School of Business, Dartmouth College, and a Distinguished Scholar in Residence at Babson College. His previous books include *Mission Critical: Realizing the Promise of Enterprise Systems*, *Working Knowledge: How Organizations Manage What They Know* (coauthored with Laurence Prusak), and *Process Innovation: Reengineering Work through Information Technology*.

John C. Beck is an Associate Partner and Senior Research Fellow at the Accenture Institute for Strategic Change. He is also a Visiting Professor at the Anderson School of Management at the University of California at Los Angeles and an Adjunct Professor at the Ivey School at the University of Western Ontario. Beck has served as Publisher of *The Asian Century* newsletter and has published more than one hundred books, articles, and business reports on the topics of e-commerce, business in Asia, strategic management, globalization, leadership, and organizational behavior.